Death Sc

The Ethnography of Political Violence

Cynthia Keppley Mahmood, Series Editor

A complete list of books in the series
is available from the publisher.

Death Squad

The Anthropology of State Terror

Edited by Jeffrey A. Sluka

PENN

University of Pennsylvania Press

Philadelphia

10 9 8 7 6 5 4 3 2 1

Published by
University of Pennsylvania Press
Philadelphia, Pennsylvania 19104-4011

Library of Congress Cataloging-in-Publication Data
Death squad : the anthropology of state terror / edited by Jeffrey A.
  Sluka.
      p.   cm. — (Ethnography of political violence)
    Includes bibliographical references and index.
    ISBN 0-8122-3523-1 (cloth : alk. paper). —
  ISBN 0-8122-1711-X (pbk. : alk. paper)
    1. Terrorism.   2. State-sponsored terrorism.   3. Death squads.
  4. Human rights.   5. Political persecution.   I. Sluka, Jeffrey A.
  II. Series.
  HV6431.D433   1999
  303.6'25—dc21   99-34602
                                                                   CIP

Contents

Illustrations

Preface

This book is the first collection of ethnographic case studies focused specifically on the anthropology of state terror. It is a positive response to Linda Green's observation that "Overwhelming empirical evidence demonstrates that state violence has been standard operating procedure in numerous contemporary societies where anthropologists have conducted fieldwork over the past three decades. Despite an alarming rise in the most blatant forms of transgression, repression and state terrorism, the topic has not captured the anthropological imagination" (1995:107). It also reflects her suggestion, after Nancy Scheper-Hughes, that one way anthropologists may overcome this failure of imagination is to construct ethnographies as "sites of resistance," "acts of solidarity," and a way to "write against terror" (Green 1995:109). The goals of the book are to bring together contemporary ethnographic studies of state terror and its impact on local-level communities, particularly the occurrence of extrajudicial state killings of political opponents and civilians through disappearances and death squad activities, and to both present and reflect upon the "state of the art" of contemporary anthropological considerations of state terror, including theoretical perspectives, methodological approaches, fieldwork experiences, and ethical dilemmas.

The book brings together an international panel of anthropologists with extensive research experience in areas marked by extreme forms of state repression and terror, who have all studied state terror from the local-level perspective of victims and survivors living in "targeted" communities. The first chapter provides a general introduction to the topic of state terror, an overview of contemporary anthropological approaches to this subject, and the outlines of an anthropological theory of state terror. This is followed by eight ethnographic case studies, exploring aspects of the complex, difficult, and disturbing human issue of state terror in Argentina, Guatemala, the Philippines, Kashmir, Punjab, the Basque Country, East Timor, and Northern Ireland. The volume does not aim to be a global survey because, unfortunately, so many countries engage in state terror that such a survey could never be compressed into a single volume. Instead, we have chosen specific illustrative cases. Besides providing a cross-cultural sample, the eight case studies reflect the traditional eclectic nature of the discipline and present a wide range of theoretical perspectives and interpretations. They also demonstrate the cultural complexities and ambiguities of terror when viewed at the local level and from the participants' point of view, and represent examples of the ways different anthropologists are trying to do good anthropology that also works for humankind by working against terror. The conclusion to the volume is by Kay B. Warren, one of the discipline's most respected authorities on conflict, terror, and resistance, who has done extensive research in Latin America.

This is risky anthropology, and all of the contributors may suffer recriminations as a result. In fact, many of them already have from their previous work. There are considerable risks for anthropologists who dare to speak, write, and act against terror, but the contributors to this volume seek to live up to the legacy of Myrna Mack, and produce anthropology that is "synonymous with courage, social consciousness, and first-rate scholarship" (Manz 1994:13).

Acknowledgments

I would like to sincerely thank all of the people who made this book possible, particularly the chapter contributors and the people and communities who participated in the research they report here. Additional heartfelt thanks are due to our understanding editors, Patricia Smith and Cynthia Mahmood, for their practical advice, thoughtful criticism, unflagging support, and great encouragement. I would also like to thank the anonymous reviewers of the manuscript for their helpful comments and suggestions. Some of the chapters published here were originally presented in the session on "The Anthropology of State Terror" at the 1996 annual conference of the American Anthropological Association (San Francisco, 20–24 November). Thanks to Bill Rolston for permission to use his photographs of Belfast murals in Chapter 5.

Bibliography

Green, Linda
    1995 "Living in a State of Fear." In *Fieldwork Under Fire.* C. Nordstrom and
    A. Robben, eds. Berkeley: University of California Press.
Manz, Beatriz
    1994 Foreword. In *Massacres in the Jungle,* by R. Falla. Boulder, Colo.: Westview
    Press.

Introduction
State Terror and Anthropology
Jeffrey A. Sluka

This chapter provides an introduction to the general topic of state terror, an overview of contemporary anthropological approaches to this subject, and the outlines of an anthropological theory of state terror, representing an attempt to begin to not only describe but also explain the immense problem of state terror in the world today.

State Terror

In political science, there has been a convention of distinguishing between state violence and antistate violence, referring to the former as "terror"[1] and the latter as "terrorism," but while there is now a massive literature on antistate terrorism, state terror has been neglected by academics,[2] the media, and governments. The reasons for this have been more political and ideological than empirical,[3] and the only compelling reasons to distinguish between terror and terrorism are because the function of one is to maintain the status quo while that of the other is to achieve political change, and because there is a huge difference in scale between them. The point has been made often and well by Noam Chomsky and Edward Herman, who distinguish between the "wholesale terror" practiced by states and the "retail terror" practiced by antistate individuals and insurgent groups (see Chomsky and Herman 1979; Herman 1982). As they have shown, if terrorism means political intimidation by violence or its threat, and if we allow the definition to include violence by states and agents of states, then we find that the major form of terrorism in the world today is that practiced by states and their agents and allies, and that, quantitatively, antistate terrorism pales into relative insignificance compared to it. The fact is that even small states have much more power to terrorize than even the most advanced antistate terrorists; for example, only state terrorists have weapons of "mass (civilian) destruction" or the ability to deprive large numbers of people of subsistence requirements and produce hunger, malnutrition, high infant mortality rates, and other chronic diseases of poverty and neglect, as means of political intimidation and control.

A good dictionary definition of terrorism that avoids the ideological subterfuge of excluding state terror is "the policy of using acts inspiring great fear as a method of ruling or of conducting political opposition" (cited in Nagengast 1994:114). But if we want a specific definition of state terror that distinguishes it from antistate terrorism, a good definition is that state terror refers to the use or threat of violence by the state or its agents or supporters, particularly against civilian individuals and populations, as a means of political intimidation and control (i.e., a means of repression).

State terror is a major and growing world problem. If politically motivated torture and murder are defined as terrorism, then it is in the large number of authoritarian states, both on the right and left, that these forms of terrorism have massively escalated in recent decades. This is violence aimed at citizens by their own governments. It is now widely acknowledged that, as Herman has shown, "The really massive and significant growth of terrorism since World War II has been that carried out by states" (1982:83). As Nagengast has observed, "Since 1945, state-sponsored violence toward ethnic and political groups has caused more deaths, injuries, and general human suffering than 'all other forms of deadly conflict, including international wars and colonial and civil wars' " (1994: 126). This rise in state terror is a direct corollary of the alarming rise in the number of authoritarian states during this period — variously characterized in contemporary literature as "shakedown" (Chomsky and Herman 1979), "strong" (Ackroyd et al. 1980), "national security" (Herman 1982), "coercive" (Hillyard and Percy-Smith 1988), "fearful" (Ali 1988), "homicidal" (Amnesty International 1992), or "outlaw" (Taylor 1993) states — who routinely employ terror and other forms of mass intimidation against their own civilian populations.

In the second half of the twentieth century, military and other authoritarian regimes came to power in virtually all of Central and South America, and in many countries in Asia, Africa, and elsewhere. During this period, terror practiced by authoritarian states has resulted in a couple of million "disappearances" and other politically motivated murders, at least several million people tortured, many millions of political refugees, scores of millions of people threatened and intimidated by the use of direct and indirect state terror, and the rise of cultures of terror in a large and ever growing number of countries around the world. The massive escalation in terror practiced by authoritarian states over the last few decades is evidenced by the reemergence of torture as a serious world problem, the rising tide of death squad murders, and the use of direct state violence to intimidate millions of people. Worldwide, human rights suffered serious setbacks in the 1970s and 1980s, and this trend has continued through the 1990s. The UN Commission on Human Rights reports that human rights violations around the world have steadily increased, particularly in Latin America and Asia. In scores of countries worldwide, the most fundamental human rights are being transgressed by government-condoned terror involving the harassment, torture, and murder of political opponents of those in power.

In its annual global human rights reports, Amnesty International has extensively documented the escalation in state terror. In 1996, among 150 countries surveyed, 82 (55 percent) were guilty of torturing and 61 (41 percent) of murdering political opponents of those in power (Amnesty International 1997). Year after year, Amnesty International has reported that the victims of state-condoned "extrajudicial killings" have included government opponents, members of ethnic and religious groups, and civilians living in areas of military operations. They were gunned down in groups and shot individually, blown up with bombs and artillery, stabbed, strangled, hacked to death, or poisoned. Many were tortured to death, and victims were often severely mutilated and sexually abused before being killed.

Amnesty International (1993) has identified the main forms of state terror as arbitrary detention, unfair trial, torture, and political murder or extrajudicial execution. Here, it is worth elaborating on torture and murder as the sine qua non of state terror.

Torture

The use of torture has grown massively, most notably in the Third World client states of the West. As noted above, in 1996 over half of the world's governments were guilty of using torture on a systematic, institutionalized basis — that is, as a "normal" mode of governance. This startling development was first highlighted by Amnesty International in its 1974 *Report on Torture*, which pointed out that torture had suddenly reemerged and reached "epidemic proportions" (1974:131). In the 1970s, about thirty-five countries worldwide practiced torture on an "administrative basis" (Chomsky and Herman 1979). By 1988 Amnesty International was reporting that over half of the world's governments were torturing or otherwise "mistreating" prisoners, and at the end of 1989 the UN Commission on Human Rights reported that the year was marked by a "resurgence of torture" by government interrogators. The use of torture has not been confined to interrogation for the purposes of extracting information or confessions, and it is often employed by "torture states" as a generalized tactic of political intimidation of opponents of government and elites. There have been increasingly widespread reports of torture of children in front of their parents, again both as a method of interrogation and of general political intimidation, and rape is also increasingly being used as a form of mass political terror (see Stiglmayer 1994; Littlewood 1997).

Political Murder

Along with torture, the proliferation of state-sanctioned extrajudicial killings, "disappearances," and death squads have also been a hallmark of the massive growth of state terror in the last quarter of the twentieth century (Amnesty International 1992). Death squads have become one of the most noteworthy aspects of contemporary, primarily right-wing, state terror. During the 1960s and 1970s, death squads emerged in at least ten states in Latin America alone, and like torture and disappearances conducted by regular state forces, also spread steadily through the Third World in the 1980s and 1990s.

In 1986 the ICIHI reported that disappearance was a sinister form of "repression in a new guise" and "still largely unknown to the general public" (1986:13). It noted that disappearances were first documented in the mid-1970s, and it was not until 1978 that the UN General Assembly first recognized the practice of disappearances as a widespread problem. In response, in 1980 the UN established the Working Group on Enforced or Involuntary Disappearances. Unfortunately, its effectiveness has been severely restricted by lack of cooperation by governments, inability to exert any pressure, and other limitations, but it is still an important organization. The UN has condemned disappearances and extrajudicial executions as grave violations of fundamental human rights, and has stated that their systematic practice represent "war crimes" against humanity.

Over the past two decades, between 200,000 and 300,000 people have been "disappeared" worldwide. In 1989, the UN Commission on Human Rights reported that the number of officially recorded disappearances had doubled over the previous year. "Disappearances" are "cases where individuals are seized by military, paramilitary, or police agents of the state [or their proxies], who secretly murder and dispose of the bodies of their victims, often after torture, always without legal process, and without acknowledgment and admitted responsibility of the state" (Herman 1982:7; see also ICIHI 1986; Amnesty International 1993:350). The members of these death squads are usually linked directly or indirectly with the regular security forces, but sometimes they are part of paramilitary "defense" forces, or civilian right-wing paramilitary groups who kill people the state wants, or doesn't mind being, killed. Either way, there is always overlap in membership and other forms of direct and indirect collusion between the death squads and the army and police, and the death squads are usually directly or indirectly under official or unofficial state control.

While death squads operate outside the law, they effectively do so with impunity and are generally and secretly fully integrated into the state's regular security network (Amnesty International 1981). The attraction of death squads is that despite being sanctioned by key sectors of the government apparatus, they are distinct enough from the official chain of command for governments to maintain a "plausible denial" of involvement with them; their "separation from the regular security forces allows systematic murder to be carried out for which the state can deny any knowledge and responsibility" (Herman 1982:117). The ICIHI has described disappearances as "the acme of despotism" (1986:40), and Hannah Arendt (cited in Herman 1982:7) has identified them as "one of the last and most terrible phases in the evolution and degeneration of totalitarian states."[4]

It is important to note who is likely to be disappeared, because they are as a rule misrepresented by those responsible as either being or supporting "terrorists" or "subversives" out to destroy the country. Terror states who practice extrajudicial execution or political assassination of their opponents have seen "subversion" in any activity or idea that challenges the status quo — including organizing peasants, unions, Bible classes, proposals for land reform, or tax increases on the rich. Anyone engaged in such activities — clergy, labor organizers or trade unionists, human rights activists, indigenous peoples and minorities asserting their rights, teachers, students, health and social workers, journalists, and so on — are defined as subversives, terrorists, traitors, or communists, and this is used as the rationalization and justification for killing them without even due process of law. No one is safe; the victims have included men, women, children, and old people, activists, relatives of activists, and witnesses of state abuses. "The target," as one U.S. diplomat described death squad operations in 1984, "is anybody with an idea in his head" (Siegel and Hackel 1988:115).[5]

In the 1990s, there have been growing reports of the emergence and spread of a new face of death squad terror in Latin America, the addition of the homeless, "delinquents," street children, and other "undesirables" to the list of other "terrorists" and "subversives." Reports have emerged particularly from Guatemala, Argentina, Brazil, Colombia, and Mexico. For example, in 1992 Amnesty International reported that "Many of the children living on the streets of Guatemala City have suffered torture, 'disappearance' and extrajudicial execution at the hands of the security forces" (1992:55). In 1996, reports emerged from Mexico City that street children living in the sewage system, "children of the drains," were being persecuted and executed by the militarized police as "delinquents." For the "children of the drains," life is literally a struggle for survival, and the police and army make sure that the struggle is a fight to the death. In 1997, Colombian security forces were accused of "social cleansing" — the murder of the homeless and poor squatters, the unemployed, street children, prostitutes, homosexuals, dissident teachers, and Indians (*An Phoblacht/Republican News*, 17 July 1997, p. 19) — in sum, all the "non-productive" ones.

"Death by Government": The State as Terrorist

Political scientist R. J. Rummel's *Death by Government* (1994), his fourth book in a series on genocide and government mass murder, was the first attempt to do a thorough accounting of the twentieth century's state-instigated mass murders, starvations, and genocides. Rummel calculated that "In total, during the first eighty years of this century, almost one hundred and seventy million men, women and children have been shot, beaten, tortured, knifed, burned, starved, frozen, crushed, or worked to death; buried alive, drowned, hung, bombed, or killed in any other of the myriad ways governments have inflicted death on unarmed helpless citizens and foreigners."[6] This is a *conservative* accounting, and Rummel notes that, because governments have been unwilling to admit such monstrous acts, "the dead could conceivably be nearly three hundred and sixty million people" (1994:9). He concludes that no other century has seen a slaughter of such magnitude, and his figures only cover the first eighty-eight years of the century, and do not include the massive death tolls in government-inspired genocides and starvations that have occurred since then in Bosnia, Somalia, Sudan, Rwanda, and other countries.

Rummel demonstrates what he terms "the sheer lethality of power," and postulates that the "belief in power as a tool" is responsible for the death toll: "It is as though our species has been devastated by a modern Black Plague. And indeed it has, but a plague of Power, not germs" (1994:9). His central theoretical conclusion stresses the relationship between power and terror: "as the arbitrary power of a regime increases massively, that is, as we move from democratic through authoritarian to totalitarian regimes, the amount of killing jumps by huge multiples" (1994:17). The more concentrated the power of the government, the more deaths; as the arbitrary power of regimes increases, the practice of terror increases: "The more power a government has, the more it can act arbitrarily according to the whims and desires of the elite, and the more it will make war on others and murder its foreign and domestic subjects. The more constrained the power of governments, the more power is diffused, checked, and balanced, the less it will aggress on others and commit [political mass murder]" (1994:1–2). Rummel argues that where absolute power exists, "interests become polarized, *a culture of violence develops*, and war and state murder follow. Where, on the other hand, power is limited and accountable, interests are cross-pressured, *a culture of nonviolence develops*, and no wars occur and comparatively few citizens are murdered by the governing elite" (1994:23–24; emphasis added).

While no form of government, including democracy, has been immune to employing mass terror, Rummel shows that totalitarian and authoritarian governments are far and away the main culprits. He therefore makes a strong argument for freedom and democracy as antidotes to terror; "the empirical and theoretical conclusion is this: The way to end war and virtually eliminate [state-sanctioned mass murder] appears to be through restricting and checking power, i.e., through *fostering democratic freedom*" (1994:27; emphasis in original).

The International Context: The Global Culture of Terror and the "American Connection"

One of the most important observations made by the leading academics who have studied state terror over the past two decades is that violent, systematic repression is never an isolated phenomenon. State terror in Third World countries is invariably linked at both instrumental and structural levels to militarism (e.g., the arms trade and military assistance) in the countries, particularly the First World ones, with which they have military and economic ties. This system is reinforced through the mutual political, economic, and military interests of the elites in both the First and Third Worlds. In an important volume, *The State as Terrorist*, Stohl and Lopez (1984:9–10) note that this view, that the state terror system operates internationally as well as domestically, and that "outside nations combine with internal trends and political actors to provide the climate, if not the stimulation, to systems of repression and/or state terror," is widely accepted among political scientists.

Michael Stohl (1984), in particular, has explored the manner in which the international political system serves as the arena in which state terror policies unfold:

States . . . have been willing in the past decade to help provide other states with the tools of the terror trade . . . the new technologies of repression are widely available and easily distributed. The United States has been an active provider of the instruments of terror and repression to Third World client states to employ on their populations and also in a number of cases to train the security services of these societies in the proper employment of these instruments. It is a lucrative trade, and the US government has been an active assistant to US corporations in the purveyance of their wares. Other Western governments similarly assisted their national corporations in this regard . . . [as did] the Soviet Union. (Stohl 1984:55)

The arms or "security" industry is the largest industry in the world, and a multibillion dollar international repression trade flourishes in providing not just arms but the whole range of technology — both hardware and software — of political control to client dictatorships and other authoritarian states.[7] In its 1996 report, Amnesty International accused powerful governments of "trading in terror" by selling arms and other "security" equipment to countries with bad human rights records, and then denying responsibility when atrocities occurred.

At the end of the 1970s, at the same time that Amnesty International and other human rights organizations were first beginning to present alarming reports of the existence of a new global "epidemic" of state torture and murder, the first academic studies also began to emerge about this, led by the pioneering work of Chomsky and Herman. In a series of important books (e.g., Chomsky and Herman 1979; Herman 1982; Chomsky 1985, 1988), they reported that the global rise in state terror was concentrated among Third World states in the U.S. "sphere of influence," and provided extensive information on the terror occurring in the United States' client states in Latin America. They showed that in the 1970s, all ten of the countries in Latin America in which death squads appeared, and twenty-six (74 percent) of the thirty-five countries in the world that used torture on an "administrative basis," were client states of the United States who received direct military and other assistance enabling them to establish and maintain authoritarian regimes prepared to resort to terror to pursue their interests and stay in power. This led Herman to conclude that "the death squad is a manifestation of U.S. influence. Torture and the death squad are as U.S.-related-American as apple pie" (1982:132).[8] Chomsky's and Herman's basic conclusion, and the thesis they have advanced in their work since then, is that the global rise in state terror has been mainly or fundamentally the result of U.S. foreign policy.

This thesis was further supported by Michael McClintock's *The American Connection* (1985), which provided additional documentation and analysis of U.S.-backed suppression of political and human rights in the Third World. In 1991, another noteworthy volume was published, *Western State Terrorism*, edited by Alexander George. This was the first book to deal substantively with the issue of not just "the U.S. connection," but the wider context of Western state-sponsored terrorism which underpins the "new world order." It provided additional wide-ranging and well-documented academic description and analysis of the forms of terror supported by the United States and some of its allies. It further supported "the fundamental thesis about terrorism: that its primary manifestations are supported, or directly carried out, by Western governments," and once again stressed the crucial point that "The plain and painful truth is that on any reasonable definition of terrorism, taken literally, the United States and its friends are the major supporters, sponsors, and perpetrators of terrorist incidents in the world today . . . many, probably most, significant instances of terrorism are supported, if not organized, by the U.S., its partners, and their client states" (1991:1–2).[9] While the ICIHI (1986:87) has taken the position that "The origin of our concern is not any one state or continent, for evil is contagious, and a spreading fire knows no borders," as Chomsky (1988) argues, the United States represents the hegemonic "culture of terrorism," providing the central model and leading example emulated by every other nation involved in state terror around the world.[10]

However, while the United States leads the way, Chomsky, among others, observes that it is not at all unique in supporting terror when it is perceived to be in its politicoeconomic interests; "every other power in the world is exactly the same" (1996:46) in their own international spheres of influence, contributing to terror through their support — financial, military, and diplomatic — of Third World regimes founded on violence. Thus, at the global level there is an international network or system of authoritarian (mostly Third World) states that employ terror as normal procedure, coupled with their (mostly First World) external or international sponsors and support system of governments and multinational corporations, particularly the arms/security industry. At the top of this system, leading by example, are the United States and its allies (particularly the United Kingdom and France), and the terror states they support, followed by other terror states outside their sphere of influence who are supported by other international patrons pursuing their own interests.

George Aditjondro (this volume) asks an important and classical anthropological question: are the incredible cross-cultural similarities we observe in the practices of state terror a case of "independent innovation" or "diffusion"? It is clear that the latter is the case, and that the structures, tactics, and technology of state terror have been diffused, in fact aggressively marketed and exported as a form of "military aid" to developing countries. A focus on state terror at the level of individual countries tends to obscure the fact that it is a global phenomenon supported by an international structure or network, and local cases are only comprehensible within this encapsulating context. Individual states which are cultures of terror are encapsulated in a global or international culture of terror within which they are nurtured, and without which they probably could not long survive — that is, they are dependent on international support for their continued existence. They are dependent variables in the equation of global terror.

Anthropology and State Terror

Political anthropologists normally concentrate on the intensive study of micropolitics at the local level, and it is our experience at the grass roots in Third World and other countries that brings us to connect with the macropolitical level of world terrorism, outlined above. Anthropologists are working today in every nation of the world, and our perspective is profoundly grounded on fieldwork among the victims — the "targeted communities" — of state terror. Because of this, we know their grievances, the political and economic realities of their existence, and the origins of the terror that has today come all too often to dominate their lives. For a long time now (since at least the 1960s), the message anthropologists have heard, particularly from the many "killing fields" in the Third World, is that the main source of the violence is the oppressive states in which they are citizens, and those who support these states. This message from the microlevel, and the participant-observation-based research anthropologists have done on state terror at the grass roots, fits hand in glove with and tends strongly to confirm the macrolevel theses presented by Chomsky and other leading academics of state terror outside of anthropology.

One of the distinguishing characteristics of the leading anthropologists who write about state terror today is that they have gone through a similar historic and biographical progression — they all evolve directly from the research experience of fieldwork with victims in communities targeted by state terror. Most of them were not originally drawn to state terror as a topic of research, but came to this in response to their experiences with victims of state violence in many places around the world — particularly the Third World. Because they felt compelled to speak and respond in some positive way, many of them became increasingly interested in resistance and the interdynamics of resistance and terror. Nonetheless, George Aditjondro (this volume) points up a hard truth about our discipline when he pointedly observes that, even though anthropologists have made "earnest attempts to defend the victims of blatant as well as structural oppression," they have

rarely taken as their duty to understand the perpetrators of human rights violations, which is more commonly seen as the duty of political scientists and human rights lawyers. This negligence is quite telling about the discipline and the community, since many anthropologists have not shunned studying rituals of non-Westernized societies, which, in the United Nations' human rights standards, are quite barbaric. So, why is it that, with some exceptions, most anthropologists have avoided studying the barbaric practices of governments, whose commandos have reinforced and refined those practices in the elite special forces' training centers in the U.S.?

The discipline is beginning to respond to this criticism and there is a shift toward writing about state terror in its own right.

Nonetheless, as noted earlier, state terror has not "captured the anthropological imagination" (Green 1995:107), and, among the well over 10,000 anthropologists worldwide, only a few dozen have chosen to study state terror. Carole Nagengast has observed that this is "in part because its methods and theory depend on months or years in the field, until recently defined as a relatively small, self-contained community that did not include the state. Also, prolonged research in a local community is difficult or impossible in times of violent strife and it is risky business to appear to take sides in situations in which the state resorts to torture, terrorism, and disappearances and in which armed opposition groups operate in a similar manner" (1994:112). This has been part of the problem; the other part is confusion and debate about how anthropologists should respond to state terror and whether they should try to actively work against it.

Despite these impediments, anthropologists have now established a considerable literature on the lived experience of human violence, and the ethnographic study of terror and resistance has become a subfield of its own. A growing number of anthropologists who work in areas characterized by violence and conflict have begun to deconstruct the insidious and pervasive effects and mechanisms of violence, terror, and resistance.[11] A number of important books — the main ones described below — represent milestones in the evolution toward an anthropology of state terror. Today, the anthropology of state terror is emerging from a previous preoccupation with resistance, and while most anthropologists writing about terror are still doing so mainly from the perspective of its victims, we are in the midst of a transition away from studying victims toward studying *perpetrators* of state violence.

Writing Against Terror

Many anthropologists are committed, even passionate, about the need to make anthropology more politically engaged, and have been "rethinking the politics of anthropology" and debating the question of how to respond to what Orin Starn describes as "the pervasiveness of injustice and terror in this late-twentieth-century world" (1994:26). Starn himself has presented a vision of a more "emancipatory politics for the discipline" and stresses "the urgency of efforts to develop our capacity to contribute to struggles for equality and justice" (1994:1). Beatriz Manz (1995:261) suggests an *antropología comprometida*: "In Latin America it means to participate in a committed way; to opt for and to side with," and offers Ricardo Falla as a notable example. As Linda Green has expressed it, "What is at stake, it seems, are the struggles between the powerful and powerless and what is at issue for anthropologists is with whom to cast their lot" (1995:107).

Among anthropologists, Michael Taussig has led the way in the analysis of terror as a cultural system, and by his seminal suggestion that anthropologists should "write back against terror" with a "poetics of destruction and reve!ation" that "fight[s] with words in and against the silence imposed by the arbiters of discourse who beat out a new reality in the cells where torturer and tortured come together" (1987:4, 9; also 1984, 1992). Taussig's work has been compelling to anthropologists who want to write against terror because of his ability to take a principled moral stance against political torture and murder, while maintaining the highest standards of anthropological research. This has become the hallmark of the emerging anthropology of state terror.

Nancy Scheper-Hughes has added another compelling voice to the chorus of calls for anthropologists to write against terror. She has argued for a politically committed, morally engaged, and ethically grounded anthropology, and that "cultural relativism, read as moral relativism, is no longer appropriate to the world in which we live, and anthropology, if it is to be worth anything at all, must be ethically grounded" (1995:409). Such an anthropology, she suggests, "could not ignore the massacres and disappearances of vulnerable people that often occur (though one would hardly know it) right in front of the anthropologist's unsteady gaze" (1995:437). Scheper-Hughes argues that anthropologists should, at the least, serve as witnesses to and reporters of human rights abuses and the suffering of the poor and oppressed. Not to do so is an "act of indifference" (1992), a hostile act, and she suggests that anthropology should exist "on two fronts: as a field of knowledge (as a 'discipline') and as a field of action, a force field, or site of struggle" (1995:419–420).

Like Taussig, Scheper-Hughes suggests that anthropological writing and monographs can be sites of resistance, acts of solidarity, and an important way to write against terror. She calls for anthropologists to "become alarmists and shock troopers — the producers of politically complicated and morally demanding texts and images capable of sinking through the layers of acceptance, complicity, and bad faith that allow the suffering and the deaths to continue without even the pained cry of recognition of Conrad's evil protagonist, Kurtz: 'The horror! The horror!'" (1995:417). In *Death Without Weeping* (1992), she reflects on her

personal engagement in recording human conditions based on participant-observation and "testimony." She suggests that it is the act of "witnessing" that lends our work its moral character (1995:419), and that
participant-observation "has a way of drawing ethnographers into spaces
of human life where they might really prefer not to go at all and, once
there, do not know how to escape except through writing, which willy-
nilly draws others there as well, making them party to the witnessing"
(1995:419).

The emerging anthropology of state terror is a relevant and politically
engaged anthropology which observes, witnesses, and records, but also
seeks to confront, expose, and oppose human rights abuses. Anthropologists who write against terror step outside the boundaries of standard
anthropological practice. Many of them have an intense commitment to
the people they have worked, lived, and sometimes suffered with, and a
very few have become action or even liberation anthropologists to support
the causes they have witnessed. They do not believe that this necessarily
undermines their scientific objectivity or ability "to tell the truth and to
expose lies," as Chomsky (1987:60) has simply but elegantly summarized
the social responsibility of intellectuals. After C. Wright Mills (1963:611),
they believe that the values and politics of anthropology should be the
values of humanism and the politics of truth.

Decolonizing Anthropology

Another reason to write against terror is that this is an important means
of "decolonizing" the discipline and moving towards a more "emancipatory" or "liberation" anthropology. As Edmund Gordon has expressed it:

As more of us reach intellectual maturity, we find the contradictions of existence
within a colonized discipline harder to bear. As the conflict between the oppressed and the oppressors intensifies worldwide, we are haunted by the recognition that we are professionals in a discipline which chose the wrong side a long
time ago. In this context it becomes imperative for ourselves and our people,
either to begin the process of definitively decolonising at least our practice of the
profession with which we have identified — or get out . . . To be an anthropology
which no longer serves the interests of the oppressors it must be one which
actively serves those of the oppressed. We must make a decolonised anthropology
positively the "anthropology of liberation." (1991:153)

Gordon suggests that decolonized anthropologists should be activists
committed to "creating and consolidating a counter-hegemonic movement through active political struggle," and that this work should be both
intellectual and activist. A sound intellectual understanding of the culture
should be "enhanced through identification and participation in political
struggle with the community. The creation of a counter-hegemony is

essentially a political act. As such, it cannot be carried on by the anthropologist alone" (1991:163). Gordon believes that

> sustained communal political activism provides a middle ground between the political economic and post-modern positions in anthropology. As a posture of full identification it places the critical anthropologist as "insider." From this perspective the structural inequalities which oppress our communities can be analyzed and strategies to combat them created and evaluated without falling prey to the ethical and analytical problems of objectification, constructed representation, omniscience and/or vanguardism, because we are writing within our own "subjectivities." (1991:163)

Many contemporary anthropologists want to be seen as allies of oppressed peoples struggling against poverty, racism, violence, and other forms of oppression, believing this to be an important step toward the decolonization of the discipline. Writing against terror is one of the most effective arenas in which anthropologists are trying to do this, and it is also one of the main sites where First and Third World anthropologists are working together.

The Ethnography of State Terror

As noted, the best anthropology of state terror has been done by scholars who have been able to write against or denounce state terror while maintaining the highest standards of anthropological research. In this section I want to briefly review some of the best examples of this — the pioneering work of E. V. Walter's classic study of despotic rule in African kingdoms, *Terror and Resistance* (1969), and some key contemporary works by anthropologists who have done research in Argentina and Guatemala — Marcelo Suarez-Orozco, Ricardo Falla, and the contributors to Robert Carmack's outstanding edited volume *Harvest of Violence* (1988). The dirty war in Argentina and the "long war" in Guatemala have become synonymous with modern reigns of terror and have stimulated the anthropology of state terror. In the 1980s, anthropologists in Latin America began to respond to the growth of state terror in that region, and this response has spread rapidly as the anthropology of state terror becomes an increasingly central concern of political anthropologists.

"Terror and Resistance"

Published in 1969, E. V. Walter's *Terror and Resistance* provides a solid source of theory for analyses of state terror and authoritarian rule. In the first systematic effort to develop a general theory of state terror, Walter studied "regimes of terror" — systems maintained by established power holders "who choose to rule by violence and fear" (1969:vii), particularly the despotic reign of the Zulu King Shaka—and presented a structural-functional and processual analysis, focusing on how terror is employed to maintain "order" and counteract "crises of integration."

Walter begins by observing that "Rule by terror, a familiar process in history, has virtually escaped systematic analysis. Working for the modern state, this old scourge of human communities destroys men [*sic*] for the same ends it once achieved as the instrument of immemorial despots. This form of power remains at the edges of rational inquiry, but the experience of recent times, punctuated by terroristic outbreaks and burdened by regimes of terror, makes the world tremble with an awareness that seeks general explanation" (1969:3).

The main function of terror identified by Walter is to maintain "order" and counteract "fissiparous tendencies" within the polity by inhibiting resistance, preventing change, and maintaining the existing political order—in short, to protect the status of the ruling elite. Terror is used as a means of political control: Its proximate aim is to instill fear, but the ultimate end is control (1969:13). Its function is "not only to punish acts of disobedience and resistance but also to sap the potential for disobedience in advance and to break the power to resist" (1969:19).[12] Walter does not say enough about the nature of the "crises of integration" that lead to terror, but does observe that one of terror's main functions is to "support tactical resistance to social and political change" (1969:10), that is, to maintain the political status quo from challenges from below.

Walter presents a dramaturgical model of the terror process, which involves three sets of actors—the source of violence, victims, and targets:

The victim perishes, but the target reacts to the spectacle or the news of that destruction with some manner of submission or accommodation—that is, by withdrawing his [*sic*] resistance or by inhibiting his potential resistance. An expanded model, closer to the realities of a political system, would have a division of labor and specialization in the source of violence. Let us call the organization which is the source, the *terror staff*, and within it distinguish between a *directorate*— men who design, initiate, control, define, and justify the terror—and the *agents of violence*—executioners, warriors, and the "king's knives," who carry out orders and perform acts of destruction. The victims and the targets may or may not have special social identities, depending on the circumstances. Everyone in the system may be a target, but the process needs a regular selection of victims, who are dispatched according to variable rates of destruction. (1969:9)

Three of Walter's main points are particularly relevant. (1) While state terror is culturally variable, it exhibits important cross-cultural regularities; "it is a universal process formed by recurrent elements and organized in systems with regular structural features" (1969:viii). (2) Terror is a familiar—even normal as opposed to abnormal or extraordinary—

process in the history of states. It is not confined to "anomalous circumstances or exotic systems," but rather is potential in all state systems. Any state "can be transformed into a system of terror" (1969:10). (3) Terror is a choice, not a necessity. Instead of a "last resort" or *ultima ratio*, it is just as likely to represent the preferred resort, a *prima ratio protestatis* (1969:26). Walter asserts that the resort to terror is not the inexorable product of historical forces or in any sense inevitable. Rather, it is a social invention — a deliberate political choice and "one option, within cultural limits, in a range of alternative patterns" (1969:292). The sources and agents of terror voluntarily choose it because they receive material and other benefits. The rest of society faces a "forced choice": The terror regime creates a context in which a person must choose between the lesser of two evils — the obvious dangers of resistance, or relative safety and the potential advantage of cooperating with the regime; "the subjective alliance he [*sic*] makes with the officials shatters the solidarity of his own social group and reinforces his active cooperation with despotic power" (1969:286–287). Scholars of state terror have long demonstrated that under conditions of terror, the slimmest inducements can enlist people to cooperate with the system, and Walter concludes that "The secret of terroristic organization in states . . . combines the process of terror with the 'forced choice' and the competitive struggle for relative advantage" (1969:288–289).

Finally, Walter identified a shared ideology of state emergency — referring in particular to "collective fantasies" (1969:340; see Suarez-Orozco below) — that justifies the terror. He further revealed his humanist agenda, which echoes in the work of the leading contemporary anthropologists of state terror, when he suggested that "it may be possible to uncover the hidden mechanisms of terror, and for practical as well as theoretical reasons, learn not only its causes and functions, but also *the secrets of its termination*" (1969:11; emphasis added).

"Harvest of Violence" in Guatemala

> From the beginning *Harvest of Violence* was for us a humanistic undertaking. We have not tried to disguise our love and concern for the Mayas and their country, or the dangers we faced in telling their story.   (Carmack 1988:vii)

The first major anthropological book to respond to the escalation of state terror in Latin America in the 1970s and 1980s was Robert Carmack's edited volume *Harvest of Violence: The Maya Indians and the Guatemalan Crisis* (1988). This was not only the first anthropology book to deal comprehensively with state terror since Walter's *Terror and Resistance*, published nearly two decades earlier; it also included the first anthropological article specifically about the operation of a death squad at the local level (Paul and Demarest 1988). All of the contributors had conducted extensive fieldwork in Guatemala, and the chapters were written in response to the genocidal "counterinsurgency" policies of the Guatemalan government to explain what had been happening to the over three million Mayans since 1976. Almost everyone the authors of *Harvest of Violence* talked to in the course of their research had personal incidents to tell about family tragedy or loss, and many said that it was only *por la gracia de Dios* (by the grace of God) that they survived. They found that people lived constantly with the memories and anxieties of past and ongoing horrors, and about the location of refugees, displaced persons, and the "disappeared." Because these memories were all-pervasive, people began to refer to them as part of a more encompassing "culture of fear" in Guatemala that emerged in the Indian population as a result of the government's policies.

In his commentary on the volume, Adams (1988:275) noted that anthropologists "have not been in the forefront in the study of violence, terror, and war," saying:

When in the late 1970s events of the kind recounted herein were increasing, anthropologists had no ready response. Communities that had hospitably received scholars were now the scenes of bloody assassinations. Refugees began to appear, and word trickled out about close friends now dead or disappeared — not merely occasional deaths, but exterminations of whole families and communities. People well known to the anthropologists, people who they knew had little reason to become involved, were killed or "disappeared" — or so it was reported — because they were allegedly "guerrillas," "Communists," or "Marxist-Leninists." When they sought further information, the events were denied and travel threatened, and Indians who had been close to the missing were afraid to discuss the matter.

Adams also noted that "Latin-American scholars such as Gabriel Aguilera Peralta, Jorge Romero Imery, Ricardo Gallindo Gallardo, and Guillermo Monzon Paz [had] analyzed the results of terrorism from daily news reports; the last three named were killed for their efforts" (1988:275–276). In Guatemala, the saying "publish or perish" became literally "publish *and* perish," and anthropologists have also been killed and threatened for their involvement on the side of the Mayan victims of indiscriminate state terror. The three leading Guatemalan anthropologists have been Victor Montejo, Myrna Mack, and Ricardo Falla. As a result of their research, Montejo, a Mayan, was forced into exile in 1982, Mack was brutally assassinated by a soldier in 1990, and Falla lives in exile after being threatened by the Guatemalan army in 1992. Among the anthropologists who have worked in Guatemala, there is a strong sense of commitment and purpose, and some of them have literally been prepared to die for it.

Anthropological research with Guatemala's indigenous people has become difficult and dangerous, but it is also from anthropologists working in Guatemala that some of the best contemporary anthropological studies of state terror and resistance have emerged (see Falla 1994; Manz 1988; Montejo 1987; Wilson 1991; Green 1995). The example set by the contributors to *Harvest of Violence* is exemplary, has been emulated, and is representative of how anthropologists have responded to state terror since its publication.

Ricardo Falla

Ricardo Falla is a Guatemalan Jesuit priest with a Ph.D. in anthropology from the University of Texas, Austin. He has been described as "A world-class scholar, author of a long and distinguished list of publications, and a person of great integrity" (*Anthropology Newsletter*, April 1993, p. 14), and is frequently identified as Guatemala's foremost anthropologist (Carmack 1988:40). Falla spent some thirteen years on and off (1966–1979) doing fieldwork in Guatemala, primarily among the Indian and ladino peasants in the Ixcan, and in 1983 and 1984 he did fieldwork mostly in the Lacandon forest refugee camps in Mexico, studying the effects of the violence on Mayan refugees. In 1992 the results were published in Guatemala as *Masacres de la Selva* (Massacres in the Jungle), where it became an instant sensation and immediately sold out. In this and other major publications, he meticulously recorded the effects of the "scorched earth" counterinsurgency policies and provided the first detailed documentation of the Guatemalan "holocaust" of the 1970s and 1980s, concentrating on repression — "disappearances, torture, selective killings, executions of several people at a time, group massacres, and massive massacres of entire villages — in a word, genocide" (1994:4).[13]

In 1994 Falla's book was published in an English version with a foreword by Beatriz Manz, who commented that Falla is

> a committed anthropologist whose work presents a challenge to a new generation of concerned social scientists throughout the world . . . Few anthropologists could have gained the confidence of the people or the personal commitment to participate and be a witness in the way that Falla did. His documentation is so careful because he wants to accurately convey his country's painful history and, above all, because he cares deeply about the people he is writing about. Falla declares his commitment to the poor and to the Indians along with his contempt for the criminal actions of the military, emphatically condemning when something "is not right." His high ethical standards and exceptional scholarship shine throughout the research. (1994:xiii)

At the time that *Masacres de la Selva* was published in 1992, Falla returned to the Ixcan to conduct pastoral work and more fieldwork. He lived there under the most difficult conditions among the "population in resistance," displaced civilians organized into several communities who had been living for the past decade under the dense rainforest cover in order to hide from the military. In this remote and dangerous locale, he assumed the name "Marcos" to avoid detection by the army. But yet another army offensive, during which three Mayan communities where Falla worked were destroyed, forced the communities to flee once again. He fled with them, and in the assault and destruction that followed the army dis-covered a hidden deposit of material belonging to the Catholic Church's pastoral team. Among the many church records left behind were Falla's diary, some field notes, and a list of names of victims that appears in *Masacres de la Selva.* "The author of the famous book, Ricardo Falla, could now be placed among the population of resistance. The army, already stung by the authenticity of the material and the credibility of the author, jumped at the opportunity to 'prove' that Falla was a guerrilla commander and thereby discredit his writings. The book became '*un libro subversivo*' " (Manz 1994:xv). Declaring Falla a "subversive" and "guerrilla *coman-dante*" is the equivalent of a death sentence in Guatemala, and Manz recounts how Falla left the Ixcan to respond to these accusations, address-ing the Guatemalan people in a full-page ad in the press:

He answered the army's accusations, not by honoring them with a denial but by declaring instead who he [was], what he [had] been doing for the past six years, and why. He simply stated he was a priest and an anthropologist, left no doubt about his commitment to the poor, and denounced the army persecution of the civilian Indian population . . . This response gave Falla an opportunity to further discredit and deflate the military, create an awareness in Guatemala and the world of the population in resistance and his own work among them, and bring to the consciousness of every Guatemalan a painful hidden reality. Falla's eloquent moral arguments contrasted sharply with the military's tired rhetoric and ab-surd charges. In reaction to the military's provocation, the Guatemalan Catho-lic Church, the Jesuit Provincial order, and the academic community — both in Guatemala and internationally — all passionately jumped to Falla's defense. (Manz 1994:xv–xvi)

Nonetheless, the danger was too great and Falla was forced to abandon the country; he remains in exile.[14]

Falla's approach, and what he has to say about the purpose and mean-ing of anthropology, is potent and inspiring. As Manz (1995:262) ob-serves, "Falla's writings and intervention in international forums are all aspects of his unique approach, which encompasses full participation, acute observation, deep commitment, and witnessing." His view of an-thropology is anthropology at its best, where it can be employed as a powerful tool to help improve the quality of peoples' lives. He believes his duties include the service he can provide to the "poor and persecuted with the scientific instrument of anthropology," and ponders, "why did I study [anthropology] if I do not put it at the service of those most in need?" (in Manz 1995:xvi). Those research skills formed the factual basis for his denunciations of the Guatemalan military and the terrible massacres in the Ixcan.

Like Scheper-Hughes, Falla is convinced that neutrality is not an option, and he warns about the dangers of claiming neutrality under the rubric of cultural relativism. While we need to understand the actions of state terrorists from a theoretical point of view, this in no way precludes offering the judgement that these actions are unjust or wrong. In an interview with Manz (1995:265–266), he said:

You have to treat the army as a social agent, with its own rules of behavior. We have to try to understand these rules as if we ourselves were subject to them. At the same time we can't remain at that level, because then why have we done that study? . . . There are some things that are just deplorable. We can't fall into a cultural relativism trap by saying, well that's the way the army is, it's a military culture, and so they do all those things, and we must understand it, and the others have a culture of fatalism and we must understand that, too, and that's the end of it. We need a set of criteria that says there are some things that are simply unconscionable . . . It is mixing anthropology with a certain sense of justice. Justice means human rights. We have to judge, especially in a context of such terrible oppression like we have in Guatemala, with the bloodbath that has taken place. We can't just remain passive and study the massacres as a product of a military culture. We can't fall into that. We're striving to give strength to the voice of a people. We have to choose sides.

Falla argues that anthropologists should act as intermediaries, lending their voices on behalf of those who have witnessed and suffered terror, serving as scribes who document what people themselves narrate as their own histories. Falla narrates or "witnesses" what the victims of state terror have told him; this essentially represents the most common approach in the contemporary anthropology of state terror.

A Psychocultural Approach to State Terror

Like Guatemala, Argentina has emerged as one of the most studied "textbook cases" of state terror. Research stimulated by the so-called dirty war during the second half of the 1970s has helped lead the way in the development of the anthropology of state terror. Examples include the work of Marcelo Suarez-Orozco (described below) and Julie Taylor (1993), who reminds us that Argentina "has the dubious distinction of adding the word *desaparecido* to the world's vocabulary." Terror is simultaneously a subjective experience (or psychic state), and the thing that terrifies — the violent event that produces the state of fear — and where in 1969 E. V.

Walter emphasized the structures and processes of terror, contemporary anthropologists have led the way in considering its subjective and psychological aspects. One of the best examples of this is the work of Marcelo Suarez-Orozco.

Suarez-Orozco's psychocultural approach to state terror represents one of the leading examples of a contemporary, postmodern ethnographic approach which succeeds in avoiding neutrality and in writing against terror, while maintaining high standards of scientific objectivity. His writings succeed in conveying to readers the perspectives of both the victims *and* perpetrators of state terror, while making no bones about who is responsible for it, and he seeks "to illustrate how, through psychologically informed ethnographic work, we can give a voice to the voiceless" (1990: 354).

In his work (see 1987, 1990, 1992), Suarez-Orozco has delineated the "grammar" or underlying structure of terror, and explored a number of key psychological aspects of political terror and resistance in dirty war and post–dirty war Argentina, which he argues reveals an "isomorphic underlying pattern to the Central American responses to political terror" (1990:354). He observes that other approaches to state terror have emphasized its instrumental and rational ("functional") aspects, and often fail to "pay sufficient attention to the irrational and expressive aspects of terror" (1992:227). An example of his evocative approach comes from an important article on state terror and the abuse of children in the dirty war:

A particular ritual devised by those running the Argentine death machinery was the torture of children in full view of their parents, and vice versa. We shall explore the meaning of such specific forms of torture. Each time an agent discharges an electrical current through the body of an infant in front of his/her parents, or through the penis or vagina of "subversives," in front of their children, a perverse poly-semantic ritual is enacted. These rituals can be explored as meaningful "texts" telling a horror story about our times. Our task here is to decode the messages, both hidden and overt, in the historical rediscovery of torture in the Argentine chambers of death. In these ghastly texts, children emerge as valuable commodities to be strategically exploited in a demented "dirty war" fought between the Security Forces and their phantom, demonic enemies. (1987:227–228)

In his writing, Suarez-Orozco uses unconventional terminology and applies concepts from clinical psychology to sociopolitical conditions. While he presents the "grammar" or structure and logic of justifications and rationalizations Latin American state terrorists have presented for the "necessity" of systematic murder and torture, he has also revealed the paranoid psychology of state terror and death squads. He describes the dirty war as "psychotic," analyzes the "hysterical denial" of the civilian population, and dissects the political "fantasies," "hallucinations," "collective delusions," and particularly the "paranoid ethos" that "afflicted" the perspective of the elite and military. In a "paranoid atmosphere," he argues, terror becomes an intrinsic part of the military's political mission.[15]

Cultures of Terror

One of the most important concepts developed and employed by anthropologists of terror and resistance is that of "cultures of terror." Suarez-Orozco (1987), for example, has described the culture of terror that evolved during the dirty war in Argentina. There, in what has turned out to be a very common pattern, what began as a counterinsurgency effort against left-wing guerrillas evolved into a culture of terror aimed at "pacifying" the civilian population as a whole:

As the military grip on civilian institutions became increasingly formalised, a new repressive horror descended on the Argentine consciousness. After its successful war with the armed left, the security forces turned their 'dirty war' apparatus upon as yet innocent but "potentially dangerous" civilians. What ensued was an unpredictable deployment of terror by the security forces and those working for them. Anyone thought to be sympathising with the left, or in any way opposing the military regime became a possible target for kidnapping. The term *desaparecido* ("disappeared one") with its unspoken connotations of death and torture, became part of the new Argentine vocabulary of sorrow. Soon everyone knew a *desaparecido*. All segments of society had become touched by the spreading terror. (1987:230)

The culture of terror concept emerges largely from three sources — research in colonial or Third World societies, particularly Latin America (e.g., Corradi et al. 1992), research on U.S. intervention in these societies (Herman 1982; Chomsky 1988), and, in anthropology, the seminal work of Michael Taussig (1984, 1987, 1992), subsequently developed by others like Suarez-Orozco and Linda Green (1995), who has written about the "culture of fear" in Guatemala. Taussig argues that where political torture and murder become endemic, cultures of terror flourish. The basic characteristics of cultures of terror is that these are societies where "order" (more precisely, the order of stratification or social inequality) and the politicoeconomic status quo can only be maintained by the permanent, massive, and systematic use or threat of violence and intimidation by the state as a means of political control. A culture of terror is an institutionalized system of permanent intimidation of the masses or subordinated communities by the elite, characterized by the use of torture and disappearances and other forms of extrajudicial "death squad" killings as standard practice. A culture of terror establishes "collective fear" as a brutal means of social control. In such a system, there is an ever present threat of repression, torture, and, ultimately, death for anyone who is actively critical of the politicoeconomic status quo: "Rumors of death lists and denunciations, gossip, and innuendos create a climate of suspicion. No one can be sure who is who. The spectacle of torture and death, of massacres and disappearances . . . became deeply inscribed in individuals and in the collective imagination through a constant sense of threat" (Green 1995:105). When fear becomes a way of life, as it did in Argentina and Guatemala, a culture of terror has emerged.

Dangers of Writing Against Terror

Most, if not all, of those who do research on state terror run the risk of suffering recriminations, even to the extent of themselves becoming targets for torture and/or death squad attacks, and all of the anthropologists I know who have taken this path have been threatened in one form or another. There is real personal danger for anthropologists who dare to speak and write against terror; by doing so, they potentially and sometimes actually bring the terror down on themselves. Anthropologists, like other social scientists and journalists[16] courageous enough to write about terror and human rights abuses, run the risk of censorship and reprisal.

The dangers emanating from state authorities include the risks of harassment, intimidation, physical assault, arrest, interrogation, torture, persecution, prosecution, imprisonment, and, ultimately, execution or assassination. Other dangers include being defined as a sympathizer with antigovernment "radicals," "activists," "subversives" or "terrorists," or being accused of giving aid and comfort to them ("the enemy"). It is most dangerous when anthropologists write about terror taking place in their own countries of origin, but the risk does not end when they leave the field or even the country where they do their fieldwork. Along with the physical dangers, other "occupational hazards" include that authorities may deny or revoke permission for their research, and that they may receive frequent, sometimes vehement criticism by other academics attacking their objectivity, accusing them of partisanship, and questioning their professional ethics (see Swedenburg 1989, 1995; and Bourgois 1991). Below, I consider examples of the physical danger and some of the epistemological dangers or difficulties inherent in the ethnography of state terror.

Physical Danger: Casualties Among Anthropologists

Anthropologists have been both indirect and direct victims of state terror and death squads; many have been threatened, and at least four have been killed "on the job" as a result of their research relating to state terror. Guatemalan anthropologist Ricardo Falla and Indonesian anthropologist George Aditjondro both live under the threat of state-sanctioned assassination if they return to their countries from exile. I know of four anthropologists who have been killed for speaking and writing against terror:

- In 1982 South African anthropologist and antiapartheid campaigner Ruth First was killed by a mail bomb in her office at Maputo University in Mozambique, generally believed to have been sent by South African secret service agents.
- In 1984 Melanesian anthropologist Arnold Ap was tortured and killed in West Papua by the Indonesian army, and his body dumped into the sea from a helicopter. The army said he was involved with the Free Papua Movement (OPM) but had "escaped," and denied responsibility for his death. (This "escape corridor" dirty trick is described in Aditjondro's chapter in this volume.)
- In 1989 South African anthropologist David Webster was shot dead from the back of a speeding van while out walking his dogs. An antiapartheid and human rights activist and lecturer at the University of Witwatersrand, he was killed by a proapartheid death squad.
- In 1990 Guatemalan anthropologist Myrna Mack was brutally murdered, stabbed twenty-seven times by a then unknown assassin, in the street as she left her research office in Guatemala City. The killer turned out to be a soldier, and her death has been linked to the army and other high officials in Guatemala.[17] Mack was well known for her work with Mayan refugees in the Ixcan, studying the effects of the brutal counterinsurgency war of the early 1980s.[18]

All four of these anthropologists were activist scholars. I do not know if they represent anthropological "martyrs"; I suspect they did not die for anthropology, but rather for the people whom they spoke out on behalf of. But because they did die *doing* anthropology—they knew the danger, and chose to continue their work and face the consequences—they are as close to martyrs as the discipline is likely to get.

Epistemological Dangers

During the academic turmoil surrounding the Vietnam War, Laura Nader (1969:289) was among the first to suggest that anthropologists should move toward "studying up"—that is, studying "the colonizers rather than the colonized, the culture of power rather than the culture of powerlessness, the culture of affluence rather than the culture of poverty." Nearly three decades later, we are still only beginning to do this. So far, the anthropological attempt to study state terrorists has focused on studying up the commanders and organizers who give the orders, rather than the rank and file who actually apply the electric cattle prods and pull the triggers. Very little fieldwork has been done with rank and file death squad members themselves,[19] but a number of anthropologists have interviewed or otherwise worked with generals and other high-ranking officials responsible for state terror. For example, Julie Taylor (1993) worked with a dissident army major; Antonius Robben (1995) interviewed a number of generals responsible for terror during the dirty war in Argentina; and Orin Starn (1994) interviewed a general responsible for death squads in Peru.

From these experiences, we are learning that ethnographic fieldwork with perpetrators of state terror involves not only the obvious physical dangers, but also a number of unique epistemological, methodological, and ethical difficulties, which we are only beginning to recognize and work our way through. We have already referred to Falla's warning (in Manz 1995) about the necessity of avoiding neutrality under the rubric of cultural relativism, and Scheper-Hughes's assertion (1995) that cultural relativism, read as moral relativism, is not appropriate in the terror-filled world in which we live. Three other emergent difficulties are ethnographic seduction, misrepresentation, and moving from prior research on resistance to new research on terror.

Ethnographic Seduction

As a result of his research with Argentine generals, Antonius Robben (1996) has warned of the dangers of "ethnographic seduction."[20] Robben simultaneously studied both victims and perpetrators of violence and state terror, and few anthropologists have had his experience: "There were days when I talked in the morning to a victim of political persecution and in the afternoon with a military officer who had been responsible for the repression. These days were stressful because they demanded radical swings in empathetic understanding" (1996:97).

Robben first realized the importance of seduction as a dimension of fieldwork "through the elaborate display of *caballerosidad* (gentleman-likeness) and the barrage of kindness and courtesy bestowed on me by several Argentine generals" (1996:73):

My military interlocutors must have known that the image I had received abroad — and which they reckoned was being confirmed in my talks with their political opponents — was one of officers torturing babies and ordering the disappearance of tens of thousands of innocent Argentine civilians. I had, of course, anticipated their denial of these serious accusations, but I did not expect to be meeting with military men who exuded great civility and displayed a considerable knowledge of literature, art, and classical music. The affability and chivalry of the officers clashed with the trial records I had read, affected my critical sensibility, and in the beginning led me astray from my research focus. It was only later that I realized that I had been engrossed in ethnographic seduction. (1995:83)

Robben interviewed one general who was under indictment for ordering disappearances and for rape and torture by the men under his command (subsequently released from criminal prosecution by a presidential decree), who saved Robben from being run over by a taxi.[21]

Robben was already sensitive to the risks to objectivity in doing research with victims of state terror, aware that it is easy in face-to-face research to be "seduced" by their obvious emotion and suffering. But he did not anticipate that this would be a problem when studying up state terrorists. He found that it was; the general and other military officers treated him well and with respect, and stressed their class affinities with him (well educated, elite, bourgeois): "Although my initial sympathy and tolerance of personal idiosyncrasies was greater with members of human rights organizations than with the armed forces, I soon met officers whose politics I detested but for whom I felt a personal liking" (1996: 99–100).

Once sensitized to this, Robben then found that he also recognized it in his subsequent meetings with bishops, human rights activists, and former guerrilla leaders, and that "each group was seductive in its own way" (1995:83). He observes that "It is much easier to acknowledge manipulation by victimizers than by victims. We have more sympathy for unmasking abusers of power than doubting the words of their victims. I have the same sympathies" (1995:84). But he argues that seduction "disarms our critical detachment" (1995:86), and that "victims may be harmed and their testimonies discredited if we report their views naively and uncritically" (1995:84).[22]

Misrepresentation: Humanizing the Inhumane?

In 1991, Orin Starn interviewed General Luis Perez Documet, who was in charge of a campaign of state terror in Peru's central highlands. Starn described the general as "a semimythical figure of fear in his part of the world. Under his rule, the mutilated bodies of suspected Shining Path sympathizers snatched off the streets of Huancayo by armed men in Jeep Cherokees would be discovered at dawn on the garbage-strewn banks of the Mantaro River. As organizer of these death squads, [he] had earned the nickname 'General Tutu' — an allusion to the skirts of a malevolent fairy who can make people vanish forever with the touch of a wand" (1994:13). When Starn later published an article in a Peru news monthly about this interview, which he believed revealed the "ugliness" of the general's rule, he was surprised to find that it was misrepresented in subsequent media reports: "Already active in human rights work in the Peruvian Andes, I worried that criticism of one of Peru's highest-ranking generals might get me kicked out of the country. It was with considerable surprise, then, that I found myself cited in several subsequent newspaper stories as a North American 'expert' who had found the command of Perez 'effective and impeccable.' The general himself, reported a Peruvian journalist friend, liked the article for portraying him on the offensive against the Maoist rebels" (1994:13). What Starn perceived as an act of writing against terror, was instead misrepresented and employed to produce the opposite effect: "I had touched up the image of a protagonist in Peru's dirty war" (1994:14).

One difficulty with studying up state terrorists is that anthropology is based on a relationship of trust and empathetic understanding and tends strongly to humanize the ethnographic "other." Humanizing state terrorists may have unanticipated negative consequences, and may be misrepresented and misapplied by the apologists of terror as a sort of defense of their position, perspectives, and actions.

From Resistance to Terror

Robben could simultaneously study agents of both terror and resistance because the dirty war was essentially over and it was safe enough to do this (though even after the end of the war, terror continues in Argentina; see Taylor 1993). If he had tried to do this *during* the dirty war it would probably have been impossible, and he possibly would have been killed. In the context of ongoing terror and conflict, it is particularly difficult and dangerous for anthropologists who have done research on victims and resistance to try to shift or expand their research to interviewing state terrorists. While those who have studied victims and resistance are under increasing pressure to study up state terrorists, the risks of doing so are frequently dramatic or extraordinary. Frank M. Afflitto has poignantly highlighted this difficulty:

More thoughts on why NOT to do research with death squad members. These people usually want something for their testimonies, such as amnesty for their crimes/actions. Some of these people, for instance, the ex-agents who want to get things off their chests, it seems to me, might be useful sources of information and willing to talk. But to me it is doubtful that an anthropologist/ethnographer can safely be in a country where death squads are active and powerful and carry out successful research that, to me, is worth the risk to one's life. Guatemalan death squads are so sick that they often kill their own operatives after periods of time of using their services so that there are no witnesses. If Guatemalan death squads kill their own lower level operatives, as it were, why would they hesitate to bop off a foreign anthropologist who had previously performed participatory action research with popular movement organizations calling, internationally, for an end to their activities, and on whom they have a file and who they tried to intimidate and more subtly play with more than once? Your case is quite similar, I am sure. There may be ways, however, to speak with former Civil Patrol people in Guatemala, for instance, who did things locally and were under army orders or pressure. But the highly-integrated people from the apparatuses who show such ruthlessness in their past actions cannot be trusted to provide immunity for political/social anthropologists. They are so low, that they may kill some innocent Guatemalan, horribly torturing him/her, just to get you to stop writing your book, collecting your data, or to turn over your data to them. Too many risks involved. (correspondence, April 1997)

Afflitto suggested that "instead of doing a book on the deadly work of ethnographies of death squads, the perpetrators, I would most certainly get my brains blown out, believe me, why don't we do a book on ethnography and participatory fieldwork in situations of state terror/death squad societies? Sounds safer, relevant, and will bring to light many of the death squad operations vicariously" (correspondence). As this volume indicates, while the trend is toward studying up state terrorists, ethnography based on fieldwork with victims and survivors is still the main approach in the anthropology of state terror.

Forensic/Physical Anthropology and Archaeology Against Terror

Cultural anthropologists have not been the only anthropologists who have sought to work against terror. Since about 1990, forensic/physical anthropologists and archaeologists have been involved in excavating mass graves and exhuming the bodies of victims of genocide, war, and state terror (e.g., death squad victims) in many places around the world, to gather evidence to corroborate verbal testimony of survivors in order to prosecute those responsible. They have worked or are working now in Guatemala, Argentina, Bolivia, Chile, and other countries in Latin America, as well as in the Philippines, Haiti, Bosnia, Croatia, Romania, Iraqi Kurdistan, and Rwanda.

The use of forensic anthropology and archaeological techniques in the context of human rights abuses is a relatively new but growing field with only a handful of international practitioners, many of them trained by Clyde Snow, the eminent forensic anthropologist from the University of Oklahoma. Snow has applied his skills to exposing atrocities committed by state agents, overseen exhumations in most of the countries where this work has been done, and trained many other forensic anthropologists from these and other countries to do this work as well. Snow observes that

The great mass murderers of our time have accounted for no more than a few hundred victims. In contrast, states that have chosen to murder their own citizens can usually count their victims by the carload lot. As for motive, the state has no peers, for it will kill its victims for a careless word, a fleeting thought, or even a poem . . . But the homicidal state shares one trait with the solitary killer — like all murderers, it trips on its own egotism and drops a trail of clues which, when properly collected, preserved, and analyzed are as damning as a signed confession left in the grave. (Cited in Amnesty International 1992:11)

During the course of their investigations, many of the members of these forensic teams have received serious death threats, and sometimes they have had to be accompanied at all times by military escorts for protection (see Anonymous 1996; Edelman 1996b; Skomal 1996; Connor 1997; Perez 1997). They have also had their own epistemological problems. For example, while in many cases remains can be identified and returned to the families, "providing a closure they would never have otherwise reached" (Connor 1997:30), there has been some criticism by families of victims that this closure is not always the one they necessarily wanted. In Argentina, the Mothers of Plaza de Mayo — an organization of women with disappeared loved ones — opposed exhumations, saying that "they want to make us mothers of dead people, we are mothers of disappeared" (cited in Suarez-Orozco 1992:246).

Nonetheless, Rebecca Saunders, who was part of a forensic team exhuming bodies in the Balkans, described the work as "very fulfilling," and explained that "It is important to prosecute those people who, through their arrogance, thought that no one would pursue them for their crimes. I am optimistic that because we now have the techniques, we will be able to demonstrate their culpability in a legal forum. This kind of legal action is the only way to forestall such crimes in the future" (Skomal 1996:6).

Toward an Anthropological Theory of State Terror

> In recent decades, parts of the world have clearly become more repressive, and presently we have no adequate explanation of why this has happened. If we believe in political freedom, we must try to understand why repression has grown and do something about it.
> (McCamant 1984:37)

Nagengast has suggested that the challenge to anthropologists is to "locate [violence] within a set of practices, discourses, and ideologies, to explain it as a way to deploy power within differential social and political relations, or as *a means that states use to buttress themselves and to maintain power*" (1994:111, emphasis added). She observes that the social order "need not be objectively precarious for the heavy hand of the state to be felt" (1994:120), but I believe that the precariousness of the social order is the main cause of the contemporary global spread of state terror. In this section, I present an outline of an anthropologically informed theory of state terror adequate to our times. I argue that the most promising approach is a power-conflict theory that focuses on the operation of elites within a global system of social stratification. As McCamant suggests, "we must focus on rulers who control the means of coercion and how they use coercion against the population to enforce their interests and belief systems. Rulers fit into a structure of power that goes from the local community to the great empires of the United States and Soviet Union" (1984:37).

It is not coincidental that the global decline in human rights and rise in state terror corresponds with the rise of the New Right in the West and the emergent global hegemony of economic neoliberalism, particularly the rise of the Reagan and Thatcher governments and their successors in the United States and the United Kingdom, and the influence this has had on their Third World client states. Starting in the early 1980s, these governments abandoned a previous emphasis in international relations on human rights and replaced it with an emphasis on combating "terrorism," and it is with the propaganda of "fighting terrorism" that states who employ terror most frequently justify their actions. The rise of cultures of terror seems to correlate almost exactly with the rise and spread of the New Right, and I believe this is the fundamental causal link explaining the monumental rise in state terrorism in the last quarter of the twentieth century. In response to increasing popular resistance resulting from the rapidly widening gap between the rich and poor all over the world, states have increasingly resorted to violence and its threat to contain this resistance and protect the economic and political domination of local and international elites.

There appear to be two major theories of why state terror has grown so rapidly in the last quarter of the twentieth century. One is a basically structural-functional theory that terror results from the inherent *weakness* of the modern state, evidenced in the growing number of states suffering "crises of integration"; they are rent by social divisions and lack "internal cohesion," and elite control and the legitimacy of the state are actively challenged. In such circumstances, there is a "functional necessity" to resort to violence to "maintain order," counteract these fissiparous tendencies, and hold the polity together. Second is a power-conflict theory that terror results from the *strength* of the state and the massive and ever increasing concentration of power in the hands of national and international elites. Strong states unafraid of the consequences of the direct application of force to achieve their ends are the result of the concentration and application of unchecked power. Terror states do not emerge because violence is necessary, but rather because elites choose to rely on it, believing that it is a rational and cost-effective means to achieve their politicoeconomic ends — namely, to preserve and advance their privilege within the system of social stratification. Terror is here conceived as primarily a strategy or weapon exploited in a system of concentrated power. Elites who resort to terror do not do it because the state is weak, but rather because they are strong and can get away with it.

In some ways, the first theory tends to blame resistance to elite domination for the terror, because it asserts that state violence is mainly a reaction to growing popular resistance and challenges to elite rule, rather than a conscious and rational strategy employed in its own right. The second theory tends to put the blame more where it belongs, with the elites who choose to rely on it. It does not argue that terror is mainly a necessary reaction to resistance, but rather is the result of unbridled power, sometimes occurring even when there is no threat to elite rule. As noted above, Rummel (1994) argues that as power increases the likelihood of its abuse increases as well. Similarly, Chomsky and Herman argue that the reason torture has reemerged as a global scourge is due to "the fact that the greatest super power on earth finds regimes that torture *useful* and thus torture thrives and the Free World has learned to look the other way" (Herman 1982:131, emphasis added). This can be said about almost every other state in the world, nearly all of whom are apparently prepared to tolerate if not actively support state terror at home and abroad when it is in their "national (read elite) interest" to do so. One important corollary of this rational, power-conflict theory of terror is the contention that the way to reduce or combat it is to make it too costly to perpetrators—to change the cost-benefit ratio. Theoretically, at least, when it is no longer "cost-effective" for elites to employ terror they will resort to other less bloody means.

These two theories of the growth of state terror—structural-functional and power-conflict—correspond to the traditional anthropological consensus and conflict theories of the evolution, function, and nature of the state (see Nagengast 1994:116). Rummel has observed that there is still a tendency to take a functional or consensus view of the state, emphasizing its role in maintaining law and order, individual security, cultural maintenance, and social welfare:

Political scientists are still writing this stuff, when we have numerous examples of governments that kill hundreds of thousands and even millions of their own citizens, enslave the rest, and abolish traditional culture . . . Then there is the common and fundamental justification of government that it exists to protect citizens against the anarchic jungle that would otherwise threaten their lives and property. Such archaic or sterile views show no appreciation of [state mass murder] and all its related horrors and suffering. They are inconsistent with a regime that stands astride society like a gang of thugs over hikers they have captured in the woods, robbing all, raping some, torturing others for fun, murdering those they don't like, and terrorizing the rest into servile obedience. This exact characterization of many past and present governments . . . hardly squares with conventional political science. (1994:25–26)

Walter's analysis in *Terror and Resistance*, while going beyond structural-functionalism, still suffers from the weaknesses of that approach. His emphasis (or bias) is on order rather than conflict,[23] and while he argues that regimes of terror are basically a functional response to "crises of integration," he fails to identify the cause or nature of these crises, which result from social stratification and its fundamental relationship to the state, and therefore his theory is insufficient as an explanation for state terror today.

Both the power of the elite and the degree of social inequality have grown hugely in the last two to three decades. It strikes me that the growth in state terror is fundamentally linked to the continuing growth in the concentration of power in the hands of the power elite, and the increase in the social inequality and stratification — the ever widening gap between rich and poor, within countries and between them — which every social observer has noted as one of the main characteristics of the global scene since the rise of the New Right in the West in the 1970s. There appears to be a direct correlation between the increasing power and wealth of the elite, the steadily increasing gap between rich and poor, and the growth of state terror, perhaps the three most obvious global characteristics of the last quarter of the twentieth century. I suggest that state terror is a dependent variable in the equation of inequality, not the independent variable many elites, governments, and establishment "terrorism experts" (see Herman and O'Sullivan 1989) claim it to be.

Social stratification is the central feature of the state and civilization, and Gerald Berreman, Morton Fried, John Bodley, and other like-minded anthropologists have emphasized it as the most dangerous feature of contemporary society. Berreman, who has dedicated his professional life to the study of systems of social inequality, has observed that social stratification "refers to the fact that some categories of people get more of the valued things in life and others get less; a few get most, and most get the rest. Some live well and long; some live poorly and briefly. There is a ranking, in other words, of access to goods, services and experiences — to what the social theorist Max Weber called 'life chances.' There are national elites and international elites; the national poor and international poor. There are rich nations and poor nations" (1980:8). Bodley has argued that social stratification is linked to all of our major contemporary human problems, and is the most fundamental characteristic of civilization "from which other critical problem-causing features are ultimately derived" (1985:217). Social stratification leads to such conflict-inducing factors as the market economy; ethnic, religious, and ideological discrimination; socioeconomic deprivation; political inequality and its correlates such as infringement of rights, injustice, and oppression; the absence of effective channels of peaceful or systemic resolution of grievances and conflicts; exploitation and alienation; and, apropos our topic, state terror to maintain and defend the order of stratification against challenges to elite rule and the social, economic, and political status quo.

These anthropologists have also stressed the link between social stratification and the state. Fried (1967:235) defines the state as "a collection of specialized institutions and agencies that maintain an order of stratification," and Berreman (1980:8) observes that "stratification and the state are one in origin; one in function — creation, protection and continuation of the powerful and privileged at the expense of the rest." Fried also notes that

It is the task of maintaining general social order that stands at the heart of the development of the state. And at the heart of the problem of maintaining general order is the need to defend the central order of stratification . . . Undoubtedly . . . one means of doing this is to indoctrinate all members of society with the belief that the social order is right or good or simply inevitable. But there has never been a state which survived on this basis alone. Every state known to history has had a physical apparatus for removing or otherwise dealing with those who failed to get the message. (1967:230–231)

Physical power alone is not sufficient to integrate a state. Integration must be based on legitimacy, not just force. The crisis of the state at the turn of the century is that as social inequality grows, the ideological bases of state legitimacy are breaking down. Increasing numbers of people — the masses — are politically alienated, and when popular legitimacy cannot be maintained by ideological means, elites rely on force — on terror — to protect and advance their interests. For the state and power elite, where consensus fails, coercion rules.

Berreman has argued that systems of social stratification are "everywhere characterised by conformity rather than consensus, by conflict rather than tranquillity, by enforcement rather than by endorsement, by resentment rather than by contentment" (1977:229), and what he observed over twenty years ago seems to be even truer today: "Naked power is being resorted to more unabashedly as the conflict becomes more evident . . . the incidence, the likelihood and the impact of overt conflict between individuals is increasing both within and between societies and nations . . . Present trends suggest a worldwide polarisation in access to power, privilege and resources — the gap between the 'haves' and the 'have nots' increases with a diminishing willingness among the poor to continue to suffer deprivation, and among the wealthy to ameliorate it" (1977:236). All the major world problems are growing at an accelerated rate, and the gap between the few who have much and the many who have little, between rich and poor, between developed nations and developing ones, is growing ever wider. Karl Marx, who argued that this was the inevitable result of free-market capitalism, referred to this process as "progressive emiseration." It should be no surprise that in an era of increasing global emiseration, states and elites have resorted increasingly to terror to contain challenges to the politicoeconomic status quo. Like other social crises, state terror is a dependent variable in the equation of inequality.

Conclusion

> Indifference is the worst enemy of human rights. Today, perhaps more than ever, the world needs an immense humanitarian upsurge if it is to resist violence and the abuse of power — a form of madness known to be contagious.   (ICIHI 1986:93)

George Aditjondro (this volume) has simply but succinctly identified the single main reason why those anthropologists who study state terror have chosen to do so: "In order to fight the beast, you have to know it first, and know it well." Anthropologists who write against terror choose sides in the sense that they are prepared to pursue the values of humanism and politics of truth, and take the position that state terror in general — but political torture and murder in particular — are completely unacceptable, unconscionable, and culturally indefensible. They argue that we cannot remain neutral; we must stand opposed to terror and actively seek ways to prevent or ameliorate it, just like other abuses which have long featured in the sad list of violations of human rights explicitly forbidden by international conventions and declarations. This is not to say we should lose our scientific objectivity or critical independence; but at the same time, not to stand on the side of the oppressed and victims of terror is to abandon anthropology as a humane and socially relevant discipline with a contribution to make to improving the human condition, particularly of those Fanon (1967) termed "the wretched of the earth," and not just of the rich and powerful, whom Mills (1959) so aptly described as "the power elite." In writing against terror, anthropologists could do worse than to be identified as "principled moralists who wish to make this world better" (D'Andrade 1995:400 n.).

Anthropological work on terror must be part of an overall political or humanist agenda of resistance to terror in the service of alleviating human suffering and misery (the Enlightenment vision). As those who have advocated the decolonization of the discipline have observed, we "chose the wrong side a long time ago" (Gordon 1991:153): This time, we need to pick the right side. By standing for human rights and against terror, we are taking an important step toward an emancipatory, decolonized anthropology appropriate to the human issues of our time. The issues are urgent, the cruelty and hypocrisy is mind-boggling, and critical views need to be heard.

The only real leverage anthropologists can hope to exercise lies in public exposure, in breaking the silence that surrounds and nurtures terror. As the ICIHI observed, "Public opinion must be kept constantly on the alert. If it is allowed to forget or become indifferent, we may lose one of the most effective forces for progress on human rights, and against the violence and periodic relapses into barbarity which can overcome civilization. It is in awareness, of the individual, of the community, of society as a whole, that the greatest hope lies" (1986:94). To help counterbalance the state and resist its use of violence, anthropologists can apply their skills to gather information about state terror and publish it as widely as possible. It is clear that public statements and the publication of reports provide at least moral and sometimes practical support for victims, dissidents, and activists, and can prevent further abuses, including torture, disappearances, and extrajudicial death squad killings. There are many concrete examples which attest to the effectiveness of such reporting and the importance of international support. As the work of Amnesty International illustrates, such actions frequently have a deterrent effect, since governments are often more sensitive to public criticism than one may believe.

Though politically and economically weak, we can cause the strong to think again; we can keep a close watch on governments, challenge them, attribute responsibility, and enhance public awareness by providing firsthand evidence, and we can serve as nerve centers for information and action. Anthropologists should also support the ratification of human rights treaties and the implementation of international human rights accords, and encourage governments to implement the Amnesty International programs for the prevention of torture, disappearances, and extrajudicial executions (see Amnesty International 1993:350–353), and other international instruments, including the UN Declaration on the Protection of All Persons from Enforced Disappearances.

To paraphrase the argument presented by Chomsky and Herman, state terrorists will continue to escalate the violence to whatever level is required to preserve elite control *if they can get away with it*. National and international elites have shown themselves to be quite comfortable with the most ruthless governments, but entirely unconcerned with the indiscriminate and wholesale torture and murder of civilians. They will only be slowed down and reversed by a serious and determined opposition. It has been demonstrated that ordinary people, organizing and acting at the grass roots, can affect policy.

While the risks are considerable, there is a significant payoff in taking the risks of decolonizing the discipline and writing against terror. For example, as Manz has observed, "Until recently few Guatemalans had ever heard of the profession of anthropology. In the innumerable press reports since Myrna Mack's assassination, however, she is always referred to as '*la antropóloga* Myrna Mack.' As a result, anthropology has become an honored, widely known and admired profession. It has become synonymous with courage, social consciousness, and first-rate scholarship" (1994: xiii). That is certainly the most positive and encouraging statement about the discipline that I have heard in a very long time, in the midst of an era when anthropologists have been severely criticized by our Third and Fourth World interlocutors. I also take great encouragement from sentiments expressed by anthropologists like Frank M. Afflitto, who wrote:

The Palestinians, when I had the opportunity to be in the Intifada for three weeks in 1989 in the West Bank, had a saying that "*Ya Tikum Al Afiyeh*," which means "May God give you strength in the struggle." Once you've seen two year olds in diapers running up to Israeli soldiers and flashing them the V for victory sign, you know that state terror has some inherent weaknesses. Death and torture may NOT be the worst of alternatives for all people in a society. Maybe some of us would rather struggle for the truth, for justice, for an end to oppression without worrying so much about what might happen to us, rather, worrying more about what will keep happening to us, collectively, if we do nothing. (correspondence, April 1997)

Notes

1. As in a "reign of terror."
2. One notable exception is genocide studies (see Horowitz 1976; Kuper 1981; Mey 1984; Chalk and Jonassohn 1990; Staub 1992; Andreopoulos 1995; Strozier and Flynn 1996). On anthropology and genocide, see Hinton (1996) and Connor (1989). Most of these scholars take a basically psychological anthropology approach. Another emerging exception is torture studies (see Agger and Jensen 1996; Gordon and Marton 1995; Duner 1998).
3. See Zulaika and Douglass (1996) for a devastating anthropological critique of the validity of the concept of "terrorism." For other critiques, see especially Herman (1982); Herman and O'Sullivan (1989); and Chomsky (1986).
4. The ICIHI (1986:39–40) explains the fundamental attraction and significance of disappearance as a technique of political terror: "Why bother with justifications which may be disputed, or with conspicuous political trials and public executions? Why incur the condemnation of the international community? Why saddle oneself with political prisoners who arouse sympathy, or executions which fan the flames of opposition and lend it a glow of martyrdom? Arranging a disappearance is a distinctly more 'refined' solution. It is quick, and leaves no trace. It allows the authorities to claim that their hands are clean. The most effective means of terror is to strike with no explanation. In this sense, the practice of disappearances represents the acme of despotism — a form of despotism which dares not say its name and which destroys the very foundations of society. To abandon the law and the most elementary moral principles, and resort instead to underhand methods, is in itself an acknowledgment of illegitimacy."

5. As one of the generals who directed the dirty war in Argentina in the 1970s and early 1980s once put it, "First we will kill all the subversives; then we will kill their collaborators; then . . . their sympathizers, then . . . those who remain indifferent; and finally we will kill the timid" (cited in Suarez-Orozco 1992:235).

6. These calculations do not include the combatants killed in wars; if these are included the figure would be over 203 million people (Rummel 1994:13).

7. On the shifting patterns of the international arms trade, see Klare 1996. Since the collapse of the Soviet Union a new post–Cold War paradigm of global arms trafficking has emerged, characterized by "the unrivalled dominance of the USA in the global arms traffic" (between 1987 and 1990 the U.S. provided 21 percent of arms transfers to Third World states; between 1991 and 1994 they accounted for 48 percent [1996:861]), and "the primacy of economic (as against ideological and geopolitical) motives for arms exports" (1996:859).

8. There is a large body of evidence that U.S. training and aid programs have directly and indirectly encouraged and promoted torture and death squads (see Omang and Neier 1985; Edelman 1996c; Haugaard 1997).

9. As noted, Latin America and Asia are the two main areas identified by Amnesty International as centers of growth of state terror, and two more of the most significant books to emerge on state terrorism are *Fear at the Edge: State Terror and Resistance in Latin America* (Corradi et al., 1992), and *The Fearful State: Power, People and Internal War in South Asia* (Ali 1993). These are written by Third World scholars, many of whom were eyewitnesses to the terror they write about.

10. Johan Galtung suggests that the New World Order can be divided into seven spheres or regions (the U.S., Europe, Japan, Russia, China, India, and Islam), six of them headed by well-known hegemonic powers. "One 'hegemon' is *prima inter pares*, the hegemons' hegemon: The United States of America" (1997: 188).

11. For example, Lan 1985; Ranger 1985; Zulaika 1988; Bourque and Warren 1989; Sluka 1989, 1995; Falla 1991; Feldman 1991; Nordstrom and Martin 1992; Stoll 1993; Warren 1993a, 1993b; Pettigrew 1995; Mahmood 1996; Nordstrom 1997; and McKenna 1997.

12. Walter cites Hannah Arendt's observation that terror atomizes people and renders them politically inert — that is, incapable of effective resistance — and argues that "The practice in authoritarian states of punishing definite acts of resistance and breaking up organizations suspected of sedition may be compared to a surgical procedure. In contrast, the process of terror, in its ideal form, may be compared to a chemical procedure. Independent social clusters and unauthorized political associations tend to dissolve in the medium of extreme fear. More than that, however, an emotional environment is created in which certain kinds of interaction cannot take place. The first efforts from which organized opposition might emerge are simply not made. The steps that might lead to confrontation with the agents of violence are never taken. Unless they are insulated in some unusual manner from the corrosive process, the people in such an environment are deprived . . . of a capacity that naturally belongs to the members of other systems — the power of resistance" (1969:26–27).

13. In *Masacres de la Selva*, Falla documents the cases of 773 civilian victims of army counterinsurgency in the Ixcan between 1975 and 1982: "The period ended with terrible massacres that were like open wounds in the living map of Guatemala, particularly in the indigenous areas of the country. There were 440 villages destroyed, according to the army, and the dead (primarily civilians) numbered between 10,000 and 20,000 by conservative estimate; more reliable statistics between 50,000 and 75,000" (Falla 1994:8).

14. The threat to Falla was reported in the April 1993 *Newsletter of the American Anthropological Association* (p. 14), and the following issue in May (p. 25) reported that the AAA Commission for Human Rights, established in December 1992 and taking its first action, had written to Guatemalan President Jorge Serrano Elias, requesting that Falla's human rights, and those of the Mayan people in the Ixcan region, be restored.

15. Paranoia is generally understood as a rigid, persistent system of delusions usually focused on a persecutory other; a longing for order; an abnormal or unreal fear.

16. Thousands of journalists have been threatened and several hundred killed worldwide over the last two or three decades for investigating and reporting state violations of human rights in their country.

17. In August 1992, the police detective investigating the case claimed to have found evidence of the involvement of the military, and was then shot as he was preparing to leave the country to testify about the case before the Inter-American Commission on Human Rights. Journalists and judicial officials working on the case were also intimidated and threatened (Amnesty International 1992:92). Later that year a former Guatemalan soldier, picked up in Long Beach by the California Highway Patrol for a traffic violation, was arrested and returned to Guatemala to face charges for Mack's murder. In February 1993, he was convicted and sentenced to thirty years in prison, and in June 1996, three high-ranking army officers were indicted and accused of ordering her assassination. This was the first time in Guatemala that an army officer had been indicted for ordering an assassination (Edelman 1996a:13). With the formal ending of the "long war," in December 1996 the Guatemalan Congress passed the Law of Reconciliation, and in January 1997, these officers, along with other state terrorists accused of human rights abuses, applied for amnesty under its provisions (Seligmann 1997:19).

18. For more about Myrna Mack, see Oglesby 1995.

19. Israeli anthropologist Nachman Ben-Yehuda has presented an analytical summary of the methodological problems and experiences he encountered during three years of research on political assassinations by Jews in Palestine and Israel, and he suggests that "similar methods could be used to study other phenomena where the information can be characterised as secret, dirty and hidden" (1990:345).

20. "Ethnographic seduction [is] a complex dynamic of conscious moves and unconscious defenses that may arise in interviews with victims and perpetrators of violence" (Robben 1996:72), which undermines critical detachment.

21. "Later I realized that his interest in the interview might have been to use me as an intellectual sparring partner for his upcoming trial" (Robben 1996:102).

22. For another example of ethnographic seduction, see the case of Sam Blake, described in Hawkins 1994:56.

23. In the structural-functional or consensus approach, conflict is evaluated positively when it contributes to maintaining or reestablishing order, and evaluated negatively when it leads to social disorder and disintegration.

Bibliography

Ackroyd, Carol, Karen Margolis, Jonathan Rosenhead, and Tim Shallice
    1980 *The Technology of Political Control.* Second revised edition. London: Pluto Press.

Adams, Richard
    1988 "Conclusion: What Can We Know About the Harvest of Violence?" In
    Harvest of Violence: The Maya Indians and the Guatemalan Crisis. R. Carmack, ed.
    Norman: University of Oklahoma Press.
Agger, Inger, and Soren Buus Jensen
    1996 *Trauma and Healing Under State Terrorism.* London: Zed Books.
Ali, S. Mahmud
    1993 *The Fearful State: Power, People and Internal War in South Asia.* London: Zed
    Books.
Amnesty International
    1997 *Amnesty International Report.* London: Amnesty International.
    1996 *Amnesty International Report.* London: Amnesty International.
    1993 *Amnesty International Report.* London: Amnesty International.
    1992 *The Americas: Human Rights Violations Against Indigenous Peoples.* London:
    Amnesty International.
    1981 *"Disappearances": A Workbook.* London: Amnesty International.
    1974 *Report on Torture.* London: Amnesty International.
Andreopoulos, George J. (ed.)
    1995 *Genocide: Conceptual and Historical Dimensions.* Philadelphia: University of
    Pennsylvania Press.
Anonymous
    1996 "Documenting the Reign of Terror." *Anthropology Newsletter*, February,
    p. 11. Washington, D.C.: American Anthropological Association.
Ben-Yehuda, Nachman
    1990 "Gathering Dark Secrets, Hidden and Dirty Information: Some Method-
    ological Notes on Studying Political Assassinations." *Qualitative Sociology*, 13:4,
    pp. 345–372.
Berreman, Gerald D.
    1980 "Are Human Rights Merely a Politicized Luxury in the World Today?"
    Anthropology and Humanism Quarterly, 5:1, pp. 2–13.
    1977 "Social Barriers: Caste, Class and Race in Cross-Cultural Perspective."
    Papers in Anthropology, 18:2, pp. 217–242.
Bodley, John H.
    1985 *Anthropology and Contemporary Human Problems.* Second edition. Menlo
    Park, Calif.: Cummings.
Bourgois, Philippe
    1991 "Confronting the Ethics of Ethnography: Lessons Learned from Field-
    work in Central America." In *Decolonizing Anthropology.* F. Harrison, ed. Wash-
    ington, D.C.: Association of Black Anthropologists, American Anthropological
    Association.
Bourque, Susan, and Kay Warren
    1989 "Democracy Without Peace: The Cultural Politics of Terror in Peru."
    Latin American Research Review, 24, pp. 7–34.
Carmack, Robert (ed.)
    1988 *Harvest of Violence: The Maya Indians and the Guatemalan Crisis.* Norman:
    University of Oklahoma Press.
Chalk, Frank, and Kurt Jonassohn
    1990 *The History and Sociology of Genocide: Analyses and Case Studies.* New Haven:
    Yale University Press.
Chomsky, Noam
    1996 "Enduring Truths, Changing Markets." *Covert Action Quarterly*, 56, p. 46.

1988 *The Culture of Terrorism.* London: Pluto Press.
1987 *The Chomsky Reader.* J. Peck, ed. New York: Pantheon Books.
1986 *Pirates and Emperors: International Terrorism in the Real World.* Claremont: Black Rose.
1985 *Turning the Tide: U.S. Intervention in Central America and the Struggle for Peace.* Boston: South End Press.

Chomsky, Noam, and Edward Herman
1979 *The Washington Connection and Third World Fascism* (*The Political Economy of Human Rights*, vol. 1). Nottingham: Spokesman.

Connor, John W.
1989 "From Ghost Dance to Death Camp: Nazi Germany as a Crisis Cult." *Ethos*, 17, pp. 259–288.

Connor, Melissa
1997 "Forensic Archaeology: An Application of Methods." *Anthropology Newsletter*, March, pp. 29–30. Washington, D.C.: American Anthropological Association.

Corradi, Juan E., Patricia Weiss Fagen, and Manuel Antonio Garretón (eds.)
1992 *Fear at the Edge: State Terror and Resistance in Latin America.* Berkeley: University of California Press.

D'Andrade, Roy
1995 "Moral Models in Anthropology." *Current Anthropology*, 36:3, pp. 399–408.

Duner, Bertil (ed.)
1998 *An End to Torture: Strategies for Its Eradication.* London: Zed Books.

Edelman, Marc
1996a "Update on Myrna Mack's Assassination." *Anthropology Newsletter*, September, p. 13. Washington, D.C.: American Anthropological Association.
1996b "Death Threats Against Forensic Anthropologists." *Anthropology Newsletter*, September, p. 13. Washington, D.C.: American Anthropological Association.
1996c "Torture and Murder Taught at the School of Americas." *Anthropology Newsletter*, November, pp. 6–7. Washington, D.C.: American Anthropological Association.

Falla, Jonathan
1991 *True Love and Bartholomew: Rebels on the Burmese Border.* Cambridge: Cambridge University Press.

Falla, Ricardo
1994 *Massacres in the Jungle: Ixcan, Guatemala, 1975–1982.* Boulder, Colo.: Westview Press. (English version of 1992, below).
1992 *Masacres de la Selva: Ixcan, Guatemala, 1975–1982.* Guatemala: Universidad de San Carlos de Guatemala.

Fanon, Frantz
1967 *The Wretched of the Earth.* Harmondsworth: Penguin Books.

Feldman, Allen
1991 *Formations of Violence: The Narrative of the Body and Political Terror in Northern Ireland.* Chicago: University of Chicago Press.

Fried, Morton H.
1967 *The Evolution of Political Society: An Essay in Political Anthropology.* New York: Random House.

Galtung, Johan
  1997 "Is There a Therapy for Pathological Cosmologies?" In *The Web of Violence: From Interpersonal to Global.* J. Turpin and C. Kurtz, eds. Urbana: University of Illinois Press.
George, Alexander (ed.)
  1991 *Western State Terrorism.* Cambridge: Polity Press.
Gordon, Edmund
  1991 "Anthropology and Liberation." In *Decolonizing Anthropology: Moving Further Toward an Anthropology of Liberation.* F. Harrison, ed. Association of Black Anthropologists. Washington, D.C.: American Anthropological Association.
Gordon, Neve, and Ruchama Marton (eds.)
  1995 *Human Rights, Medical Ethics and the Case of Israel.* London: Zed Books.
Green, Linda
  1995 "Living in a State of Fear." In *Fieldwork Under Fire: Contemporary Studies of Violence and Survival.* C. Nordstrom and A. Robben, eds. Berkeley: University of California Press.
Haugaard, Lisa
  1997 "Textbook Repression: U.S. Training Manuals Declassified." *Covert Action Quarterly*, 61, pp. 29–38.
Hawkins, Janet
  1994 "Confronting a 'Culture of Lies'." *Harvard Magazine*, September–October, pp. 49–57.
Herman, Edward S.
  1982 *The Real Terror Network: Terrorism in Fact and Propaganda.* Boston: South End Press.
Herman, Edward, and Gerry O'Sullivan
  1989 *The "Terror" Industry: The Experts and Institutions that Shape Our View of Terror.* New York: Pantheon.
Hillyard, Paddy, and Janie Percy-Smith
  1988 *The Coercive State: The Decline of Democracy in Britain.* London: Fontana.
Hinton, Alexander
  1996 "Agents of Death: Explaining the Cambodian Genocide in Terms of Psychosocial Dissonance." *American Anthropologist*, 98:4, pp. 818–831.
Horowitz, Irving Louis
  1976 *Genocide: State Power and Mass Murder.* New York: Transaction Books.
ICIHI (Independent Commission on International Humanitarian Issues)
  1986 *Disappeared: Technique of Terror.* London: Zed Books.
Klare, Michael T.
  1996 "The Arms Trade in the 1990s: Changing Patterns, Rising Dangers." *Third World Quarterly*, 17:5, pp. 857–874.
Kuper, Leo
  1981 *Genocide.* New York: Penguin Books.
Lan, David
  1985 *Guns and Rain: Guerrillas and Spirit Mediums in Zimbabwe.* Berkeley: University of California Press.
Littlewood, Roland
  1997 "Military Rape." *Anthropology Today*, 13:3, pp. 7–16.
Mahmood, Cynthia Keppley
  1996 *Fighting for Faith and Nation: Dialogues With Sikh Militants.* Philadelphia: University of Pennsylvania Press.

Manz, Beatriz
1995 "Reflections on an *Antropología Comprometida*: Conversations with Ricardo Falla." In *Fieldwork Under Fire: Contemporary Studies of Violence and Survival.* C. Nordstrom and A. Robben, eds. Berkeley: University of California Press.
1994 Foreword. In *Massacres in the Jungle,* by Ricardo Falla. Boulder, Colo.: Westview Press.
1988 *Refugees of a Hidden War: The Aftermath of Counterinsurgency in Guatemala.* Albany: State University of New York Press.
McCamant, John F.
1984 "Governance Without Blood: Social Science's Antiseptic View of Rule; or the Neglect of Political Repression." In *The State as Terrorist.* M. Stohl and G. Lopez, eds. Westport, Conn.: Greenwood.
McClintock, Michael
1985 *The American Connection, Volume One: State Terror and Popular Resistance in El Salvador.* London: Zed Books.
McKenna, Thomas
1997 *Muslim Rulers and Rebels: Everyday Politics and Armed Separatism in the Southern Philippines.* Berkeley: University of California Press.
Mey, Wolfgang (ed.)
1984 *They Are Now Burning Village After Village: Genocide in the Chittagong Hill Tracts, Bangladesh.* Copenhagen: International Work Group for Indigenous Affairs.
Mills, C. Wright
1963 *Power, Politics and People: The Collected Essays of C. Wright Mills.* I. Horowitz, ed. New York: Ballantine Books.
1959 *The Power Elite.* New York: Oxford University Press.
Montejo, Victor
1987 *Testimony: Death of a Guatemalan Village.* Willimantic, Conn.: Curbstone.
Nader, Laura
1969 "Up the Anthropologist: Perspectives Gained from Studying Up." In *Reinventing Anthropology.* D. Hymes, ed. New York: Random House.
Nagengast, Carole
1994 "Violence, Terror, and the Crisis of the State." *Annual Review of Anthropology*, 23, pp. 109–136.
Nordstrom, Carolyn
1997 *A Different Kind of War Story.* Philadelphia: University of Pennsylvania Press.
Nordstrom, Carolyn, and JoAnn Martin (eds.)
1992 *The Paths to Domination, Resistance, and Terror.* Berkeley: University of California Press.
Oglesby, Elizabeth
1995 "Myrna Mack." In *Fieldwork Under Fire: Contemporary Studies of Violence and Survival.* C. Nordstrom and A. Robben, eds. Berkeley: University of California Press.
Omang, Joanne, and Aryeh Neier
1985 *Psychological Operations in Guerrilla Warfare: The CIA's Nicaragua Manual.* New York: Random House.
Paul, Benjamin, and William Demarest
1988 "The Operation of a Death Squad in San Pedro la Laguna." In *Harvest of Violence: The Maya Indians and the Guatemalan Crisis.* R. Carmack, ed. Norman: University of Oklahoma Press.

Perez, Ramona
    1997 "Human Rights Alert in Guatemala." *Anthropology Newsletter*, November,
    p. 8. Washington, D.C.: American Anthropological Association.
Pettigrew, Joyce
    1995 *The Sikhs of the Punjab: Unheard Voices of State and Guerrilla Violence*. London:
    Zed Books.
Ranger, Terrence
    1985 *Peasant Consciousness and Guerrilla War in Zimbabwe*. London: James Cur-
    rey.
Robben, Antonius C. G. M.
    1996 "Ethnographic Seduction, Transference, and Resistance in Dialogues
    About Terror and Violence in Argentina." *Ethos*, 24:1, pp. 71–106.
    1995 "The Politics of Truth and Emotion Among Victims and Perpetrators of
    Violence." In *Fieldwork Under Fire: Contemporary Studies of Violence and Survival*.
    C. Nordstrom and A. Robben, eds. Berkeley: University of California Press.
Rummel, R. J.
    1994 *Death by Government*. New Brunswick, N.J.: Transaction Books.
Scheper-Hughes, Nancy
    1995 "The Primacy of the Ethical: Propositions for a Militant Anthropology."
    Current Anthropology, 36:3, pp. 409–420.
    1992 *Death Without Weeping: The Violence of Everyday Life in Brazil*. Berkeley:
    University of California Press.
Seligmann, Linda
    1997 "Amnesty for Accused Murderers of Anthropologist Mack?" *Anthropology
    Newsletter*, March, p. 19. Washington, D.C.: American Anthropological Asso-
    ciation.
Siegel, Daniel, and Joy Hackel
    1988 "El Salvador: Counterinsurgency Revisited." In *Low Intensity Warfare:
    Counterinsurgency, Proinsurgency, and Antiterrorism in the Eighties*. M. Klare and
    P. Kornbluh, eds. New York: Pantheon Books.
Skomal, Susan
    1996 "Under the Balkan Sun: Applied Archaeology in the Name of Justice."
    Anthropology Newsletter, November, p. 6. Washington, D.C.: American Anthro-
    pological Association.
Sluka, Jeffrey
    1995 "Domination, Resistance and Political Culture in Northern Ireland's
    Catholic-Nationalist Ghettos." *Critique of Anthropology*, 15:1, pp. 71–102.
    1989 *Hearts and Minds, Water and Fish: Popular Support for the IRA and INLA in a
    Northern Irish Ghetto*. Greenwich, Conn.: JAI Press.
Starn, Orin
    1994 "Rethinking the Politics of Anthropology: The Case of the Andes." *Cur-
    rent Anthropology*, 35:1, pp. 13–38.
Staub, Ervin
    1992 *The Roots of Evil: The Origins of Genocide and Other Group Violence*. Cam-
    bridge: Cambridge University Press.
Stiglmayer, Alexandra (ed.)
    1994 *Mass Rape: The War Against Women in Bosnia-Herzegovina*. Lincoln: Univer-
    sity of Nebraska Press.
Stohl, Michael
    1984 "International Dimensions of State Terrorism." In *The State as Terrorist*.
    M. Stohl and G. Lopez, eds. Westport, Conn.: Greenwood Press.

Stohl, Michael, and George A. Lopez (eds.)
  1984 "Introduction." *The State as Terrorist: The Dynamics of Governmental Violence and Repression.* Westport, Conn.: Greenwood Press.
Stoll, David
  1993 *Between Two Armies: In the Ixil Towns of Guatemala.* New York: Columbia University Press.
Strozier, Charles, and Michael Flynn (eds.)
  1996 *Genocide, War, and Human Survival.* Lanham, Md.: Rowman and Littlefield.
Suarez-Orozco, Marcelo
  1992 "A Grammar of Terror: Psychocultural Responses to State Terrorism in the Dirty War and Post–Dirty War Argentina." In *The Paths to Domination, Resistance, and Terror.* C. Nordstrom and J. Martin, eds. Berkeley: University of California Press.
  1990 "Speaking the Unspeakable: Toward a Psychosocial Understanding of Responses to Terror." *Ethos,* 18:3, pp. 353–383.
  1987 "The Treatment of Children in the 'Dirty War': Ideology, State Terrorism and the Abuse of Children in Argentina." In *Child Survival: Anthropological Perspectives on the Treatment and Maltreatment of Children.* N. Scheper-Hughes, ed. The Netherlands: Reidel.
Swedenburg, Ted
  1995 "With Genet in the Palestinian Field." In *Fieldwork Under Fire: Contemporary Studies of Violence and Survival.* C. Nordstrom and A. Robben, eds. Berkeley: University of California Press.
  1989 "Occupational Hazards: Palestine Ethnography." *Cultural Anthropology,* 4:3, pp. 265–272.
Taussig, Michael
  1992 "Terror as Usual: Walter Benjamin's Theory of History as a State of Siege." In *The Nervous System,* by M. Taussig. London: Routledge.
  1987 *Colonialism, Shamanism, and the Wild Man: A Study of Terror and Healing.* Chicago: University of Chicago Press.
  1984 "Culture of Terror—Space of Death: Roger Casement's Putumayo Report and the Explanation of Torture." *Comparative Studies in Society and History,* 26, pp. 467–449.
Taylor, Julie
  1993 "The Outlaw State and the Lone Rangers." In *Perilous States: Conversations on Culture, Politics, and Nation.* G. Marcus, ed. Chicago: University of Chicago Press.
Walter, E. V.
  1969 *Terror and Resistance: A Study of Political Violence with Case Studies of Some Primitive African Communities.* New York: Oxford University Press.
Warren, Kay
  1993a "Interpreting *La Violencia* in Guatemala." In *The Violence Within: Cultural and Political Opposition in Divided Nations.* K. Warren, ed. Boulder, Colo.: Westview Press.
Warren, Kay (ed.)
  1993b *The Violence Within: Cultural and Political Opposition in Divided Nations.* Boulder, Colo.: Westview Press.
Wilson, Richard
  1991 "Machine Guns and Mountain Spirits: The Cultural Effects of State Repression Among the Q'eqchi of Guatemala." *Critique of Anthropology,* 11:1, pp. 33–61.

Zulaika, Joseba
    1988 *Basque Violence: Metaphor and Sacrament.* Reno: University of Nevada Press.
Zulaika, Joseba, and William Douglass
    1996 *Terror and Taboo: The Follies, Fables, and Faces of Terrorism.* New York: Routledge.

Chapter 1
A Fictional Reality
Paramilitary Death Squads and the
Construction of State Terror in Spain

Begoña Aretxaga

State violence, especially the kind that circumambulates the law, that transgresses the law from within (questioning thus the hegemonic discourse of the state as public interest), that violence that materializes frequently in the assassinations of death squads, the torture of detainees, the disappearance of victims, and other like technologies of terror — such violence, simultaneously public and secret, is deeply wrapped in fictional plots and phantasmatic images. It is that fantasy space within which state violence operates that gives it a surreal, uncanny, and chilling feeling, a power to "unmake worlds" (Scarry 1985) as it "unmakes" bodies. No amount of political, economic, and social causality, of rational aims, goals, and interests can explain that surplus of meaning in state violence that manifests itself at the level of the feeling body as a sense, an image, a panic, or an excitement. This essay is about that surplus in state violence and the fantasies that produce and fuel it. It recounts and analyzes an episode of state terror taking place in contemporary democratic Spain, as it was narrated by some of its protagonists. Through a reading of this episode I hope to open a discussion about the play of fantasy in the articulation of political violence.

To speak of state violence necessarily entails a discussion about the state, its forms of production and reproduction, its discourses, and its imaginings. I argue in this essay that the narratives produced by the state have a fictional character, that is, they resonate with existing genres and forms of emplotment.[1] It is within — and not outside — these fictional genres that the state is imagined as subject by diverse publics in concrete locales, like the Basque Country. Thus the narratives of state violence have the effect of embodying the state by endowing it with agency and feeling. This "feeling state" incarnated in the excitements of concrete state officials opens in turn the question of how fantasy and desire articulate political imaginaries and practices of violence. What is at stake is not only how people imagine the state — and thus produce it as social fact — through a variety of discourses and practices, but also, and equally important, how state officials imagine the state and produce it through not only discourses and practices but arresting images and desires articulated in fantasy scenes. At the center of these fantasy scenes, in which the state is produced as violent excess, is the phantom of terrorism, Basque terrorism. Let me now turn to my story.

The Fetish of Democracy

At the end of December 1994 the involvement of the socialist government in paramilitary terror hit the press and became a national scandal. It triggered the largest political crisis in Spain since the attempted coup d'état in 1981 that led the socialist party to power the following year. With the socialists in power, the negotiated but troublesome transition from forty years of dictatorship to a parliamentary democracy became a symbolic fact. Not casually did the socialists rally under the slogan "Por el Cambio" (For a change) in their electoral campaign, suggesting that *they* were the key to a definite democratic turn in Spanish politics. There was, of course, a measure of bad faith in this attribution of historical agency embedded in the promise of radical political change. After all, the socialist party had been an eager protagonist in the intense negotiations that, following the death of General Francisco Franco, orchestrated the democratization of the country as a process of reform of, rather than rupture with, the Francoist state. One of the consequences of this policy of reform was that the basic structures that had embodied the Francoist state — the army, the police, the bureaucracy — remained largely unchallenged after the death of Franco. There were no resignations of former officials, no demand that responsibility be assumed, no public trials. Political "realism" seemed to triumph. Thus, the radical change the socialists espoused with great enthusiasm during the 1982 electoral campaign was already inscribed within a space of continuity with the former regime, a continuity with which they were complicit.[2] All the same, in 1982, after the failed coup d'état of Colonel Tejero that held the country hostage for more than twelve hours, the socialist government resonated with the social memories, real and inherited, of a republican time filled with the hopes of social justice and the passions of social change, a time prior to the traumatic events of the civil war and the surreal social space of a dictatorship that would last thirty-six years, marking ineluctably the lives of three generations.

I remember the elections that brought the socialist party to the government as a kind of exorcism of the past, the coming to a historical full circle, a kind of redemption that was supposed to triumph over the void represented by the silence of those Francoist decades. At once constrained and enabled by the complicities of continuity with the former regime, the new socialist government became nevertheless the repository of social desire for redemptive change, a signifier of a *real* break with the dictatorship. Even those of us — radical Basque nationalists and revolutionary leftists — who did not trust the social-democratic suit of the socialist party were in spite of ourselves excited by that intangible, emblematic power that seemed bestowed upon it like a halo by virtue of their position as government, which is to say as State. This was not just the power of State fetishism — with a capital S (Taussig 1992) — it was the power of democracy as fetish. It was a fetish produced by the forgetting of the traces that linked the Spanish democracy to the former regime (its nature as a reform of it), and its reinvention as the real Thing, democracy — an object of desire that held the promise of a new, European, modern, successful form of life.[3] The fetishization of democracy endowed the Spanish state with a new aura and new body, a sacred one that came to replace the desacralized and profaned body of the Francoist state. The legitimacy of the new state, however, depended on the continuous exercise of an act of forgetting. Thus constituted as a fantasy of modern prosperity, democracy became under the socialist government the legitimizing discourse for a wide variety of authoritarian state practices.[4] It is within this space of erasure and fantasy that I place the practices of state terror that have stubbornly persisted through the new democratic era, articulating a political imaginary filled with the mirror fantasies of Basque terrorism and the terror of the state. Let me return to the story that constituted the state as a terrorist subject.

The Dirty War

In 1983, one year after the socialist electoral victory, the assassinations of Basque radical nationalists began under the anagram of a new paramilitary organization that called itself GAL, or Antiterrorist Liberation Groups. From 1983 to 1985 the new paramilitary squad claimed the assassinations of twenty-five Basque people.[5] Most of them were Basque refugees, active or retired members of the radical nationalist guerrilla organization ETA, who were living across the frontier in the French Basque Country.[6] Some were just sympathizers with the legal political movement for Basque independence, Herri Batasuna (HB, Popular Unity).[7] Among those killed, for example, were a well-known journalist (Xavier Galdeano) and a pediatrician (Santi Brouard). In the Basque Country radical nationalists organized demonstrations to protest the dirty war.

Right-wing paramilitary groups were not new in the Basque Country. There had been a succession of them during the last decade of the Franco-ist dictatorship and the turbulent years that followed the death of General Franco. There were the Christ King soldiers, the Basque Spanish Battalion, the Accion Apostolica Antiterrorista (AAA, an emulation of the Argentinian equivalent), and the general, unnamed *incontrolados* — right-wing elements and plainclothes policemen who often emerged at popular fiestas or demonstrations and intimidated people with their guns, or attacked persons suspected of leftist or separatist sympathies. In the Basque Country it was *vox populi* that these groups were linked to the security forces and particularly to the Civil Guard, a most hated branch of the army empowered with policing functions. The complicity of the security forces in terrorist practices was, of course, never proved officially, despite a good degree of evidence.[8] Thus, when in December 1983 the GAL made its debut through radio communiqués, its menacing graffiti on the walls of towns and cities, and the razor inscription of its anagram on the bodies of terrified persons, there was a ready frame in which to place it. After all, shady assassinations of Basque citizens had been an old habit of the former state, and so was it an old habit to suspect a shady state hand behind the threat of paramilitary squads or unclaimed political violence.[9] Old habits die hard. But the old habits of dictatorship were utterly incongruent with a socialist administration that represented a sharp break with the past, that is, a new state. What, then, was this state that was new, yet linked to old practices of violence? How was one to regard this state that appeared at once in control and out of control? At once an emblem of the new order of Law and itself an outlaw?[10]

In 1987 José Amedo and Michel Dominguez, two police inspectors working for the intelligence department of the national police (the successor of the former secret police) were convicted of organizing the GAL. The response in the Basque Country was a mixture of outrage at the involvement of the security forces in the organization of political terrorism, and satisfaction at the public evidence of what had been unrecognized common knowledge. These were the first sentences dictated against the security forces. Along with Amedo and Dominguez, a number of mercenaries were arrested in France in connection with the assassinations of Basque activists living there as political refugees. Amedo and Dominguez assumed full responsibility for the creation of the GAL and the judicial case was closed.

Then, seven years later in December 1994, following a series of corruption scandals,[11] José Amedo and Michel Dominguez, the two policemen convicted of organizing the GAL, began to reveal their secrets. This revelation began by a long exclusive story published by one of the major Spanish newspapers, *El Mundo*.[12] It appeared in four parts over four days as if they were chapters of a novella. The narratives had a tremendous impact in the public political culture of a Spain already disenchanted with its democracy because of the corruption scandals. The impact was even greater in the political culture of the Basque Country, where it came to confirm the worst fears and anxieties about the haunting power of the state.[13] The stories were gripping. Coded in a genre spanning the confessional and the detective novel, they had the addictive quality of a soap opera. They contained convoluted scenarios, secret conspiracies, spy connections, and mercenary assassins, the unexpected involvement of public figures, briefcases filled with public money, documents stolen from the intelligence service that supposedly charted the dirty war, and iconic handwritten communiqués. At the center of the story were high officials of the government, the public administration, and the security forces.[14] *El Mundo* sold all its newspapers the first day. The second day there were no newspapers left in my neighborhood by ten in the morning, when my mother went to the usual corner store to buy it. She came home excited with a tale of stops along newsstands that led her from our neighborhood to a remote kiosk downtown where she finally found a copy. Along the way she gathered a long trail of street commentary in local shops and on street corners where people meet each other every day and chat about family, friends, or the latest political news.

A Scene from the Kitchen

My mother comes to the kitchen and starts reading avidly the second chapter of the story. She tells me parts of it as she goes along, peppered with additional commentary having to do with the shameless character of this, that, and the other official that had been condemning Basque activists while organizing terrorist assassinations of their own. "No tienen vergüenza" (They have no shame), she says. When she finishes, I take the paper and read the story in the same commenting way. I point out to my mother that there is not much hard evidence in the story, that there is a lot of "I heard him saying" and "I told him" and "they said that . . ." My mother looks at me with a serious and puzzling look. I know what she is thinking. I know that she is trying to decide if her daughter has become so Americanized that she cannot see obvious things anymore. She says, "everybody knows that is true." I have to justify myself; "I know," I say, "but you need something more than accusing words in a judicial process." My mother is not as interested in judicial procedure and its rules of evidence as she is in the discourse. Like other poor people growing up during the dictatorship she has a great distrust for the apparatus of justice. She thinks that evidence is not what produces social effects. "There has been plenty of evidence before," she says, "and *they* didn't do anything." *They* refers here not so much to particular government officials, but to the state. The vague yet concrete *they* is the Kafkaesque embodiment of the state in the discourse of radical nationalists. As in Kafka's *The Trial*, it is not clear who *they* are; *they* have a phantasmatic quality, yet they exist with an indisputable concreteness manifested best in the power to produce violence and death. The excitement that my mother shares with other working-class people of her neighborhood resides in the public disclosure of things known but negated, hidden behind what she imagines as the smoke screen of normality drawn by state power. It is the excitement of discovering that the powerful Wizard of Oz is just a small man, that the Kafkaesque *they* have faces and names.

* * *

The revelations about the GAL produced indeed a burst of public excitement I had not known since the coup d'état in 1981, an excitement fueled by an overflow of discourse, a snowball of political declarations and judicial confessions, negations, and public discussions about the nature of democracy and about the nature — or the bad nature — of the state. Rather than taking it as incidental, I think it is important to account for this excitement. What is the relation between the narratives and the production of affect? Between practices of violence and the structure of desire? Between the body of the state and the production of fantasy and political imaginaries?

The judicial case about the GAL, closed in 1987, reopened again after the confessions of Amedo and Dominguez. The reopened case led to a proliferation of judicial confessions and the GAL became a permanent feature in the newspapers, expected and searched for, like the local news or the sports page. Its quotidianity made a crime story still full of rumor and hearsay the very frame within which the state was envisioned and indeed materialized. It became a fictional reality where everybody was caught, within which things that happened made sense independently of the evidence that could be produced to support it, making clear that social knowledge does not necessarily rest on the rules of Cartesian logic.[15]

I want to consider those early narratives about state violence to raise questions about the ways in which the state is imagined and thus produced as a subject. I want to raise questions about the structure of political imaginaries that give body to the state, and about the magical effects of this *body politic.* I want to raise questions not only about how the state is envisioned, but also about the kind of affects that are produced within such envisionings. I want to suggest that the state, whatever that is, materializes not only through rules and bureaucratic routines (Foucault) but also through a world of fantasy thoroughly narrativized and imbued with affect, fear, and desire, that make it, in fact, a plausible reality.[16] By fantasy I do not mean here an illusory construction opposed to an empirical reality, but a kind of reality in its own right breaching the divide between consciousness and unconsciousness.[17]

A number of scholars have recently questioned the conceptualization of the state as a material, coherent entity, a concrete thing, a unified and autonomous structure or apparatus separated from what we call civil society. Following Foucault, Timothy Mitchell has argued that this notion of a self-willed, autonomous state arose with the new techniques of disciplinary power and order of things that accompanied modernity. For him, the boundary between the state and civil society is far from being as fixed as it appears to be. On the contrary, this boundary, he argues, is elusive, uncertain, and therefore unable to mark a position of real exteriority for the state. For Mitchell, "the appearance that state and society are separate things is part of the way a given financial and economic order is maintained . . . the arrangements that produced the apparent separateness of the state create the abstract effect of agency, with concrete consequences" (1991:90–91). As power relations become internalized through disciplinary techniques they take on the appearance of external structures, of an autonomous state where power relations can be localized. Thus, for Mitchell, "the state needs to be analyzed as a structural effect. It should be examined not as an actual structure, but as the powerful, metaphysical effect of practices that make such structures appear to exist" (1991:94). The fact that these practices are unbounded, often in contradiction with each other, and tension ridden, is precisely what gives the state, as Wendy Brown has noted, its paradoxical character — at once an incoherent, multifaceted ensemble of power relations and a vehicle of massive domination" (1995:174). In a similar vein, Akhil Gupta has called for an inquiry into the ways in which the state is socially produced and reproduced through an ensemble of discourses proliferating through the mass media and materializing in bureaucratic practices (1995).[18]

So too for Navaro-Yashin (1997, 1998) is the state created in a variety of social sites through civic ritual and pluralistic identification, making it impossible to discern "where the state ends, where society begins and vice versa" (1998:20). From a heterodox Marxist perspective critical of structural approaches, Phillip Abrams (1988) was the first to suggest that the state is a powerful illusion. For him the state should be approached as a mask, rather than a subject, a structure (à la Poulantzas) or an apparatus (à la Althusser), a mask that hides relations of power by legitimizing them under the guise of public interest. For Abrams, to treat the state as anything other than a mystifying mask that must be uncovered is to contribute to the reification of power relations. Yet by dismissing the state as the smoke screen of the "really real" relations of power, Abrams may fall prey to the very reification he tries to counteract, this time by endowing relations of power with a materiality separated from ideological or phantasmatic reality. Ultimately Mitchell might run into the same problem.

The fact that the state is an effect of a heterogeneous and contradictory ensemble of discourses and practices does not imply that the state does not have any reality at all, that it is only an illusion, a smoke screen that has to be dissipated. Within our modern political imagery, the state, as an autonomous subject, has become such a commonsense notion to explain reality that to say that the state does not exist is like saying in the fifteenth century that god did not exist. I had this experience myself during my fieldwork in the Basque Country when I tried to "demystify" the state in front of an audience of leftist activists. My attempt at showing that the state as an autonomous subject did not exist was received with utmost puzzlement and resistance. It runs counter to everything which constitutes the political experience in the Basque Country. My audience experienced the state with a materiality and violence that left no doubt about its *real* existence. The state might be an effect, as Mitchell argues, but is not less real because of that. The state has what we could call a phantasmatic reality, but this reality cannot be separated from some other "really real" relations of power hidden behind it, as Abrams attempts to do. It constitutes the "real" that must then be considered as inseparable from political fantasy.

Power relations cannot be considered as the empirical kernel of reality, obscured by the complicated illusions of a system of exploitation masquerading as common sense. They are not disentangled from specific political imaginaries; they are an integral part of them. The question then is not to demystify the state as an illusion, not just to identify the heterogeneous micropractices that give it materiality, the question is how the state as a phantasmatic reality operates within a political imaginary to constitute political reality and political experience and to produce concrete effects. The inquiry into such questions presupposes that we abandon an ontological notion of reality in which the "real" is opposed to representation, but also that we go beyond Foucault's stubborn refusal to consider subjectivity and affect as integral parts of power. Abrams's notion of the state as mask raises, as Taussig has suggested, the crucial anthropological question of how the mask — as mask — works, what universe of beliefs, practices, discourses, events, fears, and desires make possible its power. This is the crucial question that Abrams, however, sets aside. To investigate the power of the state as mask is to investigate the political fictions we live by and to explore, as Michael Taussig would have it, the power of its magic (1997, 1992). Such magic resides precisely in the mimetic transgression of the boundaries upon which the modern state is ideologically constituted. To support my argument let me go back now to the confessional narratives that gave body to the state as a subject of terrorist violence in the Basque Country.

Preliminaries

In October 1983, the GAL kidnapped two young men in the French Basque Country. Nobody would hear about them again until 1995, when in the midst of the scandal of the dirty war their bones were uncovered by a grave digger and examined by a forensic pathologist who identified the remains and certified that they had died as a consequence of torture. José Lasa and Josu Zabala, presumed members of ETA, became the first "disappeared" of the Spanish democracy. The investigation following the discovery of their remains implicated the governor of the Basque province of Gipuzkoa and the general of the Civil Guard Enrique Galindo, notorious for the torture of detainees. The disclosure of the torture to death of Lasa and Zabala and the direct implication of government officials gave the dirty war a macabre edge.[19]

The disappearances of Lasa and Zabala were not claimed at the time by any organization. Two days later the Spanish security forces attempted to kidnap Jose M. Larretxea, a Basque refugee and leader of the ETA VIII assembly (one of the factions of the ETA existing then that would soon become integrated in the stronger and better organized ETA military). The kidnap attempt was frustrated by the French police, who arrested in situ the team of kidnappers—a captain and three policemen from the GEO, the special antiterrorist branch of the Spanish police. The action was embarrassing for the Spanish government, which was caught red-handed performing an illegal operation in French territory. Not only was this an infringement of international law, but it demonstrated an incredible amateurism on the part of the Spanish security forces in charge of antiterrorist operations. The chief of state security tried to justify it as "a humanitarian action" aimed at forcing ETA to liberate an industrialist they held captive for ransom. The excuse was unconvincing and demonstrated a clear engagement in the logic of political transgression that characterizes counterinsurgency and antiterrorist thinking, a logic built on the interiorization of a fantastic enemy called terrorism that can only be countered with the same terrorist means. In the representations of terrorism, it is not democratic states that kidnap terrorists to be exchanged for captive citizens held by terrorists, it is the other way around.

These were the beginnings of the GAL's dirty war, but the first action to be officially claimed by the GAL, that gave it birth as a political entity, was the kidnapping of a French citizen, Segundo Marey, and it is this kidnapping that occupies the larger narrative space in the confessions of Amedo and Dominguez. This kidnapping has the status of a tale of origins that narrativizes the state as an excitable body, a loosely connected ensemble of characters and bureaucracies held together by the imaginary of terrorism, and narrates state terrorism as a Kafkaesque comedy of errors. For the foundational action of the GAL was indeed a mistake. What follows is my rendition of the story.

*   *   *

El Mundo, 17 December 1994. The scene is from 1983:

December 4. Jose Amedo waits at the frontier that separates the towns of Irún in Spain and Hendaye in France. He has cleared the way with the Civil Guard, the military police that controls the traffic of passengers, to facilitate the transit of a car expected to arrive at 7:00 P.M. Evening grows into night and the expected car does not appear. Amedo gets a telephone call from the top chief of police of the Basque province of Bizkaia. He tells him to go immediately to the little frontier post of Dantzarinea across the Basque Pyrenees. The police chief tells Amedo he has to pick up somebody waiting for him there. When he gets there a Spanish policeman tells Amedo that there is a man waiting for him and that the governor has said to go with him. The guy tells Amedo, "Let's go." It is a dark night and it is cold. They go through a twisted road up the mountain. Amedo: *"When we reach the top I get out of the car and see a big fat guy in a T-shirt and beside him an old man wearing striped pajamas, freezing."* The man coming with him is Mohamed Talbi, a mercenary of the GAL, and the fat man is Raymond Echalier, another mercenary. Both were arrested in 1987. Amedo: *"I see the three of them and I remember that Sancristobal, Alvarez, and Planchuelo,"* respectively the civil governor, the chief of police, and the director of the intelligence department, *"had told me that they were going to kidnap Mikel Lujua, a member of ETA. And then when I see this old man I said, 'But who is this?' and Talbi, one of the mercenaries, said 'Segundo Marey.'"* End of the first chapter.

Part two begins with a story of telephone conversations over the fate of Segundo Marey in the small police post of the Pyrenees between Alvarez (the chief of police) and Amedo: *"He is a mistake. Should they let him go?"* The governor, the chief of police, and the director of intelligence consult with each other. They decide to continue with the kidnapping to *"exploit it politically."* There follows a road trip from the Pyrenees to Bilbao swapping the kidnapped man from one car to another under highway tunnels until he is taken to an abandoned and derelict house in another mountain in the province of Santander. The number of people that have come in contact with the kidnapped man in this narrative is multiplying. *Segundo Marey is kept blindfolded in his pajamas for ten days in the kitchen of a derelict house with no electricity, water, or heat, guarded by two mercenaries and two police officers.* Michel Dominguez says he went to the house the day before Segundo Marey was liberated. The tone of his description is horror and disgust: *"When I saw the situation I was taken aback. The house was an old stone house totally destroyed, everything was dirty. The ceilings were half fallen, there was no furniture. Marey was on the floor, in the kitchen. His head covered with a bandage from the nose up, his eyes totally covered so he couldn't see anything. He was wearing the same pajamas he had on the day they took him. He didn't have a coat or anything, only a blanket, an army blanket. The officers watching him were fed up"* (*El Mundo*, 29 December 1994).

In the narrative of Michel Dominguez the mimesis of terrorist transgression turns into the ambivalence of unheroic abjection, at least for those at the bottom of *the state*—those who claim they were just following orders. Not so for those scheming in the offices of state buildings. The high officials that play terrorist in the governor's office get carried away with the excitement of transgression and the effect of omnipotence that it can produce. For them the war against Basque terrorists is lost from sight, to be replaced instead by a play against another state. The kidnapped man would be used to blackmail the French state, which was at the time refusing to collaborate in the antiterrorist scheming of the Spanish government.

The first communiqué signed by the GAL is handwritten by the governor himself, Julian Sancristobal, translated into French, and sent to the radio. Amedo is called into the building of the provincial police headquarters (govierno civic). *"Sancristobal comes with a piece of paper in his hands and says, 'take this and give it to the Moor [nickname of mercenary Talbi] and tell him to translate it into French and send it to the radio' . . . Julian had something already written in the paper and in front of me he added some more lines. It was a communiqué."* The communiqué would later become an important piece of evidence in the court case. In that first communiqué the GAL introduces itself and demands from France the liberation of the policemen arrested for the attempted kidnap of José Maria Larretxea in exchange for Segundo Marey who is accused now of collaboration with Basque terrorism: *"Listen, this is about the kidnap of Segundo Marey. He has been kidnapped because of his relations with ETA military, hiding terrorists, and participating in the collection of revolutionary tax. Everybody implicated will disappear like this one."* Soon after the first there was a second communiqué giving the French state an ultimatum: either they liberate the Spanish policemen arrested in France, or the French citizen Segundo Marey will be killed.

The risk of the operation grows as days go by and a better hideout is not found. Amedo says that in the course of a meeting, the governor Julian Sancristobal (promoted to chief of state security a year later) and Ricardo Garcia Damborenea (a leader of the socialist party) suggest that Segundo

Marey should be killed to avoid complications. *"They even bought the cal (limestone powder) to bury the body, "*assures Amedo. *"They were very euphoric, very* prepotente *(full of themselves), "*he says.

The socialist leader Garcia Damborenea was certainly obsessed with terrorism. In 1997 he published a short book entitled *Manual del Buen Terrorista* (Manual of the Good Terrorist). It is supposed to be a sarcastic account of the evils of Basque terrorism. Yet the participation of Garcia Damborenea in the production of terrorism endows his text with a surreal character. It is a literal call to terrorism posing as an acid parody of it, showing a fascination with terrorism disguised as self-righteous opposition. It is a chilling document in which there is no boundary between the copy and the original, between parody and the real thing, between legitimate and illegitimate violence. The figurative character of the text turns into a literalness filled with ambiguity. The book is dedicated "to the victims of intolerance" and this is particularly poignant, for, in hindsight, one wonders if the victims of state terrorism are counted in this dedication in another macabre mixture of the ironic and the literal. But let's not lose track of our story.

A few days after the second communiqué, France liberated the arrested Spanish policemen, and our statement decided to free Marey, not without implicating the minister of the interior as the one authorizing his release. The transcendence of this decision over the fate of Marey contrasts with the banality of the verbal exchange within which the narrative of the policeman places it: *"Sancristobal took one of the telephones from his desk, the one that connected directly with the ministry of the interior, and in my presence I heard him saying, "Minister, if it is OK with you we let this guy go tonight. Is that OK? OK then'."* (This was the point where I told my mother that this was pure hearsay and she thought that was beside the point.)

Marey was indeed liberated in France on 14 December 1983. The communiqué sent to the radio on that occasion was the first one signed with the anagram GAL. Dominguez says he translated it into French and sent it from a public telephone: *"Due to the rise of assassinations, kidnappings, and extortions carried out by the terrorist organization ETA on Spanish soil, planned and directed from the French territory, we have decided to eliminate this situation. The antiterrorist Groups of Liberation (GAL) founded with that goal communicate the following: (1) Every assassination carried out by the terrorists will have an appropriate response. Not a single victim will be left without response. (2) We affirm our idea of attacking French interests in Europe because the French government is responsible for permitting the terrorists to act from its territory with impunity. As a sign of goodwill and convinced by the gesture of the French government we liberate Segundo Marey, arrested by our organization because of his collaboration with the terrorists of ETA. You will receive further notice from the GAL. "*

In the narratives of the two policemen, the "political" success of the kidnapping of Segundo Marey left their artificers even more euphoric than the operation itself. They get carried away. Like the "terrorists" of ETA they too want to organize a "revolutionary tax," this time from French industrialists to intimidate French authorities into collaborating in the war against ETA.[20] Amedo: *"When the Marey affair ended Julian Sancristobal (the governor) said in a meeting: 'Ricardo [Garcia Damborenea] and I have decided to organize a scheme to pass a revolutionary tax to the French, to intimidate France. You have to bring a list of French industrialists, you can take it from a telephone book or whatever because we are going to pass the revolutionary tax to the French.'"* Dominguez says that they said that *"In this way it would look like the GAL were financing themselves. The expenses will be justified,"* and Amedo adds that *"Sancristobal, Alvarez, and Planchuelo thought that in this way the money would seem to come from a source different from the state."* They make a list of potential targets but the project does not get off the ground—it is not clear why. Instead, the GAL was funded by the public treasury through what is called "the state reserved funds," the secret nature of which served as a deterrent to public inquiry and seemed a guarantee against accountability. A large list of assassinations of Basque radical nationalists followed, managed now by the more efficient hands of the Civil Guard. The assassinations continued until 1987, when Amedo and Dominguez were arrested along with a number of mercenaries employed by them.[21]

Between Parody and Mimesis: Becoming the Imagined Terrorist

There are a number of issues that can be discussed coming from this confessional narrative. One of them is the issue of truth and the fictionalization of events. This is important for the judiciary that must attend to conventional rules of evidence. The events narrated by Amedo and Dominguez have been contested, negated, and also confirmed by an avalanche of new narratives that have gone into judicial files and cases, as well as filling the newspapers daily. The issue of truth is bound to the figure of the communiqués. The communiqués have the iconic function of conferring materiality and truth in the narratives of both policemen. Amedo and Dominguez emphasize those pieces of paper; they secretly kept copies of them, reproducing the record-keeping function of the state which they both embody as agents of the law and transgress as de facto terrorists. The communiqué also acquires in these narratives a fetishistic character—at once the icon of a fantastic reality (the secret production of terrorism in the banal setting of government offices) and the empirical matter that materializes terrorism and endows it with truth by virtue of the trace that links a concrete person to the ink letters hand-written in a tangible, reproducible paper. Dominguez makes these communiqués his downfall and the center of gravity of his implication in state terrorism.

The issue of truth is also linked to the question of conspiracy and "the papers of the CSID," the top secret papers of the secret service of the army that were supposed to contain ultimate evidence of the implication of the state in the dirty war. Prominent among them was the "*Acta funda-cional* of the GAL" that outlined the plot of the dirty war. The neissilvales of the papers deserve a degree of consideration that would exceed the limits of this article. Suffice it to say that they disappeared from the files of the CSID headquarters to reappear in the form of narrativized copy in the cell of the former director of the secret service arrested on charges of corruption. Then the papers disappeared again, and were secreted by the government against the demands of the judiciary prosecuting the case, despite the fact that the press had gotten hold of a copy and published it. The movement of these secrets, contorted to the extreme, constructed a conspiracy story as national narrative in which the papers were a ghostly reality (spoken by all, seen by none) and the ultimate evidence of state terrorism. As ultimate evidence, as materialization of a *real* that would set the political scene straight, out of the confusing maze of accusations and counteraccusations, the CSID papers became also the only chance of democratic redemption, the very *thing* that would clarify it all. Truth must be considered here as an effect of desire and not just of discourse.

The high officials that figure prominently in the story of the kidnap of Segundo Marey have been investigated and sent to jail. Most of them have come out on bail, however. The case has not been resolved, and crucial pieces of evidence contained in the CSID papers remain officially undisclosed until 1997. Up to the present the dirty war continues to be the object of great political controversy. In October 1996, Felipe González, ex–prime minister of the socialist government, declared to the press that there was not now and had never been state terrorism in Spain. It was not clear if Mr. González meant that the implication of his party and two of his administrations in illegal paramilitary assassination was an illusion, or that such complicity was a perfectly legitimate form of self-defense against the violence of Basque terrorism, and could not therefore be called state terrorism.

In March 1997, when the government finally lifted the veto on the disclosure of the CSID papers, the socialist party declared to the press that "el estado no tiene quien le defienda" (no one defends the state). The statement evoked the title of the famous novel by the Colombian writer Gabriel Garcia Marquez *El coronel no tiene quien le escriba* (No one writes to the colonel). It was, of course, concrete individuals that were put on trial, but there was little doubt that in the public discourse the protagonist was the state. Yet if the state was the defendant in the judicial cases still in process, so was the state — as the law — the subject conducting the procedures. The state was both, the law and its transgression, and it was this coexistence that revealed the nature of the truth of "stately being" (Taussig 1997). Yet in the next moment it was the state against itself, as it were, or the good, democratic state against the bad state that was resorting to authoritarian habits, as if the state had split itself in an act of psychotic disavowal in order to preserve its stately being as public interest. But for those nationalist radicals in the Basque Country who had suffered the consequences of the dirty war and considered the state their nemesis, the state was the one cooking and eating the cake — which is why people like my mother did not trust the outcome of the judicial processes.

Leaving aside the debate on the nature of democracy that the statement made by Felipe González, and indeed the whole GAL affair, triggered in Spain — a country still with the ghost of a dictatorship on its heels — González nevertheless put his finger, unwittingly, I presume, on a crucial dimension of state paramilitary violence, what Taussig (1993) has called, following Adorno and Horkheimer, "organized mimesis," the organized copy of terrorism to eliminate terrorism. Yet what is salient in the confessions of Amedo and Dominguez is the disorganized character of this "organized mimesis," its fantastic character, its amateurism that led the vice president of the current government (Francisco Alvarez Cascos) to call it "bar terrorism" (*El Pais* international, 7 November 1996).

There is an excess in these narratives of state terrorism that reveal the state more as a parody than as a mimicking agent. The kidnap of Segundo Marey reads indeed not so much as a copy of Basque terrorism but as a parody of the collective representation of Basque terrorist kidnappings. It follows the landscape that has belonged in film, novels, and folk stories to ETA — the iconic Basque city, cradle of nationalism, Bilbao; the obscure frontier passes along the Pyrenees; the hideout in the mountains (a terrain alien to the police and familiar to expert members of ETA); the communiqués; the hidden documents that chart the action; even the seal and anagram.[22] All this belongs to the genre of Basque terrorism in its different guises, to what literary critic Joseba Gabilondo (1996) has called "the national production of terrorism" to which the discourse of the mass media actively contributes. What is copied then is not terrorism but a fantasy of terrorism, as indeed the terrorist can only exist — like the savage — in a fantastic form, as a collective representation (Zulaika and Douglass 1996). What is produced in this mimetic engagement of the state (as a fictional entity) with the representation of the terrorist is exactly terrorism — dead bodies, material effects, but also affective states (exhilaration, anger, fear). And not only state terrorism but the state itself is produced in the act of producing terrorism — a nervous state subject to uncontrolled excitement.

The body of the State represented as concrete disconnected bodies inhabiting the bureaucratic space of offices is far from being the aseptic image of rational micro-practices described by Foucault, or the Kafka-esque nightmare of bureaucratic reason. On the contrary, this is a state suffused with affect; it gets excited, exhilarated at trespassing into the fantastic space of terrorism, carried away by its own fantasy of the om-nipotence attributed to the terrorist, unbounded by the rule of law, un-restrained by the parameters that define the civilized reality of parlia-mentary democracy. This body politic is a sentient body that wants to kill Marey and plots to copy the extortion system of the terrorists — they even call it by the same name, "a revolutionary tax." The State becomes the imagined terrorist; the calculated goals of eliminating terrorism are momentarily set aside. In the excitement of its own power, the state parodying the terrorist does what it cannot do by the "civilized" means of diplomatic pressure, that is, it terrorizes other, more powerful, states. Diplomacy responds to the rule of law, terrorism to that of desire, and this is where desire is let loose, unconstrained by the rule of law that systematically frustrates it by placing limits to the actions that the demo-cratic state can take against "terrorism."

Unlike other narratives of terrorism that explain it as a reaction to the frustration of a traumatic past, whether this past is personal or collective, terrorist transgression figures in these narratives of the state not as frus-tration but as mimetic desire to become the terrorist "other."[23] It repre-sents not so much a reaction to a painful past as a projection into the future; a future that is fantasized as a ticket to European modernity. Within this fantasy space the violence of Basque separatists constitutes more than a political threat, it is an obstacle to the desire to become European, that is, the desire to bear the marks of modernity and success. It must thus be eliminated at any cost. The desire to eliminate the terror-ist is the desire for the omnipotence of desire, the desire to hold the power attributed to terrorist transgression, a power that stands as an obstacle to European identity.

Mimetic identification does not demand exact reproduction. It does not matter that the kidnapped man is the wrong one, it is the power surging up from mimetic action, the enactment of the desire to become the terrorist that matters. It is the act of kidnapping, killing, extorting, producing communiqués, that makes terrorism — like the state — real and produces efficacy by binding actors to and in an alternate reality. In this theater of the state/terrorist, fantasy is as powerful as the calculated goals that originally impelled the actions of terror. As in Kafka's *The Trial*, the point is not the guilt or innocence of the target, but the construction of an alternate stage that, as Girard (1977) has noted, becomes all the more powerful because of its arbitrariness. Consider, for example, the narrative that Dominguez offers as the original moment of his involvement in the organization of the GAL. He was working in the intelligence department when one day the chief of police Francisco Alvarez comes to him *"and says that he wants to speak with me, and he says don't tell it to anybody. He calls me to his office and introduces me to Planchuelo, the director of the intelligence department. Then he looks at me and he says 'will you be capable of killing somebody?' "*

> Dominguez: *Well, just like that . . . I have never killed anybody.*
> Alvarez: *Yes . . . but will you be capable of killing?*
> Dominguez: *Well, if I had to defend my life, yes, but just killing I don't think so.*
> Alvarez: *But will you be willing to collaborate to help other people in a task that might be a bit risky?*
> Dominguez: *Well, if it is a question of collaborating, to help other people, well, I don't know, yes, I think I would, but the other thing, no.*
> Alvarez: *There has been a kidnapping and we have to free that person, the chief of intelligence will explain. You go with him.*

The nature of this dialogue, like the narratives discussed above, has the vague quality of a dream, the surreal scenario of a Kafkaesque story taking place in bureaucratic offices where things are said in ellipses. It is the banality of the scenario where the state materializes, the pedestrian manner in which state violence is dispensed with in this dialogue, that is terrifying. And yet, it is not surprising. Kafka made the office the fantastic space of modernity, where rational bureaucracy is the motive of an obscene and surreal nightmare. There is no self-willed state transpiring through the narratives of the two policemen, but disjointed offices and characters that come and go, fed by the fantasized image of a high purpose, an order, a state that needs to be protected and in whose name things are done. The state emerging through the narratives of the policemen is a disorganized body politic whose connections are loose and unclear, whose actions are shaped by the mixture of fantasy and bureaucratic rule, but whose effects are devastating in their deadly materiality. Against this disconnection radical nationalists, not unlike the state officials they oppose, make strenuous efforts to reconstitute the body of the state as an organic whole.[24]

Foucault, who brilliantly reworked the concept of power from a thing possessed to relations of force without origin, refused to consider the play of desire and fantasy in the formation of those relations of force. The result, as Garland (1990) has pointed out, is an overrationalist conception of power that does not take into account the force of subjective motivation in shaping power relations. It is interesting that Nietzsche, the source of inspiration for Foucault's theory of power, recognized the importance of subjectivity in social life and situated the force of affect, what he called *ressentiment*, at the center of struggles of power. Yet Foucault's reading of Nietzsche ignores the insights of this affective dimension (Brown 1997). Although his refusal responds to a political determination against the molding of desire by discourse (Miller 1993) and is not devoid of sense, it is limiting because it impedes our taking seriously the force of affect in the exercise of, and the resistance to power. Freud, in contrast, was acutely aware of the force of affect in social life, but refused to consider its political implications. Our political imaginaries and the violence that accompanies them are characterized by an entanglement of discourse and desire that needs to be examined rather than taken for granted, because it is this entanglement that constitutes political realities.

The confessional narratives of Amedo and Dominguez spun a political space thoroughly traversed by fantasy in which that elusive magical reality that we call the state materialized. Full of hearsay, fetishistic objects, shady and respectable characters, obscure conspiracies, and half-veiled secrets, these narratives became in Spain a common space of political representation, wherein the experience of the state became more "really real" than other "really reals" of administrative routines. Within this political imaginary the body of the state was not the only excitable one. In the Basque Country, at least, ordinary people like my mother responded to the narratives with obvious agitation translated into proliferation of talk in the streets, coffee shops, and taverns, in the production of jokes and avid reading of each new chapter of the saga that newspapers delivered unfailingly every day. I was not an exception to this excitement, and when I returned to the United States at the end of January 1995 barely a month after the two policemen published their confessions, my excitement must have been palpable to the department administrator, who asked about my stay in Spain. When I told her my tale of state terrorism, she asked, "is that good or bad?" and when I looked totally puzzled at her question she clarified, "Well," she said, "you seem so excited." I realized then that there is more to an event than can be translated across cultures. My excitement and her question delineated the chasm between our cultural worlds and our political universes.

If the excitement of the body politic described in this chapter sprang from the power of mimetic appropriation of the seductive and fearful power of the terrorist — our contemporary savage — how are we to understand the excitement of those who experienced the state as an effect on their lives? How are we to understand an excitement that reveals outrage but also undeniable enjoyment, or what Lacan calls *jouissance*? Enjoyment is the kernel of desire, no less present in political relations than in interpersonal ones (Zizek 1993). But enjoyment cannot be understood just as a universal structure outside history. Its operations must be contemplated within, not outside, the web of public representations and historical relations of power.

The enjoyment felt in the Basque Country over the public disclosure of state terrorism was the enjoyment of the voyeur. It was the enjoyment that those accused of perversion experience at the public disclosure of the perversity of those holding a position of self-righteousness. In the Basque Country those enjoying most the perversity of the body politic were those who were most outraged by it, radical nationalists. They were the ones chastised in the mass media as savages — totalitarian, dogmatic, violent, uncivilized — by those officials embodying the democratic state — the governors, the police, the socialist government. They were the ones to experience most strongly the effects of the state in the form of arbitrary arrests, tortures, assassinations. The confessions of Amedo and Dominguez were read as an exposure of the posturing of the body politic; an inversion of a discourse of democracy used to legitimize the monopoly of state violence. This "undressing" of the body politic is an unmasking of power as parody. The enjoyment produced by this exposure is not the enjoyment of appropriation but that of voyeuristic leveling. These two forms of enjoyment are not separated but are linked by a shared space of social fantasy within which relations of power can be imagined and materialized.

Perhaps state terrorism must be contemplated not as a deviation of democracy, a corruption of power or "power gone awry," but as an intrinsic part of contemporary practices of power (Taussig 1997; Tambiah 1996). These practices of power are deployed within a universe of fantasy in which the terrorist 'Other' has become the contemporary savage — at once an object of fear and fascination, subject to mimetic desire and identification — against whom the state can indulge in the excess of terrifying violence. "Violence," Zulaika and Douglass have noted, "introduces its perpetrators into a 'play-like' frame; fictional representations of terror become as factual as actual events and there is no longer the possibility of achieving consensus regarding what is 'real' and what is an 'as if' type of violence" (1996:135). As violence is intrinsic to the definition of the state[25] this "play-like" frame is the permanent state of being of the state, which is why the state is real even when it is a mask, why the state as mask is real and has power.

Notes

An embryonic version of this chapter was presented at the American Anthropological Association conference in 1996, in a panel organized by Jeffrey Sluka. I thank him for his encouragement and excellent editorial work. Subsequent versions were presented at the Center for Literary and Cultural Studies at Harvard University, the MIT series on "Peoples and States," and the departments of anthropology at Columbia University, the University of Texas — Austin, Rice University, and Princeton University. I have benefited greatly from the comments and suggestions of faculty and students at these venues. My gratitude especially to Josetxo Beriain, Hildred Geertz, Michael Hanchard, Michael Herzfeld, Jean Jackson, Yael Navaro-Yashin, Mary Steedly, Katie Stewart, Stanley Tambiah, Michael Taussig, Julie Taylor, Jacqueline Urla, Kay Warren, Kamala Wisweswaran, and Joseba Zulaika. The research for this article was made possible by grants from Wenner-Gren, the American Council for Learned Societies, and the George Lurcy Charitable and Educational Trust.

1. See Hayden White (1978), and in relation to how terrorism is constructed through emploted narratives see Zulaika and Douglass (1996).

2. The reform of the Francoist state was planned and set into action from within the Francoist state apparatus. With its foundations rooted in the violence of the former regime, the reform was born without political legitimacy. See Arriaga Landeta (1997:85).

3. Zizek (1993) has seen in the fetishization of democracy — as trademark of economic success and consumer enjoyment — one of the sources of the nationalist conflicts emerging in Eastern Europe after the fall of communism. This also applies to Spain, coming out of a reclusive dictatorship and gazing at Western Europe as an object of desire and social redemption.

4. A series of draconian antiterrorist laws, some of them unconstitutional, were passed during the democratic transition and the socialist administration. They freed the way to innumerable police abuses in the Basque Country. See Arriaga Landeta (1997).

5. In this day and age when the importance of violence seems to be measured by the digits of body counts, when genocide has become a public spectacle made unreal by the television screen, the violence that I am describing might seem trivial in comparison. But the gravity of violence is not measured by numbers. On the contrary, we should be weary of numbers, for in becoming the measure of value, the criteria by which we judge the meaning of violence, numbers become an anesthetic. The Basque Country is a small place (with barely two million inhabitants), densely populated and with a dense public sphere characterized by intense intimacy. In comparison with other parts of Spain, the Basque Country has a low crime rate. Terrorist violence (both from the state and from separatist organizations) has great impact in this intense social world. People who are killed are often well-known persons in their communities. Moreover, the violence in the Basque Country forms part of a drama that has been unfolding for thirty years with no clear resolution yet in sight. Placed in this historical context, each death triggers resonances at the political, social, cultural, and affective levels that need to be carefully considered.

6. The French Basque Country served as a place of refuge and center of operations of ETA during the dictatorship. Persecuted Basque activists could easily obtain political asylum and a colony of Basque refugees involved in ETA settled there relatively undisturbed except from intermittent paramilitary attacks until

1985, when France began to collaborate with the Spanish government in matters of Basque terrorism.

7. Herri Batasuna was formed in 1978 as a coalition of four political parties and a number of independent people. It was conceived and functioned from the start as the core of a political movement that gathers around itself a variety of social organizations such as youth, feminist, ecologist, labor union, and civic associations. HB functions now as a political party, but is still the center of a movement that largely exceeds the limits of its militants.

8. For example, see Miralles and Arques (1989) and Rubio and Cerdan (1997), probably the best journalistic investigations of the case.

9. ETA and other nationalist or leftist paramilitary groups operating in the Basque Country since the seventies have, as a rule, claimed responsibility for their actions.

10. See Julie Taylor (1993) for a fascinating discussion of military violence in Argentina as embodying an outlaw state.

11. The scandals involved the high echelons of the administration and financial world, and culminated with the implication of Luis Roldan, the general director of the Civil Guard, in a crime of embezzlement of public funds.

12. Apparently the government had promised Amedo and Dominguez a prompt release from prison and a large sum of money deposited monthly as compensation for their silence. The release kept being postponed and in 1994 the payments stopped. This is when Amedo and Dominguez became tired of "being a scapegoat" of the government and began to confess.

13. While in the rest of Spain the confessions of Amedo and Dominguez triggered a crisis over democratic practice and legitimation of the socialist government, in the Basque Country the controversy was woven around the legitimacy of the Spanish democracy itself and the confirmation of historical injury to the Basque people. Radical nationalists made of the dirty war the reason why the Basque Country had to be independent, in reasoning not altogether dissimilar to that made by the Zionist movement in seeking a state of their own.

14. See *El Mundo*, 27–30 December 1994.

15. By saying that the stories were full of rumor and hearsay I do not imply that they were false or that the whole affair of the dirty war is an invention, like the president of the socialist government, Felipe González, still claims. I mean only that, at the time, the confessional narratives offered by those involved in the orchestration of death squads were little more than oral narratives, yet seemed perfectly compelling. There is by now a body of hard evidence that proves the events of those narratives, yet, interestingly, such positive knowledge triggers much less interest and affective investment. What I mean by fictional reality is the configuration of a real that is structured like fantasy, and a fantasy, a plot, a scene that configures reality by articulating forms of knowing and social practices. Thus the line between reality and fantasy cannot be traced here. It would be mistaken to oppose fantasy to reality since they are linked by the same structure of desire.

16. See in this regard S. Moore (1993), particularly Moore's introduction and J. Borneman's "Trouble in the Kitchen: Totalitarianism, Love and Resistance to Authority." Y. Navaro Yashin (1997), and Warren (1993).

17. For a discussion of the notion of fantasy in psychoanalysis see Laplanche and Pontalis (1989).

18. Jenkins has made a similar point, calling for a consideration of newspapers as primary sources in ethnographic analyses of violence.

19. These disappearances had great impact in the Basque Country, the analysis

of which would exceed the scope of this article. They emerged as the confirmation of a sense of siege held by Basque radical nationalists, triggering a great deal of anger. For a new generation of young activists this event was the cognitive and emotional turn that delegitimized the Spanish democracy and constructed it as a foreign, authoritarian rule against which there was no option but to rebel.

20. The "revolutionary tax" is one of the defining features of the Basque guerrilla group ETA, an extortion of Basque industrialists that has been and continues to be its main source of funding. It is also one of the main headaches of both Spanish and Basque governments, which have tried unsuccessfully to undermine ETA's financial apparatus.

21. Subsequent investigations have implicated high officers of the Civil Guard, especially General Galindo, and attributed to this military body, which leads the antiterrorist fight, the bulk of the assassinations carried out under what is known as the dirty war. The Civil Guard has a history of paramilitary action against leftist and nationalist activists and a greater "expertise" in these matters than the Spanish national police. See in this respect Rubio and Cerdan (1997) and Rei (1996).

22. In their account of the GAL, journalists Antonio Rubio and Manuel Cerdan (1997) claim that the GAL had a seal. It was supposedly produced in the headquarters of the secret service of the army and represented an ax cutting the head of a snake. This seal, which the reputed journalists claim to have seen, points to a phantasmatic engagement with the idea of Basque terrorism materialized by the seal of ETA, which represents a snake curling around an ax.

23. For a fascinating analysis of mimetic violence and the desire of becoming the savage "other" see Obeyesekere (1992).

24. See as an example Rei (1996).

25. See in this respect Max Weber's definition of the state as holding the monopoly of violence. More caustically, Benjamin (1978) saw in the intrinsically violent character of the state a sign of its degeneration; and see Derrida's (1990) reading of Benjamin that situates violence at the heart of justice or law.

Bibliography

Abrams, Phillip
    1988 [1977] "Notes on the Difficulty of Studying the State." *Journal of Historical Sociology* 1:1, pp. 58–89.
Arriaga Landeta, Mikel
    1997 *Y Nosotros Que Eramos de HB.* San Sebastian, Spain: Haramburu Ed.
Benjamin, Walter
    1978 [1920] "Critique of Violence." *Reflections: Essays, Aphorisms, Autobiographical Writings.* New York: Harcourt Brace Jovanovich.
Brown, Wendy
    1995 *States of Injury: Power and Freedom in Late Modernity.* Princeton: Princeton University Press.
Derrida, Jacques
    1990 "Force of Law: The 'Mystical' Foundation of Authority." *Cardozo Law Review* 11, pp. 921–1045.
Gabilondo, Joseba
    1997 "Masculinity's Counted Days: Spanish Postnationalism, Masochist Desire, and the Rephrasing of Misogyny." *Anuano de Cine y Literatura en Español,* 3, pp. 53–72.

Garcia Damborenea, Ricardo
  1987 *Manual del Buen Terrorista*. Madrid: Cambio 16.
Garland, David
  1990 *Punishment and Modern Society: A Study in Social Theory*. Chicago: University of Chicago Press.
Girard, René
  1977 *Violence and the Sacred*. Baltimore: Johns Hopkins University Press.
Gupta, Akhil
  1995 "The Discourse of Corruption." *American Ethnologist* 22:2, pp. 375–402.
Laplanche, Jean, and Jean-Bertrand Pontalis
  1989 [1964] "Fantasy and the Origins of Sexuality." *Formations of Fantasy*. V. Burgin, J. Donald, and C. Kaplan, eds. New York: Routledge.
Miller, James
  1993 *The Passion of Michel Foucault*. New York: Simon and Schuster.
Miralles, Melchor, and Ricardo Arques
  1989 *Amedo: El Estado Contra ETA*. Madrid: Plaza and James.
Mitchell, Timothy
  1991 "The Limits of the State: Beyond the Statist Approaches and Their Critics." *American Political Science Review*, 85:1, pp. 77–95.
Moore, S. (ed.)
  1993 *Moralizing States and the Ethnography of the Present*. Washington, D.C.: American Ethnological Society.
Navaro-Yashin, Yael
  1998 "Uses and Abuses of 'State and Civil Society' in Contemporary Turkey." *New Perspectives on Turkey*, no. 18, pp. 1–22.
  1997 "Travesty and Truth: Politics of Culture and Fantasies of the State in Turkey." Ph.D. diss. Princeton University.
Obeyesekere, Gananath
  1992 " 'British Cannibals': Contemplation of an Event in the Death and Resurrection of James Cook, Explorer." *Critical Inquiry*, 18, pp. 630–654.
Rei, Pepe
  1996 *Intxaurrondo: La Trama Verde*. Tafalla: Editorial Txalaparta.
Rubio, Antonio, and Manuel Cerdan
  1997 *El Origin del GAL: "Guerra Sucia" y Crimen de Estado*. Madrid: Temas de Hoy.
Scarry, Elaine
  1985 *The Body in Pain: The Making and Unmaking of the World*. New York: Oxford University Press.
Tambiah, Stanley J.
  1996 *Leveling Crowds: Ethnonationalist Conflicts and Collective Violence in South Asia*. Berkeley: University of California Press.
Taussig, Michael
  1997 *The Magic of the State*. New York: Routledge.
  1993 *Mimesis and Alterity*. New York: Routledge.
  1992 "Maleficium: State Fetishism." In *The Nervous System*, by M. Taussig. New York: Routledge.
Taylor, Julie
  1993 "The Outlaw State and the Lone Rangers." In *Perilous States: Conversations on Culture, Politics and Nation*. G. Marcus, ed. Chicago: University of Chicago Press.
Warren, Kay B.
  1993 "Interpreting La Violencia in Guatemala: Shapes of Mayan Silence and

Resistance." In *The Violence Within: Cultural and Political Opposition in Divided Nations*, ed. Kay B. Warren. Boulder, Colo.: Westview Press, 25–56.

White, Hayden

1978 *Tropics of Discourse: Essays in Cultural Criticism.* Baltimore: Johns Hopkins University Press.

Zizek, Slavoj

1993 "Enjoy Your Nation as Yourself!" *Tarrying with the Negative: Kant, Hegel, and the Critique of Ideology.* Durham, N.C.: Duke University Press.

Zulaika, Joseba, and William Douglass

1996 *Terror and Taboo: The Follies, Fables, and Faces of Terrorism.* New York: Routledge.

Chapter 2
Trials by Fire
Dynamics of Terror in Punjab and Kashmir

Cynthia Keppley Mahmood

Two regions in the northwestern part of India have been the sites of major insurgencies over the past decade and a half. Punjab has faced an uprising by Sikh separatists aiming for the establishment of a sovereign state called Khalistan, and Kashmir a similar uprising by Muslims intent on either accession to Pakistan or an independent Kashmiri state. Counterinsurgencies in both areas have left the Indian government open to vigorous criticism by international human rights groups, in no area more strongly than in that of extrajudicial executions and enforced disappearances. No one knows the actual number of executed and "disappeared" Sikhs and Kashmiris; they number certainly in the thousands for each area, and probably in the tens of thousands for both regions combined. Those killed by Indian police, security and military personnel include militants, shelterers of militants, and separatist activists, but also include medical workers, human rights lawyers, and entirely innocent civilians. Torture and custodial rape are ubiquitous across both regions.[1]

Let me first, by way of background, lay out a few key differences and similarities between the situations in Punjab and Kashmir. Both involve religion — in one case Sikh, in the other Muslim — in what is formally a secular, but in de facto terms increasingly a Hindu, state of India. The Sikhs, however, are largely on their own in this conflict despite some probable assistance from India's longtime enemy, Pakistan, because of their geographic concentration in Punjab. The Kashmiri Muslims have, on the other hand, the leverage of transnational Islam, which provides both an actual and an imagined threat behind every Kashmiri assertion of separation from India.

Second, the Punjab conflict is largely a domestic one, centered on the secessionist movement for Khalistan. Kashmir is alternatively entirely tied up in international politics. Pakistan, India, and China have already fought several wars over it, there is a longstanding United Nations interest in and presence in Kashmir, and there is substantial juridical ambiguity about India's claim to the area at the time of Partition. Though Sikh militants would like to claim a similar ambiguity, the historical record is far less clear here than in the Kashmir case, and other nations — excepting again Pakistan — have shown minimal interest in getting involved.

Both Sikh and Kashmiri insurgencies are very recent, the Sikh one dating from 1984 and the Kashmiri one from 1989. Despite (or perhaps because of) their relative youth, both are heavily factionalized. Militant Sikh factions at least share the common goal of a sovereign state of Khalistan, while the Kashmiris are radically divided into those who hope to join Pakistan and those who would like to see an entirely independent Kashmir. The Hizb-ul Mujahideen and Harkat-ul Ansar are the two major forces supporting the former position, and the Jammu and Kashmir Liberation Front is the most important organization supporting the latter. These three, and other smaller groups, are currently united in a political coalition called the Hurriyet Conference, which holds the explicit goal of a plebiscite on Kashmir's future. The major Sikh forces (today in a state of quiescence) like the Khalistan Commando Force, the Babbar Khalsa, the Khalistan Liberation Force, the Sikh Students Federation, and the Bhindranwale Tiger Force, have always been somewhat at odds with one another despite a common ideology and military aim.

Finally, the level of support for insurgency among the population as a whole is today far more obvious in the Kashmiri than in the Sikh case. It may well be, as Khalistanis argue, that over a decade of counterinsurgency has frightened the Punjabi populace into apparent submission. It is also true that infiltration and criminalization of the Khalistani forces have alienated the people of Punjab from the "freedom fighters." But the plain fact is — whatever the reasons — that at the moment a Kashmiri guerrilla can assume a level of sympathy from civilians that a Khalistani guerrilla cannot.

Despite these important differences in the situations of India's two northwestern states, they are linked by a program of state terror emanating from New Delhi. From the viewpoint of the central government, a successful secessionist effort in either place could have a dangerous domino effect on other disaffected peripheries, perhaps pulling India's fragile union apart a mere half century after independence. In the name of national security India passed counterterrorism legislation that severely curtailed democratic rights and freedoms as well as turning a blind eye to the pervasive abuses noted year after year by the international human rights community. (Now there is a national Human Rights Commission, but its powers are severely limited.) Perhaps as important is the national mood of increasing intolerance for dissent, which has transformed India's intellectual life over the past decade and a half. Most Indians, willfully ignorant of the horrors taking place in their name, continue to chant the "mantra of democracy," as Barbara Crossette calls it (1993: 104); there is an Alice-in-Wonderland quality to the national image of pacific mysticism and tranquil coexistence.

At one point in the counterinsurgency in Punjab, so many bodies of "disappeared" Sikhs were being dumped in the state's waterways that the governor of neighboring Rajasthan had to issue a complaint that dead bodies from Punjab were clogging up his canals. In Muzaffarabad, on the Pakistani or "free" side of Kashmir, a blackboard by the banks of the Jhelum River keeps count as Kashmiri bodies float down from across the border. (When I visited in January 1997, the grim chalk tally there was at 476.) Given the deep mythic significance of India's rivers in the Hindu tradition, this defilement is especially telling. "The largest democracy on earth" has polluted its sacred waters with the bodies of tortured citizens.

That this hellish state of affairs continues to inspire "terrorism" is unsurprising. That the world continues to hear more about terrorism than about state terror is both misleading and shameful. Anthropologists who refuse complicity in this dangerous game have, however, the responsibility for elucidating just what the effects of state terror are at grassroots level as well as researching the dynamics of resistance to it. The ethnographic study of political violence, which complements the study of ideological and macroscopic factors with attention to the lived realities of human experience, has a great deal to contribute to our understanding of conflict and to the potential for its resolution.

This is not the place for a detailed review of the conflicts in Punjab and Kashmir; for these I refer the reader to accounts by Kapur (1986), Kumar (1996), Lamb (1992), Mahmood (1996), Newberg (1995), Pettigrew (1995), Schofield (1996), Thomas (1992) and Wirsing (1994). What I would like to do here, rather, is to further consider what living in an arena of conflict is actually like for residents of Punjab and Kashmir. What are the main features of state terror as it is experienced by Sikhs and Muslims of India's northwest? How are actions of resistance shaped by the environment of terror? And (not to be ignored) how do the militant movements themselves contribute to the perpetuation of that environment?

A Tale of Terror

It was a wintry January evening in Muzaffarabad when I heard Yacub's story, he lying on one cot, me on another, gazing up at the ceiling in the kind of semidarkness that prompts the putting aside of roles, that prompts intimacies and confidences. He was a young fellow, as many of them are, probably no more than eighteen, with close-cropped hair and a trim beard, jet black, and dark eyes, and clothes that seemed too big for his wiry frame. Or maybe it was simply his youth that made his clothes seem too big; could this really be one of the mujahideen, whose very name evokes a sense of the dangerous, the exotic, the heroic (in various combinations depending on one's political sympathies)? The reality, minus the intimidating weapons, in the comforting twilight of the guest house, was deceptively unlike the stereotype. Yacub was just a boy; he could be my student, in another world, or my son.

Yacub had decided to join the Hizb-ul Mujahideen — one of the largest of the guerrilla forces fighting against the government of India in Kashmir — after the town in which he lived suffered several sweeps of Indian security forces that left bloody corpses, burned houses, and raped women in its wake. He didn't know much about the political issues at stake here, he knew only that the devastation wreaked upon people he knew was tied to the fact that they were Kashmiri and that if Kashmir were removed from India this devastation would stop. The Hizb-ul Mujahideen, one of the Islamist groups, tied this issue to the fact that the Kashmiris were Muslims and that every other state in India was dominated by Hindus, and saw Islamic Pakistan, next door, as a natural ally. The Hizb-ul Mujahideen had bases over the Himalayan border — called officially the Line of Control — in Azad Kashmir, of which Muzaffarabad was the capital. Yacub quit school and set off, along with some of his young friends, to cross the mountains into Pakistan for training as a *mujahid*.

The group of youngsters had just left the last villages behind them when they came across an old man, gnarled and white-haired, pitifully trying to climb a rocky slope. "Grandfather," they said, "What are you doing here? Sit, rest, you will not make it up this mountain."

The old man sat, and recounted how Indian soldiers burst into his house one day, ripping the clothes off his grown daughter and tying both of them to a wooden post. One by one they raped and abused her as her father tried helplessly to close his eyes and ears. After the soldiers left, the old man managed to break free of his bindings, and proceeded to hunt down an ax. He came back to his daughter and said, "I can't leave you here like this. I am going to kill you, and then I am going to burn this house and all our things, and I am going to join the mujahideen and avenge your honor."

The old man had done just this, hacking his daughter to pieces with an ax and burning the entire compound, and was now on his way to "join the mujahideen."

"Grandfather," the young men said. "You can never make it over these mountains. You go back home, go to your relatives and stay with them. We will avenge the honor of your daughter for you. We will do the fighting for you."

Yacub then told how the old man did turn back, and made his way slowly back down the hillside. The young recruits, thirty-four in all, pushed on. Over the course of the next two weeks the little group ran into security patrols several times, resulting in nine deaths. Two more deaths came from cliffside falls; a third was buried in a chance avalanche. Four others froze to death during pauses on the high-altitude trails. When the remaining eighteen eventually crossed the border, five of them had severe frostbite, enough to warrant amputation of limbs. Another came down with a respiratory infection and died within weeks.

The handful of surviving would-be warriors began training for jihad.

My young bunkmate's story brings out some key features of the arena of terror, which I shall now explore in greater detail. Primary among these is the nonstrategic and nonpolitical quality of the lived experience of state violence, which often prompts a similarly nonstrategic and nonpolitical resistance. The language of strategy and politics, though most often used in the analysis of conflicts like the one in Kashmir, barely scratches the surface of the actual personal engagement of individuals in the violence that enmeshes them. The ethnographic study of this violence illuminates a different dynamic, which must be addressed as a central part of any attempt at conflict resolution.[2]

Humiliation

Let us begin with the very dramatic episode which ends with the old man putting his daughter to death with an ax. This is a move which angers us with its sexism and frustrates us with its waste. Yet it illuminates a central part of the dynamic of state terror, which aims not merely to suppress a threatening minority, but to humiliate its members so thoroughly that they are incapable not only of resistance but of basic dignity as well. The fact that Indian soldiers understood that the point of greatest vulnerability for Kashmiri Muslim men was the sexual honor of their women shows their acute awareness of the dynamics of this kind of humiliation in a campaign of terror. The defiant gesture of killing his daughter was then the old man's refusal to allow humiliation to stand in the way of resistance. This is, at any rate, how the story was taken by himself and his young Kashmiri interlocutors.

Intangibles like pride and shame are rarely part of the calculus of justice that frames most Western thinking about political order/disorder. In

Rawls's classic conception of a just society, for example (1971), each individual must at birth be assured of a fair chance in the game of social life; a person's rewards should be commensurate with his or her efforts. But this liberal notion neglects the element of compassion for the weak that in spite of political theory is a keystone of what most people intuitively consider to be a central element of human decency, as Avishai Margalit points out in his addendum to Rawls, *The Decent Society* (1996). A society which humiliates is never decent, asserts Margalit, however justly its rewards may be allocated on the basis of individual effort and agreed-upon social rules.

This attention to basic human respect sheds some new light on India's caste system, which even for those who relativistically accept the religious justification of merits accumulating over multiple lifetimes to account for the disparate life chances of Brahmins and Untouchables, contains an element of basic *indecency* in its denial of dignity to those ending up at the bottom. It is episodes of humiliation, and not poverty or reduced life chances per se, that are highlighted in the recollections of individuals who have spent their lives as Untouchables. Likewise — however contrary to expectation — it is the humiliating aspects of state terror, like the rape of one's daughter, that occupy center stage in the narrations of its victims. Such episodes, for the individuals involved, far eclipse the element of bodily pain, and overwhelm the political considerations typically at the heart of discussions of conflict.

Punjabi Sikhs, like Kashmiri Muslims, have a culture in which honor means everything. Over the course of six years' research on the Khalistani insurgency, I found that the two kinds of stories most likely to provoke both tears and anger were those involving female sexuality and those involving symbolic insults such as the cutting of hair or beard (kept long as a matter of religious principle). Interestingly, Sikh rebels turned these same tactics on one of their primary enemies, the former director general of police of Punjab, K. P. S. Gill. Although Gill has been publicly declared to be one of the top targets of the remaining Khalistani militants, when some ran into him in Belgium in 1996 they did not kill him but merely snatched his turban. When a Khalistani leader was asked about the limited nature of this assault, he replied that Gill "didn't deserve to be killed." He meant this is in the sense that this enemy was not *good enough* for a death with honor, a kind of battlefield death; he would, rather, be humiliated by having the turban, symbol of Sikh dignity, knocked from his head. And there is a powerful taunt in this gesture as well; we *could* kill you, but we do not choose to do so.

The sense of being a marked person, of waiting for the violent death that can come at any moment, underlies the state's use of random terror tactics as well. Sweeps of neighborhoods occur suddenly, often at night; people are dragged off to police stations and interrogation centers in their night clothes. One house will be hit; another spared. The over- whelming presence of security forces, as many as half a million in Punjab and Kashmir each at the heights of their respective counterinsurgencies, means that the civilians are virtually prisoners, awaiting the knock on the door, the siren at the end of the street. As Camus pointed out in his classic essay on the death penalty, "Reflections on the Guillotine" (1961), this purgatory state of being is itself a form of torture in its total sub- version of individual autonomy (a point echoed by Sister Helen Prejean [1993]). In a state under military occupation, everyone is under a sort of death sentence. Whether one is spared or not is more a matter of luck than of innocence. And in the face of this kind of uncertainty stress disorders proliferate; "Belfast nerves" manifest themselves in Amritsar and Srinagar, too, and they are as much a product of state terror as of "terrorism."

The undermining of the self that is the long-term result of existence in these conditions is the short-term goal of custodial torture as well. Schol- ars of torture have long known that although the near-universal rationale for torture is the obtaining of information, there is much more going on in the torture arena than linear means-to-end strategy. Elaine Scarry (1985) has written most effectively of bodily pain as a narrower of worlds, a constrictor of human space down to the mammalian elements of breath, hunger, elimination, sleep, warmth. Although we often say that torturers are denying the humanity of their victims, in fact the purposeful infliction of purposeless pain recognizes the humanity of the tortured in its attempt to eradicate that human element. As William Ian Miller notes, "[The torturers] know that the people they torture are humans . . . and that is why they torture them, in the hope that they can reveal them as not being what they know they are. There is no thrill in making a rat act like a rat. The thrill is in making a human act like a rat. And a human who acts like a rat justifies his torture for two contradictory reasons: because he disgraces his humanity by acting like a rat and because as a rat he is pretending to humanity, a most disgraceful and arrogant presumption for a rat" (1993: 166). No one wants to be turned into a rat. Is it surprising that subsequent to a degradation like this, a survivor's only thought is the reclamation of his or her humanity, whatever that takes?

Sikh and Kashmiri torture survivors frequently report the role of reli- gion in sustenance during custody. A link to God (Waheguru, Allah) through prayer is one way of retaining a hold on a world outside the domineering pain of torture Scarry so insightfully describes. It would not be too strong a statement to say that many Sikhs and Kashmiris have ended up "finding religion," so to speak, through their own incarceration and torture. This is not because in Indian jails they are rubbing shoulders with fanatics who unduly influence them in this direction (a typical explanation), but also because the conditions with which they are faced demand more-than-human resources.

Outsiders who visit Sikhs' homes and *gurudwaras* (places of worship) are often taken aback by the presence of posters illustrating gory scenes of torture. The same kinds of pictures form a wall-to-wall mural at a Kashmiri center I visited; they can be found in newsletters, in family photo albums, on wall calendars, and even on T-shirts. While part of the intent of such exhibition is to provoke continuing anger, there is no doubt that torture pictures are mostly received as inspiration by Sikh and Kashmiri audiences; see, they exclaim, what we are capable of overcoming! See how nothing stops us! Christ on the cross, after all, provokes both sorrow and joy — and is the continuing inspiration for some Latin American resistance movements through the image of *Cristo guerrillero*.

Religion, in having one foot always outside and beyond the immediate social order, is a key mobilizer of resistance against state oppression. Buoyant movements of religious nationalism around the globe today, while deeply frightening to those in the West nurtured on the ideal of secular liberal democracy, must be understood at least in part in terms of the orders which they resist (Juergensmeyer 1993). The state of India, in the actions it has taken against Sikh and Kashmiri insurgents, has clearly shown its awareness of the power of religiously motivated resistance. When it attacked the Golden Temple complex at Amritsar in 1984, containing the holiest shrine of the Sikhs, the ostensible aim was to rid the sacred buildings of the militants who had taken up shelter inside. But the level of force used in the attack was utterly incommensurate with this limited and eminently attainable aim. Seventy thousand troops, in conjunction with the use of tanks and chemical gas, killed not only the few dozen militants who didn't manage to escape the battleground but also hundreds (possibly thousands) of innocent pilgrims, the day of the attack being a Sikh holy day. The Akal Takht, the seat of temporal authority for the Sikhs, was reduced to rubble and the Sikh Reference Library, an irreplaceable collection of books, manuscripts, and artifacts bearing on all aspects of Sikh history, burned to the ground. Thirty-seven other shrines were attacked across Punjab on the same day. The only possible reason for this appalling level of state force against its own citizens must be that the attempt was not merely to "flush out," as they say, a handful of militants, but to destroy the fulcrum of a possible mass resistance against the state.

A similar chain of events occurred at Charar-i-Sharif and Hazratbal mosques in Kashmir. It is true that it was militants who first politicized these places of worship, as in the case of the Golden Temple complex.

But it was the state's response to this politicization that turned Charar-i-Sharif and Hazratbal into potent symbols of oppression. Insults to the body and soul of individuals, as in the torture enterprise, are paralleled by insults to the community and faith, when *gurudwaras* and mosques come under siege. No Sikh can ever forget what happened at the Golden Temple complex; Kashmiri Muslims will always be haunted by the image of Indian troops at their mosques. And these memories are concretized in the form of pictures, paintings, posters insisting again and again that such sacrilege will not be forgotten. Ruined buildings jostle with desecrated bodies for wall space in militant living environments.

Sikhs cremate their dead, while Muslims bury. This implies a somewhat different dynamic of memorialization in the two communities. For Sikhs there are typically memorial services held in honor of the heroic deceased every so often after the death, which are the occasions for cementing of continued solidarity. For Muslims, the presence of a burial site forms a geographic, rather than chronological, center for such solidarity. Both communities are deeply affronted when they are unable to treat the body of a loved one in the proper way; photos of wild dogs tearing apart the bodies of young men on the street are among the most horrifying of those that circulate. And "disappearances," common to both areas, are wounds that never heal. Human rights workers investigating the problem of disappearances have been themselves disappeared, without a trace.

Though there is a long history of rational grievance and countergrievance that on the macroscopic scale defines the evolution of conflict in Punjab and Kashmir, when one grapples with the grassroots experience of these conflicts one has to conceptualize not politics but humiliation and rage. Lots of Sikhs and Kashmiris know nothing at all about treaties, international boundaries, agricultural prices, or the allocation of electric power. For many of them, it is the visceral anger stemming from physical, emotional, and spiritual insult that prompts the taking up of arms.

Dignity

Yacub, the young Kashmiri fighter who now sits across the border in Pakistan, awaits his chance to avenge the honor of the old man whose daughter was raped. He is also now burdened with being among the survivors of the initial band of recruits who headed off across the Himalayas together, and hence carries a sense of responsibility to make his comrades' deaths meaningful as well. Why did he live, and they die? Yacub's sense of mission increases with each passing day. His own family, who advised him to finish school rather than joining the mujahideen, doesn't know where he is. He has to do something to make that sacrifice worthwhile, too.

The poignant combination of extreme youth with seriousness of purpose is quite dangerous, of course, particularly given the plethora of sophisticated weapons that have flooded South Asia since the Afghan war (thanks to the two former Cold War enemies whose battleground that became). The jihad of the Muslims and the *dharm yudh* of the Sikhs are both philosophical and military struggles, which our English rendition as "holy war" rather trivializes. These concepts have long and complex theological histories, but one thing they convey is the sense that there is more at stake in a given campaign than territory alone. There is a higher purpose, for the achievement of which life itself is no sacrifice at all. Hence the traditions of battlefield martyrdom that have impressed and terrified the enemies of Sikhs and Muslims throughout history.

I will suggest here that although the theological underpinnings of jihad and *dharm yudh* are unique, the notion that there is more of philosophy than strategy in why people fight is deserving of wider consideration. Paul Freire (1993) is exemplary among the dozens of commentators on guerrilla resistance movements for the lucidity with which he expresses the sense that acts of violence can best be understood as attempts to reclaim human dignity in otherwise inhuman situations. Note that in this conception it is the acts of violence which are themselves significant, independent of what they accomplish or fail to accomplish in strategic terms. This facet of revolutionary violence is often overlooked because it appears to be nonsensical or irrational in the linear terms with which we typically think about conflict, but it is critical. Without understanding that from the viewpoint of most guerrilla fighters what they are doing is the pinnacle not of inhumanity but of humanity (and for some, the strong awareness that this humanity is God-given), we will never be able to effectively grapple with the problem of insurgent violence.

If Sikh and Kashmiri fighters simply "wanted to die for the cause," as the insurgent-as-fanatic school of thought would have it, both separatist movements would be making far more use of suicide missions than they in fact do. (There are some cases in each, but they are few in number.) Suicide missions are highly effective, in sheer military terms. But although *willingness* to die characterizes both Sikh and Kashmiri guerrillas, the aim is a more existential one: to live and die meaningfully, to make one's life and death count not in the game of casualty tallies but in the definition of one's humanity. Martyrs are venerated not really for their deaths, which are incidental, but for their courage in living lives that denied the indignities around them.

There is no doubt that there is a certain exhilaration in having decided to live "with one's head in one's hands," as the Sikhs say; to relinquish the self in favor of a higher cause, to lose all fear of death. Khalistani fighters describe a sense of "rising spirits" that fills them with joy even as they face near-certain death in battle. Similar feelings of liberation have been described in other warrior traditions, such as the "killing laugh" of the *berserk* state in the Icelandic sagas (Miller 1993:103). A young man from Sudan who had come to join the jihad for Kashmir commented, "You can say I have come here because of a moral obligation to help my brothers in Kashmir. Maybe that is why I first came. But now I stay because I just like it. I feel great. I know that God is with me all the time and I have never been so much at peace in my life. I have literally no fear at all. I feel free because I am doing the right thing." Another young *mujahid*, this one too young for a beard, noted, "I thought I might feel afraid if I had to face the possibility of death. But once I made the decision [to join the mujahideen], not a grain of fear has come into my mind. All that has gone up in smoke. I used to be afraid of my teachers! Now, I am afraid of nothing. I have overcome my fear and I can do whatever is required now, as God is with me."

Lest it be supposed that I am valorizing the militants by including such quotes, let me hastily note that Sikh and Kashmiri guerrillas in these exalted states have been culpable for some horrific acts of violence. One of the most difficult things for me to grapple with in my study of Khalistani militants was the refusal of most of them to condemn the obvious atrocities committed by a few. For example, everyone would agree that innocent people should not be targeted in a war of national liberation. But when other militants did in fact set off bombs in urban neighborhoods, with no military or political target, few would come out and say that it was wrong. When I probed further, it became clear that the reason for this hesitation was that the evaluation of the act was in Sikh minds totally tied up with the wider evaluation of the individuals responsible. So-and-so is a good/sincere/devout/honest man, so what he did must have been all right. This inseparability of act from actor (honorable people do honorable things; dishonorable people do dishonorable things) is characteristic of heroic cultures (as per Nietzsche 1969). When people pushed to ratlike status rise up, they become supermen. They challenge the status quo at every turn, and every act of breaking the law is experienced by them and their audience as a celebration.

Zulaika and Douglass, who have long studied Basque separatists, note in their extended meditation *Terror and Taboo* that insurgent violence is frequently more "ritual" than "functional" (1996), drawing on anthropological categories. They describe well the sense of "deep play" that pervades the insurgent community, unfettered as it is by the fear of death that circumscribes the lives of most of the rest of us. Traditions of martyrdom among Irish Republicans, Tamil Tigers, Palestinians, and others are highly spiritual, and have little to do with "warfare" as we typically conceive it. Even though these groups talk in terms of the "wars" they are fighting, the centrality of morality in their struggles (the just war, the holy cause) places many of their actions outside the realm of military strategy. "The martyr is the antithesis of the soldier," comments Pettigrew (1996:129).

Let us return to K. P. S. Gill, former police chief of Punjab who had his turban knocked off in Belgium, for an illustration of this principle. After retiring from the Punjab police, Gill went on to become president of the Indian Hockey Federation. In this capacity he planned to attend the Olympic Games in Atlanta in 1996. There were obvious security concerns for the American hosts, given Gill's history vis-à-vis the Sikhs. Expatriate Sikh organizations, however, were totally committed to keeping violence out of North America. The U.S. and Canada had provided asylum to Sikh victims of state terror, and Khalistanis continued to need communities outside of India which were centers of activism. The public relations effect of any act of violence here would be disastrous. Everyone agreed that there must be no attempt to touch Gill in Atlanta, although he is a known top target generally.

These kinds of thoughts are the thoughts of soldiers, which the leaders of the Khalistani organizations basically are. They are thinking of the strategic impact of one or another course of action, and molding their behavior to that course of action with the highest chance of success. Fortunately, their rationality won out in this case. But many of those involved in the Khalistan movement are not, in fact, soldiers. In private discussions, there was a lot of talk along lines of the moral necessity of "delivering justice" to the former police chief no matter what the circumstances and no matter what the repercussions. Some were willing to martyr not only themselves but the cause, if necessary, to meet the moral challenge of bringing down the man they hold responsible for the thousands of abuses that occurred in Punjab during his watch.

The fact that "terrorist" acts are often more expressive than instrumental in nature is oddly reciprocated by the industry of counterterrorism, which despite its rhetoric of brute realism is focused on strategies that appeal philosophically but are rarely pragmatic responses to the violence they purport to address. When facing willing martyrs, heavy-handed combat approaches are of little use. When facing those whose anger stems from a sense of humiliation, using appellations like "mad dog," "coward," and so on (the list is endless) hurt rather than help. Both delegitimizing rhetoric and elevated security appeal to the mainstream (antiterrorist) audience, of course, just as the attack on the Golden Temple complex was applauded by the people of India generally and the labeling of Sikh militants as criminals was readily accepted in the mainline media. But both tactics preached to the choir; their reception among the militants, whose behavior after all one was presumably trying to affect, was nothing less than disastrous. For people who already feel their humanity is being challenged, being publicly imagined as nothing more than rats invites further attempts to prove otherwise.

So we have come full circle here, noting that acts of state terror like torture and the bombing of religious places are more than simple military tactics, that responses to them resonate with meanings far beyond the strategic, and that state responses to insurgent violence again cannot really be understood as pragmatic politics. To understand them as forms of performance or ritual, while risking trivialization of the bloodshed involved, is an important antidote to the hyperrational war discourse that merely skims the surface of the violent arena. The world of Punjabis and Kashmiris is one fraught with meanings; every action reverberates through multiple frames of cognition and emotion. Nothing less than the definition of the self is at stake — baptized, molded, and welded by fire.

The conflicts in Punjab and Kashmir are also, however, about the shaping of nations. We cannot address this without moving beyond individual experience to the notion of collective identities, shaped in point/counterpoint through oppositional conflict. So we have to shift gears here, from philosophy and psychology to a more sociological look at the role of state and resistive violence in group boundary definition.

Terror and Identity

Barbara Crossette's plaintive interrogative with regard to India must be taken seriously: more Indians are killed *each year* by their own police and security apparatus than were killed during the entire seventeen-year dictatorship of Pinochet in Chile, but why is there no domestic outcry (1993: 104)? The failure of Indians to protest this situation cannot be chalked up to apathy or amorality; that much is clear from their mobilization around other causes. Rather, their complicity must be understood in terms of the fact that Sikhs and Muslims have come to be defined as traitors to the Indian nation, conceptualized increasingly around its Hindu heritage, and the seemingly just punishment for treason is death. India, as a young and weak state torn up by centrifugal forces of linguistic, ethnic, and religious diversity, asserts its boundaries boldly (if extrajudicially) by eradicating those who step outside the line. This is a common scenario all over the world, as the geographic spread of the chapters in this volume tragically attests. And the "fearful state" tactics of such frail collectivities (after Ali 1993) are mirrored in the separatists' own organizations and strategies, which are likewise focused on the delineation of boundaries through the twin concepts of nationalism and treason. They are aiming for their own states, and like the state of India extrajudicially execute traitors. The phenomenon of death squad activities in arenas of conflict can be, then, a window into the ideological framework of nations and national identities — a framework which shapes discourse, and death, on both sides.

The "Black Cat" phenomenon in Punjab and Kashmir points illustratively to the role that terror tactics play in the heightened awareness of group identity nurtured in the militant movements. The phrase stems from the Indian police and security forces' use of what is called a CAT or "concealed apprehension technique," in which a former militant who has been bribed or persuaded to betray his comrades wears a black hood over his head and face and points out those to be targeted for elimination. The Black Cat commandos are a particularly feared and despised element of separatist militancy in both Punjab and Kashmir. Someone who has become a "cat" or informer is a key target for militant reprisals, of course. And there is a particular venom against "cats" as compared to other informers or enemies, because they have been part of, then betrayed, the imagined nations of Khalistan or Kashmir. Militants from all groups are utterly unapologetic about the equation of treason with death in these cases.

The Black Cat as a hooded and anonymous figure is particularly repellent, however — more of an untouchable than a mere enemy — and the vehemence of reprisals against "cats" invites further consideration. The covering of the face of the Black Cat precludes the man-to-man kind of confrontation that is celebrated in the insurgent movements. "You have to look someone in the eye and tell him what he did wrong, then punish him," a member of the Khalistan Commando Force told me. Joyce Pettigrew (1995) remarks on the tradition of public challenging that characterized the early phases of the Sikh insurgency, in which a fighter would call out his identity and dare his adversaries to respond. This goes beyond the merely strategic elimination of an enemy or a betrayer. It speaks to a need to give voice to a new reality, in which guerrillas are not terrorists sneaking around in the dark but freedom fighters boldly defining their turf and establishing new boundaries. You have crossed the line of this new nation, you are a traitor, and now I will kill you. The Black Cat, in evading this confrontation and definition by his anonymity, frustrates nationalist aspirations that depend on the articulation of nationhood and treason in the act of punishment. He trades in ambiguity, and is, hence, tabooed. Paradoxically, an enemy who will come out and fight — even if he is likely to win — helps in the definition of nationhood that the militants seek. The Black Cat is not a hero; he is an antihero, and despised.

We can all understand, if not sympathize with, a logic which posits a nation (of India, or of Khalistan or Kashmir) then punishes those who would bring it down with death — accompanying those deaths with proclamations that make publicly clear what the symbolism of the boundary means. But there is an added factor in the Sikh and Kashmiri insurgencies that muddies these waters further, and that is the equation of religious community with nation in at least some versions of the envisioned new states. We have already looked at the important role of spirituality in how individuals respond to terror and in how they define themselves in an environment of terror, as well as how the state uses attacks on religion as a form of degradation and delegitimization. But the insurgent movements as wholes have taken on the cause of defending religion as well. Sikh militant groups in Punjab have targeted not only Indian police and security forces, and not only those among their own who have betrayed the cause by becoming informers, but also civilians remiss in upholding the tenets of the Sikh religion or in celebrating the Punjabi language. Kashmiris have not only fought against the military occupiers of their towns and cities, but also against local Hindus, many of whom have now fled Kashmir as refugees, prompting accusations of "ethnic cleansing." In both Punjab and Kashmir, puritan elements of the Sikh and Muslim religious communities have forcefully attempted to impose a particular moral code on their populations of support, which has not only antagonized many of them but has also enhanced the image of the militants as "fundamentalists." Not only are they "terrorists," but "fundamentalists," too. Who can sympathize with them?

Liberals in the rest of India find themselves in a position of ambivalence; they condemn the human rights abuses that have certainly been perpetrated on the Sikhs and Kashmiris, they may stand in solidarity with some of their political grievances, but they fear a nonsecular outcome of the struggles they are witnessing. Dipankar Gupta noted after the brutal massacre of several thousand Sikhs in Delhi in 1984, "Bleeding-heart liberals weren't sure whether they should bleed with the Sikhs" (Gupta 1985). A dozen years later, they still aren't sure. Most dare not speak out too loudly about death squads and disappearances in Kashmir, for fear that stance may be taken as solidarity with those same Muslims who demonstrated against Salman Rushdie in the streets in Srinagar.

Sikhs who are defining an eventual Khalistan as a religious homeland face big questions about the relationship between the Akal Takht, the seat of religious authority for the Sikhs, and the government of a state which, after all, will include more than just Sikhs within its boundaries. Kashmiris are already facing similar issues in the division of their independence movement into the Islamist Hizb-ul Mujahideen, Harkat-ul Ansar, and other organizations, and the secular Jammu and Kashmir Liberation Front (JKLF), which envision very different futures for Kashmir. It is the rallying of the discontented and dispossessed around the banner of religion, which occurs to a greater or lesser extent among most of the Sikh and Kashmiri groups, which prompts the greatest skepticism on the part of not only secular Indians but Westerners as well. If you make the *panth*, the Sikh community, equivalent to the nation, will those opting out of or not included in the *panth* have a place? If you conceive of the *ummah*, the community of Muslims, as a sovereign collectivity, will you end up with *fatwas* against those who reject membership, defined then as traitors to the nation? Are we going to face another Iran in Kashmir?

That these kinds of fears are fueling a renewed revitalization of the Hindu majority in India is not surprising. Over the past few years there has been a decline in support for the secular, umbrella-like, Congress party and polarized support for a variety of regional, caste-based, or religiously based parties including preeminently the Hindu nationalist BJP. The middle ground which has held India shakily together is in a fragile state, and may evaporate altogether. The fact that some BJP leaders — who receive substantial electoral majorities — have explicitly equated being a Hindu with being an Indian, and hence not being a Hindu as being a traitor, is an ominous one. Anti-Muslim gangs in one of the Bombay riots called out the slogan "Pakistan or death," a frightening contortion of the early Muslim nationalist theme that led to the creation of Pakistan. This time, the mobs were not Muslims offering themselves for martyrdom, but Hindus demanding the expulsion or execution of a whole community conceived as traitorous to the national polity. And the tide has turned against India's Christians as well; beheadings of priests and rapes of nuns have been greeted in the national press by much sorrow, but also by suggestions that the perpetrators were heroes saving the Hindu nation from contamination.

Although the notion of mimesis applied to violent conflict can have the unfortunate effect of making all sides seem equally right or wrong, there is certainly a symbiosis in the definitions of nations we have seen on the Indian subcontinent since decolonization. Sikhs and Kashmiris are now expressing their grievances against the state of India not in terms of compromise solutions like the acceptance of the Anandpur Sahib Resolution in the Sikh case and the implementation of Article 370 of the Indian Constitution in the Kashmiri case, but in terms of the utter rejection of one national entity and the creation of a new one. Escalating cycles of killings and revenge killings on both sides make the boundaries between those imagined nations clearer and clearer, and the possibility of any negotiated solution more and more remote. The language of self-determination, widely recognized in international arenas, has eclipsed all other possible discourses regarding Punjab and Kashmir. At the same time, the consolidation of resistance against state oppression in terms of the Sikh and Muslim religions has led to a Hindu backlash that is having repercussions throughout India and may yet lead to a redefinition of the Indian state.

The humiliation / dignity dialectic that plays so large a role in individual experiences of terror and resistance is entangled, then, in evolving notions of national identity on both sides. The two arenas feed on each other, as each new atrocity provokes further outrage and serves as justification for further acts of violence. How to stop this cycle? I only wish I had the answer. The first step, however, must be to realistically assess what participation in conflict actually means to the people involved. No amount of negotiation over borders, in itself, can resolve issues of humiliation, dignity, and identity which are the axes of the lived experience of violence in India's tragic northwestern rim. For the ethnographer, bearing witness to this experience is both theoretically and politically mandated.

A serious distortion in Western Indology is created by the tendency to concentrate on one region, one religious group, or one conflict arena at a time. The fact is that Punjab, Kashmir, Assam, Tamil Nadu, and every place else in India are part of a single political order. It speaks to the great success of those who dominate that order that rebellions against it are couched in particularistic terms that can quite effectively be dealt with from the center on a case by case basis. A more insidious form of success is the fact that the academic vision of India has been refracted into similarly particularistic visions, which in asking why Sikhs are rebelling, why Kashmiris are rebelling, why tribals are rebelling, and so on seems to put the burden of explanation on the rebels rather than the order against which they all chafe. A more unified resistance would be deeply threatening for New Delhi; the more universalistic academic perspective on the Indian state and its malcontents now developing across a range of disciplines is revolutionary in its implications. As the late historian Herbert Gutman commented about the various progressive histories of the United States — working-class history, women's history, African-American history, and so on — when are all these going to add up to a different vision of *American* history? (Gutman 1981; and see Bonner et al. 1994.) When does the study of ethnonationalist movements within states lead to a rethinking of the nation-state itself (Tambiah 1996)?

In a 1994 speech, a leader of the Dalit movement (Dalit means "oppressed," and is the term of choice for politically aware Untouchables) chastised anthropology for its historical complicity in perpetuating caste ideology in the name of relativism. Many Western academics could also be accused of keeping their eyes shut in the face of a dangerous turn in the Indian national mood over the past few decades, one which Paul Brass likens to the "murderous, pre-fascist stage" of 1930s Germany (1994: 353–354). Tragically, state terror per se is not where it stops in India; Brass is correct in noting that what we are seeing is not just the imposition of a repressive regime but a wider cultural development that might well be termed protofascism. Urban pogroms against Sikhs and Muslims that have repeatedly taken place involved not just small bands of hired thugs but large numbers of people, and, furthermore, were never widely protested or repudiated by the Indian citizenry as a whole. The non-Hindu groups who were the targets of these pogroms are rapidly being defined out of the national self-image; they are, to use Orlando Patterson's fortuitous phrase, "socially dead" (Patterson 1991). Like the demonization of the Jews preceding the Holocaust, there is a hallucinatory quality to mainstream Indian conceptions of Sikhs and Muslims — and other, less visible minorities, too. In the worst rhetoric, that of right-wing Hindu organizations, they are cancers in the body politic that must be rooted out for India to flourish. Consider Bal Thackeray of the Hindu chauvinist group Shiv Sena, in power in Bombay (renamed by them as the pre-Muslim Mumbai), who when asked if the Muslims were beginning to feel like the Jews in Nazi Germany said that if they behaved like the Jews in Nazi Germany, then there is nothing wrong if they are treated as the Jews were in Nazi Germany (Mehta 1997:120).

The electoral success of the Shiv Sena, and the penetration of the martial Hindu organization RSS into all levels of the popular Hindu party BJP, shows that these groups which were once perceived as peripheral to the contemporary Indian psyche have become quite mainstream. Anti-Sikh and anti-Muslim rhetoric that would be considered "hate speech" in most Western countries is tolerated in major media outlets in India. The parallels with what Goldhagen has called "eliminationist anti-Semitism" in prewar Germany are stunning, not only in the ordinariness of sentiments of hostility toward the non-Hindu minorities and the celebration of Hindu purity as the foundation of Indian nationalism, but in the hegemonic quality of the entire discourse (see Goldhagen 1996). Academia is not immune here, even Western academia with its long-term romance with a harmonious and tranquil India and its long-term enmity with turbaned and bearded crusaders. (Bill Kunstler, the civil rights attorney who had defended Martin Luther King and other Black activists, by the end of his life was defending Muslims and Sikhs [see Kunstler 1994].) We have to be wary of our seduction and our prejudices here, and pay attention to the evidence before our eyes that India is not what we would like to imagine.

There is a lot at stake in India: most of us admire the beauty of its philosophical heritage; its attempts to create a democratic secular state against all odds; its gloriously plural cultural worlds. There is a lot to fear in the insurgent movements that have recently sprung up; no guarantees at all that what they would create would be better. (Pakistan and Bangladesh are no utopias, either.) But, the least we can do here is what we as anthropologists do best: listen, observe, teach, and write about people living very different lives with compassion, honesty, respect, and courage.

It is a limited project, but one that faces us with a certain urgency as shots continue to be fired across the borders of the communities we once so confidently described, and as the people we study and learn from continue to bleed.

Notes

1. For reports on the human rights situation see Amnesty International 1998, 1997a, 1997b, 1996a, 1996b, 1995, 1994, 1993, 1991; Asia Watch and Physicians for Human Rights 1993a, 1993b; Asia Watch 1991a, 1991b; Human Rights Watch 1996, 1995, 1994; Human Rights Watch and Physicians for Human Rights 1994; International Commission of Jurists 1995; Physicians for Human Rights and Asia Watch 1993.

2. The details of the above story have been slightly altered for the protection of the individuals involved. "Yacub" is a pseudonym.

Bibliography

Ali, S. Mahmud
   1993 *The Fearful State: Power, People and Internal War in South Asia.* London: Zed Books.
Amnesty International
   1998 *A Mockery of Justice: The Case Concerning the "Disappearance" of Human Rights Defender Jaswant Singh Khalra Severely Undermined.* London: Amnesty International.
   1997a *Appeal to Armed Opposition Groups in Jammu and Kashmir to Abide by Humanitarian Law.* London: Amnesty International.
   1997b *Jammu and Kashmir: Remembering Jalil Andrabi.* London: Amnesty International.
   1996a *Harjit Singh: The Continuing Pursuit of Justice.* London: Amnesty International.
   1996b *Human Rights Abuses in the Election Period in Jammu and Kashmir.* London: Amnesty International.
   1995 *Punjab Police: Beyond the Bounds of Law.* London: Amnesty International.
   1994 *The Terrorism and Disruptive Activities (Prevention) Act: The Lack of "Scrupulous Care."* London: Amnesty International.
   1993 *"An Unnatural Fate": Disappearances and Impunity in Punjab and Kashmir.* New York: Amnesty International.
   1991 *Human Rights Violations in Punjab: Use and Abuse of the Law.* London: Amnesty International.
Asia Watch
   1991a *Punjab in Crisis: Human Rights in India.* New York: Asia Watch.
   1991b *Human Rights in India: Kashmir Under Siege.* New York: Asia Watch.
Asia Watch and Physicians for Human Rights
   1993a *The Human Rights Crisis in Kashmir: A Pattern of Impunity.* New York: Asia Watch and Physicians for Human Rights.
   1993b *Rape in Kashmir: A Crime of War.* New York: Asia Watch and Physicians for Human Rights.

Bonner, Arthur, Suranjit Kumar Saha, Ali Asghar Engineer, and Gerard Hueze
1994 *Democracy in India: A Hollow Shell.* Lanham, Md.: American University Press.
Brass, Paul
1994 *The Politics of India Since Independence.* Second edition. The New Cambridge History of India Series, vol. 4. New York: Cambridge University Press.
Camus, Albert
1961 *Resistance, Rebellion, and Death.* Translated by Justin O'Brien. New York: Alfred A. Knopf.
Crossette, Barbara
1993 *India: Facing the Twenty-First Century.* Bloomington: Indiana University Press.
Freire, Paulo
1993 *Pedagogy of the Oppressed.* Translated by Myra Bergman Ramos. New York: Continuum.
Goldhagen, Daniel Jonah
1996 *Hitler's Willing Executioners: Ordinary Germans and the Holocaust.* New York: Vintage Books.
Gupta, Dipankar
1985 "The Communalising of Punjab, 1980–85." *Economic and Political Weekly,* 13 July.
Gutman, Herbert
1981 "What Ever Happened to History?" *Nation,* 21 November.
Human Rights Watch
1996 *India's Secret Army in Kashmir: New Pattern of Abuses Emerges in the Conflict.* New York: Human Rights Watch.
1995 *Encounter in Philibit: Summary Executions of Sikhs.* New York: Human Rights Watch.
1994 *Arms and Abuses in Indian Punjab and Kashmir.* New York: Human Rights Watch.
Human Rights Watch and Physicians for Human Rights
1994 *Dead Silence: The Legacy of Abuses in Punjab.* New York: Human Rights Watch.
International Commission of Jurists
1995 *Human Rights in Kashmir.* Geneva: International Commission of Jurists.
Juergensmeyer, Mark
1993 *The New Cold War: Religious Nationalism Confronts the Secular State.* Berkeley: University of California Press.
Kapur, Rajiv
1986 *Sikh Separatism: The Politics of Faith.* London: Allen and Unwin.
Kumar, Ram Nayaran
1996 *The Sikh Unrest and the Indian State.* New Delhi: Ajanta Publications.
Kunstler, William M.
1994 *My Life as a Radical Lawyer.* New York: Citadel Press.
Lamb, Alistair
1992 *Kashmir: A Disputed Legacy, 1846–1990.* Karachi: Oxford University Press.
Mahmood, Cynthia Keppley
1996 *Fighting for Faith and Nation: Dialogues with Sikh Militants.* Philadelphia: University of Pennsylvania Press.
Margalit, Avishai
1996 *The Decent Society.* New York: Cambridge University Press.

Mehta, Suketu
  1997 "Mumbai." *Granta* 57, pp. 97–126.
Miller, William Ian
  1993 *Humiliation, and Other Essays on Honor, Social Discomfort, and Violence.* Ithaca: Cornell University Press.
Newberg, Paula R.
  1995 *Double Betrayal: Repression and Insurgency in Kashmir.* Washington, D.C.: Carnegie Endowment for Peace.
Nietzsche, Friedrich
  1969 *On the Genealogy of Morals.* Translated by Walter Kaufmann. New York: Vintage Books.
Patterson, Orlando
  1991 *Freedom in the Making of Western Culture.* New York: Basic Books.
Pettigrew, Joyce (ed.)
  1996 *Martyrdom and Political Resistance: Essays from Asia and Europe.* Comparative Asian Studies Series, no. 18. Amsterdam: VU University Press.
  1995 *The Sikhs of the Punjab: Unheard Voices of State and Guerrilla Violence.* London: Zed Books.
Physicians for Human Rights and Asia Watch
  1993 *The Crackdown in Kashmir: Torture of Detainees and Assaults on the Medical Community.* New York: Physicians for Human Rights and Asia Watch.
Prejean, Sister Helen
  1993 *Dead Man Walking: An Eyewitness Account of the Death Penalty in the United States.* New York: Random House.
Rawls, John
  1971 *A Theory of Justice.* Cambridge, Mass.: Belknap Press.
Scarry, Elaine
  1985 *The Body in Pain: The Making and Unmaking of the World.* New York: Oxford University Press.
Schofield, Victoria
  1996 *Kashmir in the Crossfire.* London: I. B. Tauris.
Tambiah, Stanley J.
  1996 *Leveling Crowds: Ethnonationalist Conflicts and Collective Violence in South Asia.* Berkeley: University of California Press.
Thomas, Raju (ed.)
  1992 *Perspectives on Kashmir: The Roots of Conflict in South Asia.* Boulder, Colo.: Westview Press.
Wirsing, Robert
  1994 *India, Pakistan, and the Kashmir Dispute: On Regional Conflict and Its Resolution.* London: Macmillan.
Zulaika, Joseba, and William Douglass
  1996 *Terror and Taboo: The Follies, Fables, and Faces of Terrorism.* New York: Routledge.

Chapter 3
State Terror in the Netherworld
Disappearance and Reburial in Argentina

Antonius C. G. M. Robben

The funeral procession advanced slowly through the Jewish cemetery of La Tablada, a town on the outskirts of Buenos Aires. The old rabbi, together with the father of the deceased and four escorts, pulled the iron cart with its coffin in measured paces to each new crossroad. A halt. A glance to the left. A glance to the right. The front wheel of the bier spun round and round its axis, resisting the resolute hand of the rabbi. Another halt, more glances. The procession progressed from one juncture to another as if to mark the stages of a life climbing to the final resting place where death and reconciliation meet at last.

When the procession arrived at its destination, the coffin was lifted off the cart and placed on two crooked beams that rested across the pit. Ropes were pulled under the coffin, beams were removed, and the casket was lowered into the grave. The father appeared stoic during the entire ceremony from synagogue to burial, while the mother of the deceased cried inconsolably. The lawyer Emilio Mignone spoke a eulogy in the name of various human rights groups. He had not known Marcelo Gelman when he was alive, he said, but he remembered well the day his mother announced his disappearance. Mignone had known so many others who shared Marcelo's ideals and who had also disappeared, like his own daughter Monica.

Marcelo Gelman was a twenty-year-old journalist when he disappeared with his nineteen-year-old pregnant wife María Claudia Iruretagoyena on 24 August 1976. Marcelo was abducted by a task force of the Army Intelligence Service, most likely for being the son of Juan Gelman, a high-ranking member of the Montoneros guerrilla organization.[1] At dawn on 14 October, a corporal of the coast guard observed how several men were throwing large objects into the river San Fernando. He notified his superiors. The river was dragged for hours until eight oil drums were found. Each drum contained a corpse in an advanced state of putrefaction. The bodies of six men and two women were recovered. Most of them had been killed by a gun shot to the head. Fingerprints were taken, but no positive identification was made. The eight bodies were buried by the coast guard as unidentified corpses on 21 October 1976. The remains were finally exhumed and identified in October 1989. Marcelo Gelman was one of them, but his wife María Claudia still remains missing (Cohen Salama 1992:233–242).[2]

As the first flowers showered on the grave, one person shouted, "Comrade Marcelo! Present!" Numerous people raised a clenched fist in communist salute. One person yelled, "Only with blood can spilled blood be paid!" More flowers fell on the grave. The sobs of the bystanders grew louder. Juan Gelman, Marcelo's father, removed a tear from his right eye, turned around slowly and walked away with his ex-wife, Berta Schubaroff.

On 1 October 1989, three months before the funeral of Marcelo Gelman, another reburial had occurred. After resting for 112 years at the Catholic cemetery of Southampton, Brigadier General Juan Manuel de Rosas was placed in his family's tomb at the Recoleta cemetery in the heart of Buenos Aires. The event was of great historical significance. Rosas had fled Argentina on board a British vessel in 1852 after his defeat at the battle of Caseros. Ever since, he had been depicted as the tyrant whose twenty-four-year rule was known simply as "the terror." In the 1930s, a movement of historical revisionism arose that emphasized Rosas's patriotism and claimed that official history had misrepresented him. A public call for the repatriation of the remains of Rosas was made in 1934. The political spirit of Rosas was reinvigorated, and nineteenth-century animosities between Unitarists and Federalists became fomented again in the confrontation of liberals and nationalists.[3] Rosas's name also became linked to the ten-year populist government of Juan Domingo Perón during the mid–twentieth century as liberal opponents condemned his government as "the second tyranny."[4] A congressional debate about Rosas's remains was held in the mid-1970s. Repatriation was approved but not carried out because of the political violence preceding the 1976 coup d'état. The 1989 reburial of Rosas by the Peronist president Carlos Menem was therefore full of historic reference.

Symbolizing national reconciliation, the funeral procession with the remains of Rosas was escorted by two groups of horsemen representing the Federalist and Unitarist armies that had fought one another during the nineteenth-century civil wars. Descendants of Rosas and those of several of his onetime enemies Paz, Viamonte, Lavalle, and Urquiza were present at the interment at the Recoleta national cemetery.[5] "Today we bury more than one hundred years of black legend, of darkness, of history written with inaccuracies," so spoke the priest Alberto Ezcurra in his homily (*La Nación*, 2 October 1989). President Carlos Menem had said the preceding day that "Nobody, absolutely nobody has the legitimate right to continue to arrest our development because of bygone events, for history cannot be a heavy load, an insupportable burden, a painful memory or a petty opinion. History must be a chain of union, stronger than frustration, than war, than death" (*La Prensa*, 1 October 1989).[6] According to Menem, the political repatriation of Rosas served to close the wounds of the past that had continued to fester in the Argentine nation for more than a century. However, it was clear to everyone in Argentina that Menem's more pressing political objective was to relegate the fresh memories of the 1976–1982 dirty war to history. One week after Rosas's reburial, president Menem pardoned 277 military officers and former guerrillas, among whom was Juan Gelman, Marcelo's father. Former president Raúl Alfonsín expressed his doubts about Menem's success at bringing about a national reconciliation: "One cannot decree the amnesia of an entire society because every time anyone tried to sweep the past under the carpet, the past returned with a vengeance" (*La Nación*, 10 October 1989).[7]

Despite the different circumstances surrounding the funerals of Juan Manuel de Rosas and Marcelo Gelman — the glory and honor bestowed upon the first and the controversy surrounding the exhumation of the last — both public ceremonies reveal the central importance of human remains and their reburial in Argentine political culture. Their importance arises from the belief in the influence of the dead on the world of the living, and the obligation to bury comrades-in-arms with full honors. These two political reasons add to a general human care for the dead and the emotional need for mourning. This cultural complex was exploited by the military junta in their dirty war against the guerrilla insurgency and left-wing sectors of Argentine society. State terror in Argentina between 1976 and 1982 was as much inflicted on the dead as on the living. The bodies of the victims of military repression were incinerated, dumped at sea, or buried in mass graves by counterinsurgency task forces. Between 10,000 and 30,000 people disappeared during the seven-year military rule. This paper analyzes the ongoing anxiety about the spirit of the enemy dead, the acts of resistance by relatives of the disappeared, and the concealment and funerary obstruction of the victims of Argentina's dirty war as means to extend state terror into the hereafter.

Disappearance as Terror

Torture and disappearance are not the cruel realities of war, and the targeting of tens of thousands of civilians of the political left was not inevitable. Counterinsurgency is also possible with the help of military courts and due process. A confidential 1980 status report by the American embassy in Buenos Aires to the State Department in Washington said about the junta's preference for disappearances: "Disappearance is still the standard tactic for the Argentine security forces in dealing with captured terrorists. The military's commitment to this method is profoundly rooted in elements that range from effectiveness through expediency to cultural bias. We doubt whether international sanctions and opprobrium will, in themselves, cause the government to change the tactic and grant captured terrorists due process" (quoted in Guest 1990: 430).

The rationale of turning disappearance into the principal repressive tactic was revealed in a rare interview with the Supreme Court of the Armed Forces. Upon my provocative question why the junta had not executed the guerrillas publicly, instead of making them disappear, a brigadier general answered while the other judges nodded in agreement: "If one would have done what you have asked then there would have been immediate revenge, not only on the executioner or those who presided over the trial but also on their families. That is to say, the terror had also infused terror among the armed forces, and they responded with terror. This is the tremendous problem, the tremendous tragedy of this war" (interview, 20 December 1989).

Argentine society became terror-stricken. The terror was intended to debilitate people politically and emotionally without them ever fathoming the magnitude of the force that hit them. The armed forces had divided the country into five large zones, each subdivided into subzones. The subzones were divided into areas, and the areas might be further subdivided into subareas. The areas and subareas were the operational territories of the task forces (*grupos de tarea*). The special task forces stood generally under the command of the army or the navy. The air force participated to a far lesser extent in the repressive apparatus. The regular forces did not participate in the actual abductions, although army units might seal off a neighborhood and provide logistical support. The disappearances were generally carried out by small task forces of five or six men, under the command of a lieutenant, who pertained to the various intelligence services of the armed forces. Typically, they would first ask for a "green light" from the local police station to prevent the police from responding to distress calls from any concerned neighbor. Next, the assault gang would force its way into a home under the cover of darkness, threaten and beat the inhabitants into submission, blindfold their victim, and leave in unmarked private cars (CONADEP 1986:11–13; Mittelbach 1986).

The special task forces would take the abducted persons to the 365 secret detention centers, which were usually located in Argentina's police stations. Only one-quarter of the centers were situated at military installations. The abducted were never publicly acknowledged as detainees or prisoners once they disappeared into these so-called "pits" (*pozos*) or "black holes" (*chupaderos*). Some were released into exile, but most of them were assassinated. The corpses were cremated or interred clandestinely as unidentified bodies in municipal cemeteries. They were also abandoned at roadsides, thrown in rivers, and even flung from planes at sea under sedation (García 1995:461–470; Verbitsky 1995).

The disappearance of guerrillas sowed great uncertainty among the revolutionary organizations. They were severely hampered in their operations when they did not know whether their combatants were dead or alive, had defected or deserted, were held up in traffic, or were being tortured for information about surprise attacks and upcoming meetings. It also allowed intelligence officers to take the disappeared detainees on missions to identify their comrades at border posts, railway stations, airports, and bus stops. Some pointed out complete strangers so that a comrade could leave unnoticed. They hoped that the innocence of the unsuspected victim would soon be discovered, and that his torture would end.

The Argentine military leaders believed furthermore that historical judgment could be decisively influenced if there was no body to mourn, dead to commemorate, or epitaph to read. The disappearance of the corpses was motivated by a strategic concern about the political future of the armed forces. Eventually the military would have to hand power to a democratic government, and they knew that without a corpus delicti future criminal prosecution would be impossible.

The disappearances were also ordered to prevent the mobilization of international public opinion. A lesson was learned from the adverse reactions to the mass arrests during Pinochet's first years in power, and from the public execution of convicted members of the ETA during the Franco dictatorship.

However, it was not just the fear of international protests, operational advantages, or historical judgment that made the military choose disappearance as their principal method of repression. The disappearances were directed at the core of Argentine society. They converted the torture of detainees into the anguish of friends, colleagues, relatives, and family members. Disappearances had, and continue to have, very complex effects. People knew that torture was a common practice in Argentina among the security forces. Since many relatives were present at the abductions—60 percent of the disappeared were detained in the home—they feared that the abducted were being tortured (CONADEP 1986:11). Yet, they were helpless because the authorities denied having them in custody. Tormenting thoughts about the suffering of the disappeared person haunted those left behind. The term "home front" seldom had a more sinister double meaning.

Unlike the public display and dismemberment of enemy corpses in nineteenth-century Argentina, the disappearances of the 1970s had their greatest effect within the homes of their victims. Michel Foucault has described how the spectacle of torture in eighteenth-century France served to assert the power of the king. The public confession and dismemberment of criminals demonstrated to the people that the law was the will of the divine ruler, and that anyone who violated that law was an enemy of the sovereign and had to be punished by the sword. However, despite this awesome display of force, it also showed spectators the limits of power. "A body effaced, reduced to dust and thrown to the winds, a body destroyed piece by piece by the infinite power of the sovereign constituted not only the ideal, but the real limit of punishment" (Foucault 1979:50). The sovereign's power did not reach beyond the dust of the assassin, making it finite and therefore, according to Foucault, vulnerable.

The disappearances in Argentina were so terrifying exactly because they were not public but intensely private. Violent death was taken away from the eye and control of the people, confined to the secrecy of the detention centers, and spread through society. Fear of the military did not diminish as it was taken out of the public arena but it increased, through the conversion from public into secret into private. The continued absence of the disappeared son, daughter, husband, or wife etched a silhouette in the homes of surviving family members that had lasting political and psychological effects (see APDH 1987; ICIHI 1986; Kordan et al. 1988). The disappearances absorbed the political consciousness of the relatives into a desperate search (see Hagelin 1984; Herrera 1987). The social problems of Argentine society that had impelled people to become politically active dwarfed in comparison to the disappearance of loved ones. The initial paralysis made place for political protest. In a convoluted way, the repressive attempt to silence the political opposition in Argentina had the reverse effect. Human rights organizations emerged during the military dictatorship that dedicated all their political energy to public protest.

Even though many relatives had a premonition that the disappeared had been killed, it was difficult to reconcile oneself with such fatality. There was no body to grieve over, and the mourning process was intertwined with guilt feelings. Mourning meant abandoning the disappeared and surrendering to the conditions created by the military junta. This suffering dispersed in all directions of people's existence. The victimized relatives felt guilty about their suffering, and had to justify their public protests, while the victimizers claimed innocence in the absence of a corpse. Victory and omnipotence were instilled as defeat and fear. Disappearance extended war and torture into civil society and the hereafter.

The strategy of obliterating all physical traces of the disappeared continued with different means after the guerrilla insurgency had been defeated and the overall military repression of Argentine society began to lessen. Two official attempts were made to have the disappeared pronounced dead in absence of a corpse. The military junta issued a law in September 1979 that declared all persons presumed dead who had disappeared between 6 November 1974 and 6 September 1979. They hoped that this decree would end the insistent appeals by human rights organizations. After their 1982 defeat in the Falklands/Malvinas War, the ruling military junta was forced to step down and hand power to the interim government of General Reynoldo Bignone. This interim government published a final report in April 1983 about the 1976–1982 dictatorship and declared once again all disappeared as presumed dead (San Martino de Dromi 1988:343, 360; *Somos*, 1983, no. 346, p. 15).

At the same time, General Bignone secretly ordered the destruction of all documentation related to persons who had been detained during the 1976–1982 dictatorship, thus preventing the verification of the presumption of death made in their official report. When Raúl Alfonsín assumed power in December 1983, he installed a commission to inquire into the whereabouts of the disappeared. This commission stated in a letter to Alfonsín that its task was "hindered by an essential lack of documentary information regarding the specific operational orders of the repression, the identification of those arrested, prosecuted, sentenced, freed or killed, and the places where they were held or should have been given a decent burial" (CONADEP 1986:264).

I have now given tactical, strategic, legal, and political reasons for making the corpses of political detainees disappear, but what is the cultural significance? What is the cultural bias, referred to in the 1980 report of the American embassy in Buenos Aires, that made the Argentine military prefer the practice of disappearance? And why did the military continue to conceal the disappeared after the dirty war had ended? The French anthropologist Robert Hertz (1960:83) has said that "It is the action of society on the body that gives full reality to the imagined drama of the soul" or, in the rephrasing of Huntington and Metcalf (1979:14), "the fate of the body is a model for the fate of the soul." Thus, a study of how Argentine culture has conceived of the spirit of deceased political opponents can reveal why disappearance became the preferred repressive tactic. How have enemy corpses been treated in other violent domestic conflicts in Argentina?

Reburial at Recoleta National Cemetery

The abuse of the corpses of political opponents is not a recent practice in Argentina. Defeat and terror in nineteenth-century Argentina were intimately tied to the destination of the corpse. Decapitation and the display of their heads on public squares became the fate of many commanders. It was an extreme humiliation that defiled the personal honor of the fallen leader, and damaged the collective honor of his family and political following. The beheading and subsequent exhibition of the trophy were particularly dishonorable because they placed the victim on the level of the native American Indians who often befell the same fate in Argentina. It also symbolized the political dismemberment of the fallen leader from his supporters, and the power of the new rulers. The importance of honor, charisma, and clientalism in these times made decapitation, rather than execution, imprisonment, or exile, the preferred practice of victory. Godoy Cruz, for instance, exhibited the head of the Federalist leader Felipe Alvarez to "serve as a warning to those who have been led astray by his example" (quoted in Halperín Donghi 1975:380). The Chilean caudillo Carrera, who had taken refuge in Argentina, was eventually captured on 31 August 1821 and executed four days later after a summary trial. His head and right arm were sent on display to Mendoza, and his left arm to San Juan (CGE 1974:283). Felipe Alvarez and Francisco Ramírez were decapitated in the same year. The latter's head was placed in an iron cage and put on display in a church in Santa Fé (Rock 1987:97).

The flight of a party of ragged cavalrymen in 1841 with the decaying body of General Lavalle to prevent it from falling into the hands of General Oribe's enemy troops has become legendary. Ernesto Sábato described their getaway in his novel *On Heroes and Tombs* as follows: "Thirty-five leagues to go still. Three days' march at full gallop, with the corpse that stinks and distills the liquids of putrefaction, with sharpshooters in the rear guard covering their retreat, comrades who perhaps have little by little been decimated, run through with lances, or had their throats slit. From Jujuy to Huacalera: twenty-four leagues. Only thirty-five leagues to go now, they tell themselves. Only four or five days' march, with God's help" (Sábato 1990:472). As the days pass and the stench becomes unbearable, the men decide to remove the bloated flesh, and preserve the general's bones and heart. It would take two full decades before the remains of General Lavalle were repatriated and reburied with national honor at Recoleta cemetery (Frias 1884).

There was a widespread conviction in the nineteenth century, grounded in the Catholic belief that the soul survives after death, that human remains carried a spiritual power that could affect the world of the living. The belief in this spiritual force (*virtus*) can be traced back to medieval times when the remains of saints became relics for the believers (Angenendt 1994:155–158; Snoek 1995:11–20). Just as saints were believed to heal medieval worshippers because their relics contained a life force, so the remains of slain commanders in nineteenth-century Argentina continued to provide strength to their comrades and inflict harm on their enemies. The mutilation of enemy corpses was regarded as a way to disperse, although not to destroy, the spiritual force of the deceased.[8]

This same fear of the spirit of the dead can also be found in the terrible curse placed on Juan Manuel de Rosas by José Mármol from his exile in Montevideo on 25 May 1843: "Not even the dust from your bones will America have" (Mármol 1894:58). A similar belief is expressed by Sarmiento about Facundo Quiroga, a caudillo who together with Rosas was vilified in Sarmiento's literary indictment *Civilization and Barbarism*. Sarmiento went so far as to evoke the spirit of Facundo Quiroga to reveal the ills of the Argentine nation: "Terrible shadow of Facundo! I am going to conjure you up so that, shaking the blood-stained dust from your ashes, you will arise to explain to us the secret life and internal convulsions that tear at the entrails of a noble people! You possess the secret! Reveal it to us! . . . Facundo has not died; he is alive in the popular traditions, in the Argentine politics and revolutions; in Rosas, his heir, his alter ego: his soul has passed to this other mold, more finished and perfect" (Sarmiento 1986:7–8). The belief that the spirit of a dead person could pass into a living person turned the corpse into an object of contestation, and its ultimate destination became a matter of great political significance. Sarmiento's fear about the continued influence of Facundo's spirit on Argentine political life seemed to come true. One year after his assassination in 1835 at Barranco Yaco, Facundo's remains were exhumed from the cemetery of Córdoba at the express order of Rosas. The bones were cleansed, disinfected, perfumed, and reburied in Buenos Aires (*Buenos Aires Nos Cuenta*, no. 5, pp. 20–22).[9] What had been despised could now be revered and honored. The same spiritual force that used to be feared was now believed to be beneficial to the nation. At Recoleta cemetery Facundo joined the many military commanders who had fought in the nineteenth-century civil wars. The remains of other illustrious Argentines who died in places such as Washington, Paris, Montevideo, and Santiago de Chile — many of them in exile and some others by accident — were also exhumed and reburied at Recoleta. In this way, the cemetery became eventually the pantheon of the nation, and the life force of those buried there continued to infuse Argentine society.

Just as Durkheim has said that society worshipped itself in religion, so the Argentine nation seemed to represent and celebrate itself at the Recoleta cemetery. To be reburied at Recoleta meant to achieve immortality in the eyes of the Argentine people. This immortality was achieved by the ceremonial reburial and, as a consequence, by the continued presence of the reburied person's ossified remains and eternal spirit in the public place. Their life force became embodied in the people who visited the grave, while its political effects were determined by the strength of conviction of their ideological adherents.

At first sight, Recoleta seems very much like a late eighteenth-century Parisian cemetery. "[The memorials] were to be 'a source of emulation for posterity' to inspire visitors to the cemetery to equal or excel the deeds or accomplishments of their predecessors. The cemetery, then, was to become a school of virtue" (Etlin 1984:43). Yet, Recoleta turns into a disturbing source of incessant political conflict when understood within the context of the place of the dead in the world of the living. Mortal enemies are buried next to one another, and victims rest in the same cemetery as their assassins. Facundo is buried there together with his slayers. Rosas rests there, and so do Sarmiento, Mármol, and many other adversaries he had forced into exile. Their reburial at Recoleta did not represent their reconciliation in death but the reinvigoration of their ideas. These ceremonial reburials encouraged political adversaries to believe that the ideological battles of the past had not yet been decided and that their opposed political spirits still resonated among the Argentine people. Recoleta cemetery became in this way as much a source as a metaphor of continued political strife in Argentina.

Repatriation and Reburial in the Twentieth Century

The Argentine political obsession with corpses and their spirits continued well into the twentieth century, albeit different in form and meaning. Beheading became replaced by disappearance as the practice of terror and intimidation inflicted on political opponents and surviving relatives. The disappearance of the body of Evita Duarte de Perón, one of the most prominent and charismatic figures in twentieth-century Argentine politics, illustrates the preoccupation with the dead body in Argentine political culture.[10] Her embalmed body was missing for more than a decade and its bizarre wanderings can be compared to those of General Lavalle in the nineteenth century.

Evita died on 26 July 1952. For two weeks, an estimated 65,000 mourners a day passed by her body in state at the headquarters of the labor union confederation CGT in Buenos Aires. After months of dedicated work, the body was preserved in a perfect state by a Spanish embalmer. A 1955 coup d'état ended the official Evita cult and the glorification of Perón. Their names were removed from buildings, streets, squares, and public works. Evita's embalmed body was taken from the trade union headquarters under protest of its embalmer, Doctor Ara. Lieutenant Colonel Moore

Koenig, who was in charge of the operation, responds in the fictionalized account *Santa Evita* by Eloy Martínez: "You know very well what is at stake . . . It is not the cadaver of that woman but the destiny of Argentina. Or both, which to many people seems the same. Look how the dead and useless body of Eva Duarte has become confused with the country . . . [By] embalming it, you moved history from its place. You left history inside. You realize that whoever has this woman, has the country in its fist?" (Martínez 1995:34).

It would take more than two decades before the corpse of Eva Perón came to rest in a tomb at Recoleta cemetery. The officers entrusted in 1955 with the disappearance of the body were at a loss about what to do. At this point, fact and fiction become entwined in a complex tangle. However, it can be documented from several sources that the mummified body was shipped out of the country in 1957. Eloy Martínez tells the uncorroborated story that a number of identical coffins, all but one containing wax casts of the real body, were sent to different places in the world to conceal the true whereabouts of Evita's remains.

In 1970, a commando force of Montoneros guerrillas first kidnapped and later executed General Aramburu. Aramburu had been responsible for the overthrow of Perón in 1955. His summary execution was perceived by many Peronists as a deed of justice. The disappearance and profanation of Evita's body were among the list of charges. One year later, a public notary handed President Lanusse a letter written by General Aramburu in 1957 stating that Evita's corpse had been buried secretly in Milan. Supposedly, the body was first flown to Buenos Aires for examination, and then returned to Perón, who was living in exile in Madrid at the time. The embalmed body remained in his house for several years. Purportedly, the spiritist López Rega burned candles and spoke incantations as María Estela, Perón's third wife, lay atop the coffin to receive Evita's spiritual energy. The nineteenth-century belief in the life force of human remains continued unshaken in occultist circles, and was even embraced by the future head of state.

Perón returned to Argentina in 1973 to head the government as president with his wife as vice president. Perón died in 1974 and was succeeded by María Estela Martínez de Perón. In mid-October 1974, a Montoneros task force kidnapped the body of General Aramburu from the Recoleta cemetery as ransom for Evita's embalmed corpse, which had remained in Perón's Spanish residence. Aramburu's coffin was returned a few hours after Evita's body was repatriated on 17 November 1974 (Gillespie 1982:183). Perón's widow, María Estela, placed Evita next to the embalmed body of Perón at her presidential residence in Olivos. When the military overthrew María Estela Martínez de Perón in March 1976, they handed Evita's body to her two sisters, who reburied her at the family tomb at Recoleta cemetery (Andersen 1993:121; Martínez 1995; Page 1983:344, 424–425, 500; *Somos*, 1984, no. 415, pp. 46–49; Taylor 1979: 69–71).

The strange journey of Evita's body has the quality of a phantasmagorical story, were it not that the documented wanderings of the embalmed body and the disputes over its resting place reveal the continued importance of human remains and their burial in Argentine political culture. The 1934 and 1975 attempts to retrieve the remains of Juan Manuel de Rosas from Great Britain provide additional proof of the importance of the body, the spirit, and their reburial in Argentine political culture.[11]

The political right considered the repatriation of the remains of Rosas in 1934 as an appeal to authoritarian rule. These fervent Rosistas were convinced that world capitalism and parliamentary democracy were in a major crisis. Fascism would replace these outdated systems in the entire world. Just as Rosas had pacified the country after decades of civil war, so a new strong leader would protect Argentina against the threat of communism. As one of the proponents of repatriation said in 1934, "It has been exactly one hundred years since we gave birth to this same illness, and it was precisely the iron hand of Rosas which ended the dissolute anarchy" (Manuel Gálvez, quoted in Barletta and Amézola 1992:26–27). The opponents of repatriation feared the reincarnation of Rosas's political spirit in his right-wing heirs: "The most serious is not to bring the ashes, but to bring his spirit. . . . Bringing his remains would not mean anything, if it would not imply giving amnesty to a tyrant. The Argentine people must know that to give him amnesty is to make way for his imitators. History is not only a science concerned with texts, but history is also the spirit of times in the heart of generations. To bring his remains is to awaken the spirit that gave them life" (Ricardo Rojas, quoted in Barletta and Amézola 1992:30–31). The repatriation of Rosas's remains was debated with great intensity in the Argentine press but never became official policy.

The issue of repatriation arose again four decades later, but the political discourse changed. Whereas the 1934 debate evolved around the rehabilitation of Rosas and his political ideas, the 1973–1974 congressional debates were embedded in a general discourse about the similarities between Perón and Rosas. Both leaders had been forced into exile, had protected the sovereignty of Argentina against imperialist incursions, and had ruled with the support of the popular masses. Just as in the mid-1950s, the opponents of repatriation continued to denounce Perón as the "second tyrant" who thrived on mob rule and a hostile attitude toward the United States. The Rosista historian José María Rosa rebutted that "The hatred towards Rosas . . . is the best homage to his memory, because it demonstrates that his political ideas are still current" (quoted in Barletta and Amézola 1992:45). The repatriation of Rosas's remains was approved by Congress in October 1974 and authorized by the government of María Estela de Perón in June 1975. The diplomatic efforts by the Argentine embassy in Great Britain were suspended three months later because of the spiraling political violence in Argentina (Barletta and Amézola 1992:40–41).

The twentieth-century belief in the survival after death of political ideas evoked by the presence of human remains is a continuation of the nineteenth-century religious conviction that enemy corpses may possess a vengeful spiritual force, but there is a noticeable shift in meaning. In the nineteenth century, there was a belief in the spirit as a supernatural energy — a soul or *virtus* — which could pass between organic substances. In the twentieth century, the spirit becomes a metaphor for the ideas associated with the remains of the deceased. Notwithstanding this reinterpretation of the spirit, the cultural focus and political rituals that surround it have remained remarkably similar. Victors in both centuries believe that reburial would turn the enemy dead into martyrs and invigorate their spirit, so they resorted to mutilation and disappearance as repressive practices.

This treatment of enemy corpses betrays the continued cultural belief in a relation between body and spirit, and the great significance of a proper funeral. If reburial symbolizes the transition of the soul from the land of the living to the land of the dead ancestors, as Hertz (1960:78–81) has argued, then the unceremonial burial of the hidden corpses of tens of thousands of Argentines implies that the spirits of the deceased must be still wandering through the misty passage between life and death. The great efforts that went into reburying Juan Lavalle, Juan Manuel de Rosas, Evita Perón, and many other illustrious Argentines at Recoleta cemetery provide a cultural explanation why surviving relatives searched for the remains of the victims of Argentine state terror in the 1970s.

Contested Exhumations and Revolutionary Protest

The first evidence of the mass executions that had occurred during the dirty war surfaced in late October 1982, only months after the Falklands/Malvinas War. Eighty-eight unmarked graves with an estimated four hundred unidentified bodies were found at the park cemetery of Grand Bourg near Buenos Aires. The gruesome discovery was made during the exhumation of the skeletal remains of the union leader Miguel Angel Sosa, who had disappeared in 1976. On the evening of 25 May 1976, his naked body was found floating in the Reconquista River. It showed obvious signs of torture. The police established Sosa's identity, did not notify his relatives, and buried him as an unidentified corpse. The

1982 exhumation was made at the request of relatives who had been tipped off in 1981 by an employee of the ministry of the interior (Cohen Salama 1992:60–62; *Somos*, 1982, no. 319, p. 11). The effect of the discovery on the Argentine public was devastating. There was both disbelief and anger. Soon, more mass graves were opened and the bullet-ridden skulls were exhibited on the edge of their makeshift graves in what was called a "horror show." The display of piles of bones and perforated skulls revealed to the stunned Argentines the horrors of the military regime as well as their own mortality and the chance that they could have very well met the same fate.

The Madres de Plaza de Mayo, a human rights organization consisting of hundreds of mothers of the disappeared, believed in October 1982 that the exhumations would give the disappeared a name and an identity.[12] At last, the hastily interred bodies would be wrested from anonymity and given a proper burial. As new mass graves continued to be opened, but the identification of the victims failed to be made because of improperly performed exhumations that destroyed crucial evidence, the Madres began to raise questions about the sense of these disinterments. Its president, Hebe de Bonafini, expressed in January 1984 the conviction that "there is sufficient proof to send a great number of those guilty of this horror to prison," but she had doubts about the political will to prosecute them (*Humor*, 1982, no. 92, p. 47; *Somos*, 1984, no. 382, p. 20). The Madres' faith in the justice system declined further when the Alfonsín government decided that the nine commanders of the three military juntas of 1976–1982 were to be tried under martial law by the Supreme Court of the Armed Forces. The Madres continued their rounds around the Plaza de Mayo on Thursday afternoons at 3:30 as they had been doing since April 1977.[13] They placed white scarves on their heads, walked arm in arm, and talked to the sympathizers who continued to join their thirty-minute protest.

Sometime during the second half of 1984, the Madres de Plaza de Mayo began to formulate their opposition to the exhumations, and this was the principal cause of their separation into two independent organizations in 1986.[14] Reflecting on the intense soul-searching in 1984 about which position to take on the exhumations, Hebe de Bonafini has said: "It cost us weeks and weeks of meetings at which there were many tears and much despair, because the profound Catholic formation of our people creates almost a need to have a dead body, a burial, and a Mass" (*Madres*, 1987, no. 37, p. 10).[15] Despite the anguish, the de Bonafini group decided to keep the wounds inflicted by the disappearances open to resist a national process of forgetting. "It has been eleven years of suffering, eleven years that have not been relieved in any sense. Many want the wound to dry so that we will forget. We want it to continue bleeding, because this is the only way that one continues to have strength to fight . . . But, above all, it is necessary that this wound bleeds so that the assassins will be condemned, as they deserve, and that what has happened will not happen again. This is the commitment in the defense of life which the Madres have taken upon themselves" (*Madres*, 1987, no. 29, p. 1).

In December 1984, the de Bonafini group condemned the exhumations as a government scheme to have them accept the presumption of death of all disappeared. The Madres demanded that first the assassins had to be identified before any further exhumations were to be carried out (*Madres*, 1984, no. 1, p. 2). Their position was strengthened by a parcel received on 13 November 1984 by Mrs. Rubinstein, whose daughter Patricia had disappeared on 7 February 1977. An accompanying letter from the so-called Condor Legion read: "Dear Madam: As the culmination of the incessant search for your daughter Patricia, we have decided to send you only part of what remains of her, but which shall undoubtedly satisfy your yearning to reunite earlier with your dear daughter than foreseen by Jehovah" (*Madres*, 1984, no. 1, p. 15). A forensic examination determined that the bones belonged to a man between twenty and forty years of age. In the eyes of the Madres, the perpetrators were using the fate of the disappeared as a bargaining chip. If a deal could be struck that would end all legal prosecution and public protests, then they would be willing to reveal the makeshift resting places of the disappeared.

A new argument against forensic investigations arose in 1986. The de Bonafini group protested against proposed legislation to impose a statute of limitations on the ongoing depositions against military officers accused of human rights violations. They argued that since an exhumation only determined the cause of death, but did not identify the executioner, any future prosecution would become impossible because of a ten-year statute of limitations. Only by providing a legal status to disappearance, comparable to a kidnapping, could legal action be taken against the guilty without any time restrictions (*Madres*, 1986, no. 19, p. 16). By mid-1986, belief in the prosecution of the hundreds of military officers accused of serious violations was declining rapidly. The government had prepared legislation to impose a final date on the presentation of court depositions (*ley de Punto Final*), while the outcome of the trial against the nine junta members had not satisfied the Madres. Their ideas about forensic investigations had changed from personal hope to legal justice, and ended in disillusionment and defiance. Their opposition to the exhumations turned from a legal into a political argument.

The leading figures of the de Bonafini group were of course well aware of the psychological toll of the enduring uncertainty and had a team of psychotherapists at hand to provide assistance. The Madres never opposed individual exhumations when asked for by relatives, but they remained firmly against the opening of mass graves and the performance of unsolicited identifications. They realized that the recuperation of the remains would allow relatives to grieve for their dead, but they regarded the deliberate setting in motion of this mourning process as a sinister ploy to achieve resignation and depoliticization among the surviving relatives. Mourning would break the solidarity of the Madres and produce a reconciliatory attitude. Continued political protest weighed more heavily than individual relief because anxiety was the hinge of memory and oblivion.

Since 1988, the issue of exhumations fell in the background of attention, with the exception of late 1989 when the remains of Marcelo Gelman were being exhumed. "We know that they are exhuming cadavers. We are against these exhumations because we don't want our children to die. Our children cannot be enclosed in tombs, because they are free and revolutionary" (Hebe de Bonafini, *Página 12*, 22 December 1989). The inhibition of mourning is supposed to transform the continued anguish into a fight for the ideals of their disappeared sons and daughters. The Madres want to keep the disappeared alive by leaving their remains unidentified in mass graves, and divulge their ideals instead. "They have interred their bodies it doesn't matter where, but their spirit, their solidarity, and their love for the people can never be buried and forgotten" (Hebe de Bonafini, *Madres*, 1989, no. 58, p. 11). Reburial would confine them to the world of the dead, instead of allowing their spirit to influence the dealings of the living, very much as friend and foe believed that the spirit of Evita, Facundo, and Rosas could influence the affairs of the world.

The position of the Madres of the de Bonafini group is remarkable. They did not only go against the cultural grain of Argentine society with its profound Catholic formation, as they themselves realized very well, but they also radically changed the political significance of reburials and the spiritual meaning of the human remains. Body, spirit, and funeral were dissociated. The ossified remains lost their meaning, and so did their reburial. The spirit as metaphor for political ideas was exalted as the only thing worthy of survival in the embodiment of kindred political spirits.

In 1988, as most military officers accused of gross human rights violations had become immune to prosecution as a result of the June 1987 Due Obedience Law (*ley de Obediencia Debida*), the de Bonafini group started on a path of ideological radicalization that made them embrace the political project attributed to the disappeared. They denounced the political system as corrupt and ethically bankrupt, and talked about the need to form grassroots organizations in factories, schools, universities, and poor neighborhoods because "there will be no liberation without revolution. Our children took this road. Today the Madres follow it. Tomorrow it will be the entire population. In order not to forget, not to forgive, not to succumb and to fight for victory" (Hebe de Bonafini, *Madres*, 1988, no. 43, p. 16). By late 1988, the idea arose that the Madres have to "socialize their maternity" (*Madres*, 1988, no. 48, p. 17) and adopt the suffering of all victims of political violence in the world. "When we understood that our children were not going to appear, we socialized motherhood and felt that we are the mothers of everybody, that all are our children" (Hebe de Bonafini, *Madres*, 1989, no. 53, p. 17). Pressing social problems such as widespread poverty, declining social services, high unemployment, poor benefits for the aged, government corruption, police brutality, and the privatization of state companies have become a political platform to pursue the revolutionary ideals of their disappeared children.

The development of the arguments against exhumation and reburial demonstrates a continuous refinement of the understanding of the consequences of state terror and its many ramifications in the political life of the Argentines. In the eyes of the Madres de Plaza de Mayo, reburials become synonymous with spiritual and physical death. Reburials destroy the living memory of the disappeared, and inter them in an enclosed remembrance. The Madres fear that the disappeared will be forgotten, and that they will be relegated to an increasingly more distant past, to the time of the dictatorship and the dirty war. Instead, they try to keep the spirit of their disappeared children alive by reincarnating their political ideals. This position led the Madres to condemn the exhumation of Marcelo Gelman: "With these tactics they implement the obliteration and reconciliation demanded by the assassins, the Church and a few Montoneros. These tactics are repudiated by the people" (*Sur*, 7 January 1990). The de Bonafini group of Madres condemns the very exhumations that could give them an answer to their original plea about the whereabouts of the disappeared.

Reburial and Reconciliation

The relatives of exhumed and identified missing persons have generally felt a great sense of relief at finally being able to reunite with the remains of their loved ones. Berta Schubaroff expressed this sentiment at seeing her son's remains in the following way: "I felt that I was emotional because I found my son. I kissed him again. I kissed all his bones, touched him, caressed him. But the emotion confounded with the pain, because once I found him, he turned out to be dead. So I cried the death of my son, and those thirteen years of search vanished. I can't relate anymore to this period" (quoted in Cohen Salama 1992:249). Juan Gelman confessed to similar sentiments a few weeks later: "I feel that I have been able to rescue him from the fog" (quoted in Cohen Salama 1992:250). But what did he rescue from the fog? His son's remains or his spirit? The remembrance of the political assassination or his son's ideals? Was Juan Gelman talking about the fog that drifts between the land of the living and the land of the dead? Or was he referring to similar state terror practices during World War II, in particular the 1941 *Nacht und Nebel* (night and fog) decree with which General Keitel ordered the disappearance of the Jews on the eastern front? A similar historical spirit may have persuaded Berta Schubaroff to bury her son in a Jewish cemetery out of vindication, even though she never practiced the Jewish faith. She had become conscious of her Jewish heritage when she learnt that her son's tormentors had treated him as a "shit Jew" (*judío de mierda*), and she therefore wanted to demonstrate her forgotten identity openly through a Jewish reburial (Cohen Salama 1992:250).

The feelings of Marcelo Gelman's parents, their sense of having rescued their son in medias res, and the detachment from the thirteen-year search experienced upon caressing the bones, are feared by the de Bonafini group of Madres. Most human rights organizations, however, have become convinced of the judicial, historical, political, and psychological importance of forensic investigations. Exhumations provide evidence for legal prosecution, give historical proof of the human rights violations committed by the military, and can provide forensic evidence about disappeared women who gave birth in captivity. Exhumations also make reburials possible that allow surviving relatives to begin a process of mourning. Reburials rehabilitate the disappeared because the public ceremony gives a deference to the deceased which had been denied by the military, precisely because they believed that they were subversive of society and thus undeserving of its public respect.

Robert Hertz has argued that reburials serve three general purposes: "to give burial to the remains of the deceased, to ensure the soul peace and access to the land of the dead, and finally to free the living from the obligations of mourning" (Hertz 1960:54). These purposes seem to have been served in Argentina as much for the nineteenth-century generals and statesmen who came to rest at Recoleta cemetery as for the nearly two hundred disappeared who were exhumed, identified, and finally reburied. The torn fabric of society is restored by funerary rituals, the deceased are reconciled with their forebears, and their souls come to rest in sacred ground, only to be recaptured periodically in commemorations. However, the violent death suffered by the disappeared and their political role in Argentine history accord them a special position that continues to infuse society with potential conflict. Reburials turn from rituals of remembrance into acts of restoration for their comrades-in-faith, and into acts of defiance and public provocation for their political opponents. It is this political significance which caused the persistent efforts to repatriate Juan Manuel de Rosas and rebury him at Recoleta cemetery, and which gave political meaning to the reburial of Marcelo Gelman at La Tablada Jewish cemetery. The fight about the remains of victims of violence thus becomes a struggle about the survival of their political spirit and the reconstruction of their legacy to Argentine history and society.

The belief in the eternity of the spirit, the imperishability of the bones, and the human need to mourn the dead are indeed as deeply engrained in Argentine society as they are in most cultures. The political practice of obstructing funerary rituals prevents people from coming to terms with their dead and from reconciling eventually with their opponents. This continued effort to hold the surviving relatives hostage to their anguish led one group of the Madres de Plaza de Mayo to forego all claims to the human remains—instead of clinging to the desperate hope to ever recover them—and to appropriate the political ideals of the disappeared. Political animosities have thus become further entrenched, and continue to kindle the memory of past humiliations and injustices. State terror will only come to an end when the perpetrators of violence acknowledge their common humanity with their victims—the living as well as the dead—and by returning the dead for proper reburial.

Notes

Research in Buenos Aires, Argentina, from April 1989 until August 1991 was made possible by grants from the National Science Foundation and the Harry Frank Guggenheim Foundation. I thank Walter van Beek and Jeffrey Sluka for their perceptive comments.

1. Juan Gelman was until 1978 a leading member of the Montoneros guerrilla organization. He left Buenos Aires in 1975 after receiving death threats from the Argentine Anticommunist Alliance (AAA), a right-wing paramilitary organization run from the ministry of social welfare headed by López Rega, the right hand of Perón's widow María Estela Martínez de Perón.

2. María Claudia Iruretagoyena was seven months pregnant when she was abducted, and she was still seen alive on October 7, about one week after her husband Marcelo had already been killed. Her mother-in-law Berta Schubaroff became a member of the Grandmothers of the Plaza de Mayo (Abuelas de Plaza de Mayo), and continued to search for a surviving grandchild.

3. In the nineteenth century, the Unitarists pursued a strong central government under the hegemony of the port city of Buenos Aires. They wanted to continue to enrich themselves with the profitable foreign trade, and the import and export tax revenues. The Federalists desired a federal government which would give greater political autonomy to the provinces, and protect the rudimentary local industries against foreign imports. Rosas championed the Federalist

cause, but his ouster in 1852 reestablished the dominance of Buenos Aires. In the twentieth century, the Unitarist ideas lived on in liberal politicians who wanted to open the Argentine economy to foreign investment, while the Federalist ideas were embraced by protectionist nationalists.

4. An official decree from 14 August 1956 ordered the publication of a "black book about the second tyranny" that would divulge to the Argentine people the corruption and misgovernment of Perón. This book outlines in detail the historical analogies between Rosas and Perón (Comisión de Afirmación 1987:25–34).

5. Rosas died in 1877 and entered the clause in his testament that his remains could only be reburied in Argentina if a 1857 sentence would be revoked that had declared him to be a traitor to the country (*Buenos Aires Nos Cuenta*, no. 13, p. 107; Martínez 1978:115–127).

6. The reburial of Rosas had been carefully orchestrated. Three weeks before the historic event, on 11 September, Menem had attended the commemoration in the province of San Juan of the 101st anniversary of the death of Domingo Sarmiento. Sarmiento and Rosas had been archrivals for decades. Rosas had forced Sarmiento into exile for championing the Unitarist cause, while Sarmiento had reviled the Federalist Rosas in his memorable denouncement *Civilization and Barbarism* (Sarmiento 1986).

7. The pardoned officers consisted of military commanders who had been indicted for human rights violations, junta members convicted for waging the 1982 Falklands/Malvinas War, and the leaders of several military mutinies in 1986 and 1987. The members of the 1976–1982 military juntas who had been convicted for their repressive regime and the disappearances of the 1970s remained in prison, but were pardoned in December 1990.

8. It is plausible to assume that the desecration of the corpse was also related to the Catholic belief in Purgatory and the survival of the soul after death. The mutilated were believed to suffer horribly as they were cleansed of their earthly sins. Natalie Zemon Davis comes to the same doctrinal explanation in her interpretation of the mutilation of corpses by Catholic crowds during the sixteenth-century religious wars against the Huguenots in France. Protestant crowds were particularly keen on torturing Catholic priests, but were indifferent to the corpse, possibly because "the souls of the dead experience immediately Christ's presence or the torments of the damned, and thus the dead body is no longer so dangerous or important an object to the living" (Davis 1975:179). On the other hand, the exhumation, mutilation, and public display of the mummified remains of priests, nuns, and saints during the Spanish civil war was an iconoclastic attack by the Republican left on the conservative Church and the Nationalists (Lincoln 1989: 117–127). Mutilation must be distinguished from the medieval practice of multiplying saintly relics through dismemberment (*dismembratio*) (Snoek 1995:22–24).

9. In 1708, a small chapel was built at the present location of the cemetery for the order of the Holy Recollect (*Santa Recolección*). The barefoot friars who lived in reclusive meditation were called *recoletos*, and the church that was erected in 1732 was popularly called Recoleta. Deceased members of important families and brotherhoods were buried inside the church, while others were laid to rest in the adjoining holy ground.

10. The body of Juan Domingo Perón was also not left undisturbed. In July 1987, someone broke into Perón's tomb at Chacarita cemetery and stole the hands from the corpse, the very hands Perón used to raise in his characteristic pose during his speeches from the balcony of the presidential palace as he received the cheers and chants of the Peronist masses.

11. Commissions to recover the remains of Rosas were also installed in 1917 and 1954, but these attempts did not reach congress (Barletta and Amézola 1992:50).

12. The following books provide historical background to the Madres de Plaza de Mayo: Bousquet (1984); Diago (1988); Fisher (1989); Guzman Bouvard (1994); Oria (1987); and Sánchez (1985).

13. The first protest was held on Saturday afternoon, 13 April 1977, but was moved initially to Friday and soon to Thursday afternoons. The city was deserted on Saturdays, and Friday was believed to be an unlucky day (Simpson and Bennett 1985:157–158).

14. The group that split itself off from the main organization called itself the Linea Fundadora (Founding Line) because several of its members belonged to the original group of fourteen women who began the public protest in 1977. They cooperated with the CONADEP investigation and supported the exhumations. The main group, which continued under the name Madres de Plaza de Mayo, condemned any cooperation with the government as a political concession and opposed the exhumations.

15. Elena Nicoletti, a member of the psychological team of the Madres, has argued that the Madres have rejected all mortuary rituals of Western culture because these rites cannot initiate a genuine mourning process in the absence of any certainty about the fate of the disappeared (Nicoletti 1988:116).

Bibliography

Andersen, Martin Edwin
    1993 *Dossier Secreto: Argentina's Desaparecidos and the Myth of the "Dirty War."* Boulder, Colo.: Westview Press.
Angenendt, Arnold
    1994 *Heilige und Reliquien: Die Geschichte ihres Kultes von frühen Christentum bis zur Gegenwart.* Munich: Beck Verlag.
APDH
    1987 *La Desaparición: Crimen Contra la Humanidad.* Buenos Aires: Asamblea Permanente por los Derechos Humanos.
Barletta, Ana María, and Gonzalo de Amézola
    1992 "Repatriación: Modelo para armar. Tres fechas en la repatriación de los restos de Juan Manuel de Rosas (1934–1974–1989)." *Estudios e Investigaciones,* 12, pp. 7–61. La Plata: Universidad Nacional de la Plata.
Bousquet, Jean-Pierre
    1984 *Las Locas de la Plaza de Mayo.* Córdoba: Fundación para la Democracia en Argentina.
CGE (Comando General del Ejército)
    1974 *Política Seguida con el Aborigen (1820–1852).* Buenos Aires: Círculo Militar.
Cohen Salama, Mauricio
    1992 *Tumbas anónimas.* Buenos Aires: Catálogos.
Comisión de Afirmación de la Revolución Libertadora
    1987 *Libro Negro de la Segunda Tiranía.* Fourth edition. Buenos Aires.
CONADEP
    1986 *Nunca Más: The Report of the Argentine National Commission on the Disappeared.* New York: Farrar, Straus and Giroux.

Davis, Natalie Zemon
    1975 *Society and Culture in Early Modern France.* Stanford: Stanford University Press.
Diago, Alejandro
    1988 *Conversando con las Madres de Plaza de Mayo: Hebe de Bonafini, Memória y Esperanza.* Buenos Aires: Ediciones Dialectica.
Etlin, Richard A.
    1984 *The Architecture of Death: The Transformation of the Cemetery in Eighteenth-Century Paris.* Cambridge: MIT Press.
Fisher, Jo
    1989 *Mothers of the Disappeared.* Boston: South End Press.
Foucault, Michel
    1979 *Discipline and Punish: The Birth of the Prison.* New York: Vintage Books.
Frias, Félix
    1884 *Escritos y Discursos.* Vol. 3. Buenos Aires: Imprenta y Libreria de Mayo.
García, Prudencio
    1995 *El Drama de la Autonomía Militar: Argentina Bajo las Juntas Militares.* Madrid: Alianza Editores.
Gillespie, Richard
    1982 *Soldiers of Perón: Argentina's Montoneros.* Oxford: Clarendon Press.
Guest, Iain
    1990 *Behind the Disappearances: Argentina's Dirty War Against Human Rights and the United Nations.* Philadelphia: University of Pennsylvania Press.
Guzman Bouvard, Marguerite
    1994 *Revolutionizing Motherhood: The Mothers of the Plaza de Mayo.* Wilmington, Del.: Scholarly Resources.
Hagelin, Ragnar
    1984 *Mi Hija Dagmar.* Buenos Aires: Sudamericana/Planeta.
Halperín Donghi, Tulio
    1975 *Politics, Economics and Society in Argentina in the Revolutionary Period.* Cambridge: Cambridge University Press.
Herrera, Matilde
    1987 *José.* Buenos Aires: Editorial Contrapunto.
Hertz, Robert
    1960 *Death and the Right Hand.* Aberdeen: Cohen and West.
Huntington, Richard, and Peter Metcalf
    1979 *Celebrations of Death: The Anthropology of Mortuary Ritual.* Cambridge: Cambridge University Press.
ICIHI (Independent Commission on International Humanitarian Issues)
    1986 *Disappeared!* London: Zed Books.
Kordan, Diana R., Lucila I. Edelman, D. M. Lagos, et al.
    1988 *Psychological Effects of Political Repression.* Buenos Aires: Sudamericana/Planeta.
Lincoln, Bruce
    1989 *Discourse and the Construction of Society: Comparative Studies of Myth, Ritual, and Classification.* New York: Oxford University Press.
Mármol, José
    1894 *Obra Poéticas y Dramáticas.* Paris: Bouret.
Martínez, Tomás Eloy
    1995 *Santa Evita.* Buenos Aires: Planeta.
    1978 *Lugar Común la Muerte.* Caracas: Monte Avila Editores.

Mittelbach, Federico
    1986 *Informe sobre Desaparecidos*. Buenos Aires: Ediciones de la Urraca.
Nicoletti, Elena
    1988 "Missing People: Defect of Signifying Ritual and Clinical Consequences."
    In *Psychological Effects of Political Repression*. D. Kordon et al., eds. Buenos Aires:
    Sudamericana / Planeta.
Oria, Piera Paola
    1987 *De la Casa a la Plaza*. Buenos Aires: Editorial Nueva America.
Page, Joseph A.
    1983 *Perón: A Biography*. New York: Random House.
Rock, David
    1987 *Argentina, 1516–1987: From Spanish Colonization to Alfonsín*. Berkeley: Uni-
    versity of California Press.
Sábato, Ernesto
    1990 *On Heroes and Tombs*. London: Jonathan Cape. (First published 1961).
Sánchez, Matilde
    1985 *Histórias de Vida: Hebe de Bonafini*. Buenos Aires: Fraterna / Del Nuevo
    Extremo.
San Martino de Dromi, María Laura
    1988 *Historia política Argentina (1955–1988)*. Buenos Aires: Editorial Astrea de
    Alfredo y Ricardo Depalma.
Sarmiento, Domingo F.
    1986 *Facundo o Civilización y Barbarie*. Buenos Aires: Biblioteca Ayacucho y
    Hyspamérica Ediciones Argentina S.A. (First published 1845).
Simpson, John, and Jana Bennett
    1985 *The Disappeared and the Mothers of the Plaza: The Story of the 11,000 Argenti-
    nians Who Vanished*. New York: St. Martin's Press.
Snoek, G. J. C.
    1995 *Medieval Piety from Relics to the Eucharist: A Process of Mutual Interaction*.
    Leiden: E. J. Brill.
Taylor, J. M.
    1979 *Eva Perón: The Myths of a Woman*. Chicago: University of Chicago Press.
Verbitsky, Horacio
    1995 *El Vuelo*. Buenos Aires: Planeta.

Newspapers and Periodicals
    Buenos Aires Nos Cuenta
    Humor
    La Nación
    La Prensa
    Madres de Plaza de Mayo
    Página 12
    Somos
    Sur

Chapter 4
The Homogenizing Effects of State-Sponsored Terrorism
The Case of Guatemala

Frank M. Afflitto

Y cuando se haga
el entusiasta recuento
de nuestro tiempo, . . .
. . . saldremos gananciosos
los que más hemos
sufrido de él . . .

[And when the enthusiastic recounting of our time is
made . . .
we will prevail,
those of us
who have most suffered from it . . .]

(Castillo 1989:59)

Conflicting yet perhaps complementary ethnographic literature has been generated regarding the nature of community and organizational responses to threats to the right to life in Guatemala. In pursuing such a line of investigation, I conducted participatory action research (see Whyte et al. 1991) with Guatemalan "popular" movement organizations in the early 1900s. Interview data were collected from eighty popular movement respondents in Guatemala during two participatory field research periods (1990 and 1992) and bear witness to the existence of terrorism against the civilian population perpetrated by forces linked to the Guatemalan state. Such terrorism is particularly visible in cases of enforced disappearances and extrajudicial executions. While Guatemalan state-sponsored terrorism as exercised through its centrally organized death squad apparatus has most often been identified as the author of these structural, systematic threats to the right to life, other threats have also been frequently identified, including economic, health, and other social conditions.

For example, a natural disaster which was a direct threat to life for tens of thousands of Guatemalans was the 1976 earthquake. It was identified as a "class earthquake" due to its direct effects on the loss of life and housing of the poorest urban and rural, Mayan and mestizo sectors of the Guatemalan population. The social aftershocks of the earthquake consisted of popular movement political mobilization which cut across ethnic lines as well as the rural/urban dichotomy. This was due to the fact that movement organizers recognized the earthquake as having uniformly affected the poorest sectors of Guatemalan society. This recognition served as an impetus for activists to organize around their homogeneous situation of victims and survivors (Morrison and May 1994:118). This same analytical paradigm of the homogenization of cross-ethnic, cross-geographic individuals into a popular (mass-based) political opposition movement with relatively unified demands serves as the thesis of this chapter.

While recent authors have commented on the cross-ethnic divisiveness in the Guatemalan popular movement (see Hale 1994), this chapter argues that the effects of state-sponsored death squad terror have served as an impetus for bringing together Guatemalans. This coming together has blurred ethnic, geographic, and even class lines in serving to form a popular movement involved in a process of homogenization of political, sociolegal resistance activities.

Respondent Identification of Guatemalan State-Sponsored Terror

My interviews and participatory fieldwork reveal the existence of a state-sponsored culture of terror. The majority of works on Guatemalan state-sponsored terror have tended to address the disruptive aspects of such terror on communal and organizational levels (e.g., *Barricada Internacional* 1986; Davis 1988; Davis and Hodson 1982; Figueroa Ibarra 1991). My research has, however, led me to the value of focusing on a singular realization. This realization is that, despite intraorganizational discord and interorganizational disparities in political agendas, the decades-long death-squad-perpetrated terror orchestrated by state security forces has brought people together from all walks of Guatemalan life in their demands for an end to impunity and in their unceasing clamor for justice.

The very nature and function of state-sponsored terrorism is to inhibit the growth and development of political movements opposed to the state and its national project (see Figueroa Ibarra 1991; Weiss Fagen 1992).

State terror's existence, through the use of death squads as extralegal security and penal forces, is intentionally shrouded in semiclandestinity under a guise of independence from official law enforcement activities. Essentially, the state utilizes the death squad forces in order to hide its responsibility for lethal political repression.

The Enforced Disappearance of Persons

Guatemala is world-renowned for the state's use of the disappearance of persons as a weapon of terror, as well as a mechanism in the evasion of accountability for political repression. In fact, Guatemala is cited as the first nation in the Americas to systematically employ the enforced disappearance of persons (ACAFADE 1989, 1990, 1991); it is the nation where the verb "to disappear" was coined (Simon 1987:14). It is also not generally known that Guatemala's disappeared persons, alone, account for approximately 50 percent of all of Latin America's disappeared persons (FEDEFAM 1992), surpassing Argentina, Peru, and Chile in sheer numbers, as well as El Salvador, although political repression in El Salvador has been consistently deemed more newsworthy than that in neighboring Guatemala. One Mayan respondent poignantly described this terror practice, "It's as if they've burned a hair. Because on a burnt hair, not even ash is left. Nothing. Nothing. And that's how it is." Another indigenous informant described in detail the reasons for disappearing persons in Guatemala:

I believe that here, all the world knows, the entire population knows that the disappearances, or enforced disappearances, exist because the poor, the agriculturalists, the indigenous people rose up. No longer did they let themselves be exploited. They demanded their rights. They organized in ways to ask for better salaries. That's why they sequestered them. Because we know of the groups . . . the small groups that have taken control of Guatemala's riches. They're not capable of letting go of even one red cent towards a better salary, never mind of improving working conditions in the fields. Do you know what I mean? So, it's because of that that they believe to organize themselves, to get together to discuss good ideas and to speak with the population in general about reality, about what God wants of us, or about what God wants of His children . . . it's not convenient to them. Right? Because then the people would be somehow improving their lot. Then the people would know their rights. So that's the motive for sequestering, disappearing the *compañeros*, who are the ones who orient us or the ones who speak out the most. Because, many times, for example . . . my husband . . . what he mostly did was to speak about reality . . . that it wasn't God who wanted us to be poor, marginalized, discriminated against in the different corners of the country. That this impoverishment is what's been done by a group of persons, a group of men that have grabbed the large tracts of land and the riches of Guatemala. That's why it's not convenient to them. So then, the solution for them was to disappear him, or kill him. Assassinate him so that others wouldn't follow him. That's what I think is the reason for why there are many disappearances in our country.

4.1. Santiago Atitlán, Sololá, Guatemala, 8 December 1990. Mainly mestizo trade union and public university student organizations, along with Mayan terror-survivor organizations, join together with 45,000 Tz'utujil Mayans six days after an army-perpetrated massacre in their community. Here, Tz'utujil residents await the beginning of the demonstration on the cathedral steps under a banner which reads "For Peace, No More Hunger or Repression." Photo by Frank M. Afflitto.

In addition to expressly counterorganizational reasons for disappearing persons were reasons respondents stated which might sound ludicrous to many of us unaware of the atmosphere of terror, insecurity, and mistrust fostered by systematic state-sponsored violence. One mother described the disappearance of her daugher as due to the fact that this daughter was a Catholic churchgoer. "Before the disappearance, people said about her . . . 'What's she doing at church?' . . . 'Subversive' they said about her. And it wasn't true."

The wife of a disappeared Kaqchikel Mayan described how her husband was nabbed by army regulars on election day, thrown into the back of a jeep with his hands tied behind his back, and repeatedly beaten in the chest with rifle butts in front of townspeople and all those from the surrounding villages who had come down from the hills to vote. Townspeople who pleaded for his release were threatened with the same, and his wife was told to go home, that it was "a simple search that we are doing. Your husband will arrive in the afternoon." She stated that she "went home, afraid, because I knew all that was happening, and it hurt me so. And he never returned." She believes that her husband was disappeared because of misinformation provided by envious townspeople who did not want (other) Indians to get ahead: "There in the village, they didn't like him because he would come from his studies at the public university, attending classes bit by bit. He worked *and* studied. So then, the other villagers didn't like this, because they said 'What's he up to?' But all he was doing was working as a teacher and getting his bachelor's degree. They ratted on him [i.e., falsely accused him of 'subversive' activity]."

Extrajudicial Executions: The Death Squad as Judge, Jury, and Executioner

While the enforced disappearance of persons leaves family and community members in a chronic state of intense uncertainty regarding their fate, the later reappearance of highly mutilated corpses in public places instills fear of the known, rather than of the unknown. In the cases of detention, torture, execution, and subsequent reappearance, the message of state terror is not so much one of evasion of accountability for its own political crimes. Rather, the message sought through extrajudicial execution is one of omnipotence. Mutilated corpses, with their "sentences" inscribed on their bodies (see Foucault 1979:34, 47), spread the message that resistance to the state's national project is futile, and that the price for such resistance is high.

One indigenous woman detailed how her husband was grabbed from a Catholic Mass only to be shot outside and left dead, near the church. Scared churchgoers pleaded for his release as the plainclothes gunmen began to beat him in the midst of the religious service; they were told to silence themselves or expect the same. The widow described how the death squad "only said that I not shout any more . . . 'Because we'll be right back, and we'll come back to finish you *all* off'!"

They threw him down right there [in the church] and they jumped on him and hit him. They beat him down to the floor and they said to him . . . they asked many things of him there. And he said to them "Who knows . . . I don't know him," he told them. And they jumped on him right there. I screamed as well, from the back of the church, and I said to them "Leave my husband alone! Leave my husband! He doesn't owe[1] anything!" I told them. "Shut up!" they told me. "We're going to do you first!" And from there, they showed me that when the bullet came out of the gun barrel, that it was going to enter *me* first, right here [points to self]. They took him away walking up the road. And they came to kill him in the road. I believe it was the *judiciales* [judicial police, police intelligence division], because I did not know them. They were masked. They had arms. Yes.

Some "sentences" are carried out in public, the victims being tortured for intelligence information and their bodies left outside for public scrutiny as everyone returns from religious services or the local market. They are also carried out in private so as to shroud responsibility, while the mutilated bodies are then left for family and community members to discover and to receive the unambiguous message of the apparent omnipotence of the killers.

A mestiza woman described finding her student leader relative and his close friend in unbelievable states of physical mutilation after allegedly being sequestered by the National Police:

From the beginning, we began going up and down, searching. We went to the police station and to the army base. And, like the news was always saying, well . . . some dead person appeared here, another cadaver here, another one there . . . we traveled around various parts of the country to confirm whether or not it was our family member . . . one of those cadavers. And personally, that made a deep impression on me, because always, you look at those things [cadavers] and it's like "Holy Jesus! Could *that* be him?!?!, or not?" He was found with his face bashed in. His skull was split open. Stab marks in the back. Five bullet holes in his chest. There were signs on his hands and feet that he had received electric shocks. He had no fingernails, and there were certain parts of his skin lifted out. You know, without skin [flayed]. He didn't have one ear. The other *compañero* was "done in" in a very severe manner. Because, to him . . . they split his entire face into two pieces. And his testicles were outside the skin, because they had flayed off all the skin. Off of his abdomen, too. They were *peeled* you might say, judging by viewing the ways that they had cut them. And they were naked. Just tossed like sacks by the side of the road.

Another relative of the two assassinated university student leaders stated that "I never thought that they were going to give him that class of death."

Up until this date [three years later] it keeps hurting me . . . because the death they gave him was not just. They broke him entirely into little pieces. They cut away the top layer of his abdomen. They *broke* him! He had perforations in his back that were not from gunshots; rather, from some type of crane, or meathook or drill, like the kind you use to bore holes into wood. I think it had to have been the army, because . . . let's just say that they had a list. There was a list of those who were the . . . let's say, of those who were in the association of which they [two murdered student leaders] were a part. Of a certain number of members of this student committee, they had already taken away almost half of them. They took away the two of them [student leaders]. Only a few others of this student association are still alive. To top it all off, in the place where he appeared, like within five kilometers from there, if it's even that much, there's an army camp. Between my father and my sisters, we said to ourselves, we asked ourselves . . . "Why didn't they [the army] intervene if they had the ability to see, from there, that they had come to throw him away there?" And on that very day, in the place where my relative appeared, there was a general sweep of the area by the Guardia de Hacienda [Treasury Police], the army and the National Police. This sweep took place at like four in the morning and he was already thrown down there.

Homogenizing Effects of State-Directed Death Squad Terror

The *De Profundis* Community

The popular movement organizations with whom I conducted participatory fieldwork were principally member organizations of the UASP (Unidad y Acción Sindical y Popular; Popular and Trade Unionist Action and Unity). The UASP, founded in 1988, is largely comprised of communities of survivors of the political and ethnically genocidal violence that has been enacted by state apparatuses since a well-documented CIA-sponsored coup in 1954 (see Immerman 1982; McClintock 1985). This prolonged period of genocidal terror has been largely based on an army-dominated political worldview which reveres the anticommunist deity of death squad violence as a strategy for national stability.

Survivors of state-sponsored terrorism have formed organizations designed to address their concerns and the concerns of constituencies that have survived similar atrocities. They are herein referred to as *de profundis* communities. The term *de profundis* means "a profound and especially agonized expression of despair and misery," according to Merriam-Webster (1993). The *de profundis* communities of survivors of counterinsurgent civil war and death squad terror have arisen out of violent repression and the cloak of impunity that shrouds, in a near uniform manner, the perpetrators of such violence. These are communities of organizations which have originated through a process of being direct or indirect recipients of the state-fostered perpetration of profound despair and misery (Falla 1992).

These *de profundis* political resistance organizations, embodied, at the time, by the UASP-affiliated organizations of Los Sectores Surgidos de la Represión y la Impunidad (The Sectors Arisen out of Repression and Impunity) are actually emergent, pan-Guatemalan communities, whose coming together is based on similar experiences as targets of state-sponsored terrorism. Such pan-communal homogenization has been possible due to a singular causal mechanism for the articulation of their demands and agendas for social transformation. This mechanism is the indignant, profound, and agonized expression of misery based upon having survived, and continuing to serve as potential targets of, state-sponsored terrorism. The development of these communities of resistance does not only counter the intended disruptive effects of state-sponsored terrorism. Such community development is also a step towards nation building based on a national project apart from that envisioned by the state terror system and its proponents.

From initial chance encounters at morgues, police stations, and army barracks in search of the missing, or in investigating the responsibility for the murder of those found dead, there has grown a common sense of purpose, and hence, a pan-Guatemalan identity. This de profundis identity has been assumed by a mestizo plantation worker from Escuintla, a mestiza lower-middle-class housewife from the capital city, a preliterate, predominantly monolingual rural Kaqchikel Mayan woman, an urban mestizo trade unionist, and a K'iche' Mayan university instructor, in citing only a few key examples. As one respondent stated:

It's a pity that blood had to raise the consciousness of the people. Because this blow [assassinated uncle] that was dealt us made more vivid and real all the violations of human rights that were going on in the country. Because we'd always heard about those kinds of things. We'd always see them on television and everything, but we had never *lived* it. And we had never seen it up so close. I have encountered *compañeras* that have traumas just like this. The army has killed their fathers or killed their mothers. They have raped their sisters. *Compañeros* who have lived in the flesh what it's like to be detained. We have seen other young people who have these kinds of problems, here in the university. It's principally the people from the countryside. Because . . . I have study mates of mine that come from faraway places. And there, for being places that are more enclosed, or isolated, this type of violence occurs more. Because out there, it's the army who rules. And they do and undo just as they please. And the police, themselves, as well.

The *De Profundis* Community as Political Resistance Community

The fundamental, unifying strengths of these communities lie in their denial of the existence of an impartial (i.e., justice is blind) law, and in the empowerment of the disenfranchised through sociolegally based resistance. Such empowerment has taken the form of more democratic, grassroots participation in political mobilization of a kind that has been lacking in Guatemala's contemporary history of military-dominated social life. This political participation, through which the defenses of rights and the pressuring of demands are channeled via a process of vocalization and organizationally based struggle, involves the most traditionally peripheral yet numerous societal sectors, such as the indigenous Mayan majority, women, the slum-dwelling poor, youth, orphans, and preliterate persons.

The homogenization of previously disparate social sectors into a *de profundis* community has contributed to the establishment of a socio-

4.2. Guatemala City, Guatemala, 15 December 1990. Survivors and potential targets of death squad activity, Mayans and mestizos, proclaim "We Promote Life" as the antithesis of state terror. Demonstrators were asked to cover their faces with the banner before the photo was taken. Photo by Frank M. Afflitto.

legal response to the system of impunity and judicial ineffectiveness at the level of political resistance to the state and its death squad-perpetrated terrorism. The parallel legal system and extralegal surrogate penalties of death squad violence are countered by the *de profundis* movement's assertion of the right to life and the right to know.

While the right to life may be viewed rather straightforwardly, the right to know is twofold. Not only are the survivors and targets of terror demanding the right to know the whereabouts of their disappeared loved ones and community members, but they are simultaneously demanding an official recognition of the state's role in the formation and propagation of the death squad apparatus responsible for the 50,000-plus enforced disappearances. (The numbers have grown since attending a Catholic Mass became a perceived communist threat to Guatemalan national security.)[2]

Organizational demands for the respect of these two fundamental rights have created another parallel legal center, apart from that of the surrogate penalty of death squad violence. This new parallel legality grew out of the procedural inefficiency based on impunity and the related threat to life of attorneys, plaintiffs, and witnesses ("We hired a lawyer. They killed him"), and is comprised of the gathering of evidence of the existence of death squad and security force violence through testimonies by movement members. These parallel law centers are where *de profundis* community members pass judgment on state-sponsored authorities as being those guilty of terrorism through the propagation of death squad violence. While the desire for punishment may not be uniform across respondents and organizations, the assignment of guilt largely is. This evidence-gathering and judging community is actually performing duties that the Guatemalan criminal justice system has traditionally been too cowardly and corrupt to perform.

The *de profundis* community, while born out of misery and despair, does not exist to wallow in its collective victimization. Its *raison d'être* is to combat and defeat the envirogenic conditions which have brought about, and continue to propagate, the death-squad-led misery and sorrow which have served as their organizational rallying points (Falla 1992). Thus, the emergent community identity that has typified the past two decades of organizational and coalitional development in sectors of the popular movement has become a pan-Guatemalan identity that has not only been symbolically and politically represented, at least in part, by coalitions like Los Sectores Surgidos. It is also a community identity which has simultaneously, if not always intentionally, (re)defined concepts of modernization, nationhood, and community identity itself for movement activists and their varied constituencies.

Homogenization as an Important Passage Toward an Alternative Model of Nation Building

The emergence of communities of resistance not only counters the intended disruptive effects of state-sponsored terrorism through unification. An essential aspect of the emergent communities' importance rests on the idea that such unification is a step toward nation building. The organizational struggles of *de profundis* communities act in the building of a Guatemalan nationhood. As these disparate groups come together and recognize each other as targets and survivors of the same suffering by the same hand, they form into communities. When they look past their sufferings to a positive, altered vision of society, they become Guatemalans, and they are nation-building. The incidental result of these organizational activities ultimately represents an alternative model of a Guatemalan nation-state.

A pluralist model of a Guatemalan nation-state as formulated by participants in the communities of survivors of state-sponsored violence presents liberating aspects. The army-led, terror-defended model of nationhood is an "imposed" model (Pulparampil 1975:20). Although the army's counterinsurgent model of nationhood is ostensibly an empty shell of a pan-Guatemalan national identity, it has been a threat to the communal existence of especially Indian Guatemala. Such a state-fostered, pan-Guatemalan identity, due to its imposed anti-Indianist "ladinization" (Jonas 1991:104) as a prerequisite for modernization and development has not been a liberating paradigm for the popular classes nor for the Mayan majority.

What this terror-backed national identity has attempted in Guatemala is the "Magyarization" (Macartney 1968:116) of nation-state relations by which disparate tribal and community identities are to be subsumed under one armed sector's designs. This is an imposed model of nationhood which denies federalist and autonomist ethnopolitical aspirations through the extensive use of state-sponsored violence. Under these circumstances, to simply *be* an Indian is a subversive statement, a symbol of backwardness, as it were. ("They look at us and see that we are indigenous . . . they say that the indigenous people don't know anything.")

Conclusion

Edgar Barillas et al. (1988) observe that one cannot effectively comprehend community and ethnic identity in Guatemala, nor Guatemala's ethnopolitical contradictions, without locating them firmly in nation-state social relations. I have argued here that these nation-state social relations are based on the widespread use of terror as a weapon against political and ethnic community development. While this terror-inspired counterinsurgency project has had the intended atomizing effect on Guatemalan social life, it has also aimed for a simultaneous global effect, that is, the consolidation of all spheres of life — especially rural life — under the state's military and political apparatuses (Smith 1990).

In citing the conflictive conditions of Indian-state relations in Guatemala, anthropologist Carol A. Smith (1990) reflects that, in order for Indian culture(s) to survive state-sponsored attempts at elimination, they will have to survive in different forms. According to Smith (1990:282), one possible form through which such survival could take place is through "the development of a pan-Indian identity" that would reflect "a distinct multicultural nation . . . with its own political agenda." The emergent community identity of survivors of state-sponsored terrorism is just such a pan-Indian, as well as pan-Guatemalan, identity.

Survivor-based justice claims in Guatemala contribute to establishing the social bases of an alternative, popular justice system, counterpoised to the ongoing reign of armed impunity. A pluralist national unity, based on the common experiences of broad sectors of Guatemalan society through community identification as survivors of state-sponsored violence, is a cultural expression of nationhood which symbolically and organizationally undermines the ideology of terror. Such a *de profundis* community identity, when linked to political, sociolegal resistance and projected onto a positive conception of Guatemalan society, serves as an antithetical global vision to terror's continued attempts at dominating nation-state relations.

Notes

An earlier version of this chapter was presented at the Pacific Coast Council on Latin American Studies conference in October 1993 in Orange, California.

1. This notion of "owing" something is coined from my Guatemalan fieldwork. It is not owing in the sense of a debt, as one might perceive the term in standard English. Here, the verb *deber* "to owe" is in reference to being guilty of political or criminal misconduct.

2. Interviews and fieldwork with respondents, in addition to works by other authors, indicate that the Catholic Church may have been singled out for political repression at the height of the counterinsurgency in the 1980s. Catholic catechists, for their prestigious and well-respected positions in rural and poor communities, were murdered or disappeared with appalling frequency. The advent of liberation theology and the incorporation of social justice concerns in the evangelizing of groups like Catholic Action may have contributed to the repression against the Catholic community, as social justice is the equivalent to subversion in dogmatic Guatemalan state counterinsurgency doctrine.

Bibliography

ACAFADE (Asociación Centroamericana de Familiares de Detenidos-Desaparecidos)
    1991 *Desaparecidos en Centroamérica 1990*. San José, Costa Rica: ACAFADE.
    1990 *Desaparecidos en Centroamérica 1989*. San José, Costa Rica: ACAFADE.
    1989 *Desaparecidos en Centroamérica 1988*. San José, Costa Rica: ACAFADE.
Barillas, Edgar, with Adolfo Herrera, Marta López, Lesbia Ortiz, and Olga Pérez de Lara
    1988 *Formación Nacional y Realidad Etnica en Guatemala: Propuesta Teórico Metodológica para su Análisis. Temas de Debate*, vol. 1. Guatemala, Guatemala: Instituto de Investigaciones Históricas, Antropológicas y Arqueológicas.
Barricada Internacional
    1986 "Heridas Que No Cierran. Represión Deja Sus Marcas en los Niños Guatemaltecos." 22 May, p. 7.
Castillo, Otto René
    1989 *Para Que No Cayera la Esperanza*. Tegucigalpa, Honduras: Editorial Guaymuras.
Davis, Shelton H.
    1988 "Introduction: Sowing the Seeds of Violence." In *Harvest of Violence: The Maya Indians and the Guatemalan Crisis*. Robert Carmack, ed. Norman: University of Oklahoma Press.

Davis, Shelton H., and Julie Hodson
   1982 *Witnesses to Political Violence in Guatemala: The Suppression of a Rural Development Movement.* Boston: Oxfam America.
Falla, Ricardo
   1992 *Masacres de la Selva: Ixcán, Guatemala, 1975–1982.* Guatemala: Editorial Universitaria.
FEDEFAM (Federación de Familiares de Detenidos-Desaparecidos)
   1992 *Periodical Bulletin.* Caracas, Venezuela: FEDEFAM.
Figueroa Ibarra, Carlos
   1991 *El Recurso del Miedo: Ensayo sobre el Estado y el Terror en Guatemala.* San José, Costa Rica: Editorial Universitaria Centroamericana.
Foucault, Michel
   1979 *Discipline and Punish: The Birth of the Prison.* New York: Vintage Books.
Hale, Charles R.
   1994 "Between Che Guevara and the Pachamama: Mestizos, Indians and Identity Politics in the Anti-Quincentenary Campaign." *Critique of Anthropology*, 14:1, pp. 9–39.
Immerman, Richard H.
   1982 *The CIA in Guatemala: the Foreign Policy of Intervention.* Austin: University of Texas Press.
Jonas, Susanne
   1991 *The Battle for Guatemala: Rebels, Death Squads, and U.S. Power.* Boulder, Colo.: Westview Press.
Macartney, Carlile Aylmer
   1968 *National States and National Minorities.* New York: Russell and Russell.
McClintock, Michael
   1985 *The American Connection Volume II: State Terror and Popular Resistance in Guatemala.* London: Zed Books.
Morrison, Andrew R., and Rachel A. May
   1994 "Escape from Terror: Violence and Migration in Post-Revolutionary Guatemala." *Latin American Research Review*, 29:2, pp. 111–132.
Pulparampil, John K.
   1975 *Models of Nation Building A Critical Appraisal.* New Delhi: N. V. Publications.
Simon, Jean-Marie
   1987 *Guatemala Eternal Spring—Eternal Tyranny.* New York: W. W. Norton.
Smith, Carol A.
   1990 "Conclusion: History and Revolution in Guatemala." In *Guatemalan Indians and the State.* Carol Smith with the assistance of Marilyn Moors, eds. Austin: University of Texas Press.
Weiss Fagen, Patricia
   1992 "Repression and State Security." In *Fear at the Edge: State Terror and Resistance in Latin America.* Juan Corradi, Patricia Weiss Fagen and Manuel Garretón, eds. Berkeley: University of California Press.
Whyte, William Foote, Davydd J. Greenwood, and Peter Lazes
   1991 "Participatory Action Research: Through Practice to Science in Social Research." In *Participatory Action Research.* William Foote Whyte, ed. Newbury Park, Calif.: Sage Publications.

Chapter 5
"For God and Ulster"
The Culture of Terror and Loyalist
Death Squads in Northern Ireland

Jeffrey A. Sluka

He said if I was ready to swear the oath for it, he could join me into the organization there and then. I said I was ready, so he told me to put my hand on the gun which was on the bible, and repeat certain words after him. They were to the effect that for the rest of my life I'd be loyal to the organization, to God and to Ulster. Those were the things that I swore allegiance to, three things in that order. His next words to me were I was now a member of the organization for the rest of my life, and the only way I'd ever get out of it was in a box. I'm not sure if I should have told you that much.

(Loyalist death squad member interviewed by Tony Parker, cited in *An Phoblacht/Republican News*, 3 June 1993, p. 15)

Catholic Abducted, Shot
(*Evening Post*, 14 May 1997)

Belfast, May 13. — The body of a 62-year-old Roman Catholic was found on a Northern Ireland country road today after what police said was a sectarian murder. He was abducted from a club of the Gaelic Athletic Association (GAA), an Irish Nationalist and Catholic sports group, last night and shot after a struggle, police at Randalstown said. It was thought to be the third sectarian killing this year after the shooting of a Catholic father of nine in Belfast in April and the beating to death of a Catholic in Portadown earlier this month. No group immediately claimed responsibility for the killing but Protestant Loyalists were under suspicion.

This chapter addresses one important aspect of the culture of British state terror in Northern Ireland — Loyalist death squad attacks against the Catholic-Nationalist minority[1] — and is an attempt to write against terror through a critical "new anthropology" combining perspectives from progressive streams in the discipline. These include action (see van Willigen 1993:57–75), public interest (Davis and Mathews 1979), collaborative (Kuhlmann 1992), liberation (Huizer 1979; Gordon 1991), advocacy (Paine 1985), and human rights (Downing and Kushner 1988; Messer 1993) anthropology, and commitment, after C. Wright Mills and Noam Chomsky, to the values of humanism and the politics of truth (see, for example, Mills 1963:599–613; Chomsky 1969:23–126, 323–359). In writing it, I am not implying that all the violence in Northern Ireland has been one-sided. The Irish Republican Army (IRA) and Irish National Liberation Army (INLA) have publicly stated that they are engaged in armed conflict, and their actions have been widely and publicly documented and condemned by the British, Irish, American, and other governments; politicians; Catholic and Protestant clergy; and the media. However, beginning in 1972, there has been a vicious, continued campaign of sectarian assassination against Catholics in Northern Ireland waged by Loyalist paramilitary groups (the Ulster Defense Association [UDA] and Ulster Volunteer Force [UVF]) and their associated death squads (the Ulster Freedom Fighters [UFF], Red Hand Commandos, Protestant Action Force, etc.), which have killed nearly seven hundred innocent Catholic civilians — the largest category of casualties in the war. Thousands of other Catholics have survived Loyalist attempts to murder them. The existence of this campaign has never been publicly acknowledged as an integral part of their counterinsurgency strategy by the British authorities, who have ignored it, downplayed it, and actively misrepresented it to influence the media and public, both at home and abroad. The official position of the British authorities is that there is no state terror in Northern Ireland, and certainly no death squads. When pressed, they admit that there is Loyalist terror against Catholics, but insist that they have nothing to do with it. When pressed with evidence such as the fact that hundreds of members of the security forces have been convicted of involvement with Loyalist paramilitaries, they claim that this collusion is informal — individual acts by rogue soldiers and policemen — and not a reflection of government policy or military strategy. All of these are political lies. In this chapter, I seek to tell the truth about Loyalist death squads and expose these lies.

What I say here is based on nearly two decades of research specialization on Catholic-Nationalist political culture and the war in Northern Ireland, particularly two years, divided among three periods, living and conducting participant-observation-based fieldwork in the Catholic-Nationalist working-class urban village ghettos in west and north Belfast, which represent the major battlegrounds or "killing fields" of the war. In

1981–1982, I lived and worked for a year in Divis Flats and the Clonnard/ Kashmir area of the lower Falls Road district in west Belfast, areas renowned as battlegrounds of the Troubles, the diminuting euphemism frequently used to refer to the war. In 1991, I spent six months in the Antrim Road district, in the center of what is termed the "murder mile" because of the large number of Catholics who have been killed there by Loyalist paramilitaries and death squads. In 1995–1996, I spent another six months living in the New Lodge district. Both the Antrim Road and New Lodge districts are in north Belfast, which has borne more suffering and where more people have been killed than in any other part of Northern Ireland — including the largest number of sectarian murders. Since 1969, more than six hundred people — nearly one in five of those killed in the war — have been killed in north Belfast, an area of not more than a few square miles.[2] The New Lodge has been the hardest hit community in the war.[3] New Lodge Road itself, which runs through the center of the district, is statistically the most dangerous street in Northern Ireland, and the most dangerous single point has been the intersection of New Lodge Road with Antrim Road, where ten people have been killed (Kelters and Thornton 1993). I lived in Spamount Street, one street over from New Lodge Road, on the edge of the district near where it intersects with Tiger's Bay, a staunchly Loyalist, Protestant working-class district and a main point of entry and attack for Loyalist death squads. The house I lived in had been attacked three times. During all of the times I have lived and done research in Belfast I was, like any other resident of the Catholic ghettos, presumed to be a Catholic and under constant threat of random sectarian assassination by Loyalist death squads. I have personally experienced the constant fear and tension that is a normal part of life and the culture of terror (Taussig 1984) in these ghettos.[4]

During my first two periods of fieldwork in Belfast, I often asked people what *they* thought I should do research on and write about, and almost invariably the answer was the same — that I should tell the world about the people who they said were the forgotten victims of the war, the many hundreds of innocent Catholic civilians killed in sectarian attacks, that is, selected for political assassination for no other reason than that the religion they practiced was different from that of their killers.[5] This chapter represents my response to that suggestion. I have researched the Loyalist death squads because the research participants I am indebted to in my fieldwork in Belfast wanted such research done, and because I wanted, in sympathy with them, to write against the terror that blighted their lives.

Besides my own independent research, I have relied on research and documentation provided by a number of credible local and international organizations which have for many years produced meticulous and com-

5.1. Where death squads roam: New Lodge Road — the most dangerous location in Northern Ireland, despite massive security forces surveillance of the
area, including the British army observation post on top of Templar House
tower block (on left), helicopters, cameras, and constant foot and mobile patrols by British troops and militarized police. Relatives for Justice and other
human rights groups have asked, "How do RUC and British Army bases fail to
detect or deter Loyalist murder gangs when they enter Catholic areas since they
are equipped with sophisticated surveillance apparatus?" (Relatives for Justice
1995:1). Photo by Jeffrey Sluka.

prehensive reports documenting state terror in Northern Ireland — Silent
Too Long, Relatives for Justice, Clergy for Justice,[6] the Campaign for the
Right to Truth,[7] the Committee for the Administration of Justice,[8] the
Center for Research and Documentation,[9] Sinn Fein, and Amnesty International. I have relied on these sources not only for information but also
for enlightenment and inspiration. In particular, I have relied on the two
community-based "popular" organizations formed by relatives of innocent Catholics killed by the security forces and Loyalist assassins — Silent
Too Long and Relatives for Justice — which I worked with, respectively, in
1981 and 1995–1996. Silent Too Long was formed at the end of 1981 with
four objectives:

(1) To create unity and support amongst relatives who have suffered at the hands
of Loyalists and security forces and who want to tell their side of it. Also to show

that the 2000 plus people killed in the troubles [up to the end of 1981] were not all killed by the IRA as stated by the British Government. (2) To have the UDA banned, this force has openly boasted about their involvement in the murder of Catholics.[10] (3) To show that the Security Forces have murdered with immunity from the law. (4) To show that there has been dual membership and collusion between members of Loyalist paramilitary groups and the Security Forces. (Silent Too Long 1982:3)

Relatives for Justice was formed a decade later in 1991 to focus attention on the use of state terror by the British government:

For twenty-five years the counter insurgency methods of the British government in Northern Ireland have involved a Shoot-to-Kill policy, in direct ambushes when both innocent victims and suspects have been shot dead without warning,[11] and in a sinister indirect campaign of murder which involved manipulation of Loyalist paramilitaries who were provided with security information and who then killed with the knowledge that they were free from prosecution. This policy was pursued by small groups of RUC [Royal Ulster Constabulary] personnel, the British Army, and the secret intelligence network of MI5 and MI6. A section of the Northern Ireland administration is aware of the policy, protects it by withholding information, insincere cosmetic investigation, non-prosecution and curbing of inquests. The families and friends of the victims not only suffer the insult of cover-ups and lies but they often become targets for harassment and abuse from the British Army and the RUC. They seek redress in publicising the truth to the world and will not cease to bring their grievances before government and international human rights bodies. (Relatives for Justice 1995:1)

In 1993 Relatives for Justice published a report on British shoot-to-kill operations and the history of collusion between the security forces and Loyalist death squads, which was republished in an updated and expanded form in 1995. This lists the victims murdered by Loyalist paramilitaries from March 1990 to October 1994, and (where known) the organization responsible for the murder, the weapon used, where the gunmen's mode of transport was obtained and abandoned after the killing, incidents of leaking of secret intelligence files, and the relatively rare arrest, charging, and conviction of perpetrators, who have included serving and former members of the security forces. The 1995 report also details the number of sectarian killings in which South African weaponry, secured by Loyalist death squads with the help of British military intelligence, have been used (see below).

While the research reported here represents the victims' perspective,[12] if the essence of objectivity is gathering the available evidence and letting it lead to the conclusions, than the ethnographic overview of Loyalist death squads in the culture of terror presented here is an objective view consistent with the facts on the ground in Northern Ireland. Nonethe-

5.2. Union Jack behind head and skull of Loyalist assassin, Beechmount Avenue (Falls Road), Belfast. From Rolston (1995).

less, I think there is no academic or other dishonor in being prepared to stand with the victims of oppression and state terror.

Two Campaigns of Violence

Between the beginning of the war in 1969 and the IRA cease-fire declared at the end of 1994, a total of 3,168 people were killed as a result of political violence in Northern Ireland. The fatalities break down into the following categories (figures derived from O'Duffy 1995:772):

Security Forces	*1,045*	*(33%)*
Republicans	314	(9.9%)
Loyalists	89	(2.8%)
Catholic Civilians	*1,067*	*(33.7%)*
Protestant Civilians	571	(18%)
Political Activists	45	(1.4%)
Unclassified	37	(1.2%)

The breakdown of those responsible for the 1,067 Catholic civilians killed is the following:

By Republicans	192	(18%)
By Loyalists	662	(62%)
By Security Forces	144	(13.5%)[13]
Unclassified	69	(6.5%)

It should also be noted that of the 571 Protestant civilians killed, 114 (20 percent) were killed by Loyalists, usually mistaken for being Catholics.[14]

What these casualty figures show is that (1) statistically, those most at risk of death in the conflict in Northern Ireland are innocent Catholic civilians, over 800 of whom have been killed by the security forces and Loyalists, and (2) the two largest categories of fatalities are members of the security forces killed by Republican guerrillas and Catholic civilians killed by Loyalist paramilitaries. This supports the assertion made by Silent Too Long, and Catholics in general, but generally ignored by the media because of effective British propaganda, that there are two campaigns of violence in Northern Ireland, essentially the Republican (IRA and INLA) war against the British state and security forces, and the security forces' and Loyalist paramilitaries' war, not just against militant Republicans, but against the Catholic civilian population as a whole.

Death Squads in Northern Ireland

When commenting on Loyalist killings, the British government has consistently claimed that they are a reaction to IRA violence, thereby partially exonerating Loyalists from blame and suggesting that such killings are not linked to British policy or counterinsurgency strategy. This view, presented by both the British authorities and Unionist politicians in Northern Ireland, has a history that is not based solely in the present conflict; it predates it, going back to the establishment of the Northern Ireland state and beyond (see O'Brien 1989). Catholics have always been terrorized by Protestants since British settlers were first planted in Ulster in the middle of the seventeenth century, and the same tactic has been employed by the British government's official and unofficial forces since the establishment of Northern Ireland in 1920. It long predates the reemergence of the IRA in 1969.[15]

In the history of Northern Ireland, whenever Loyalists have perceived any sign of political advance for Nationalists, they have attacked and killed randomly selected Catholics and otherwise terrorized the Catholic minority.[16] The Protestant-controlled "Orange State" (Farrell 1980) established by the partition of Ireland was born in the midst of massive sectarian violence which began in July 1920 and lasted until the end of 1922. This pogrom by Loyalist extremists and mobs, as Catholic history records it, was supported by Unionist politicians and the state security forces, the Royal Ulster Constabulary and part-time Special Constabulary. The pogrom systematically drove Nationalist workers from employment in Belfast's shipyards, hounded Nationalist businessmen from Protestant areas by burning their premises, invaded Catholic districts, and killed innocent Catholics in sectarian attacks. During this period there were 452 killings in Belfast, 267 Catholics and 185 Protestants,[17] and many of the Protestant deaths were the result of the British army firing into Loyalist mobs attacking Catholics. Almost nine thousand Catholics were forced from their places of employment and around twenty-five thousand driven or burned out of their homes. For the next fifty years, until replaced by direct rule from Westminster in 1972, successive Unionist governments relied on the combined violence of state forces and Loyalist sectarian attacks on Catholics to instill fear in the Catholic minority as a means of political control, with the ultimate aim of maintaining partition and the union of Northern Ireland and Great Britain, and preventing Catholic-Nationalist aspirations for a united Ireland.[18]

The war in Northern Ireland began in 1969, precipitated by Loyalist mobs again attacking Catholic districts in Belfast and Derry. (It is an irony of history that almost no one remembers that the British army was first called back into Northern Ireland to protect Catholic districts from Protestant mobs.)[19] As the IRA military campaign escalated following the introduction of internment in 1971, the Loyalist paramilitaries grew apace and responded by launching a campaign of sectarian attacks and random assassinations of Catholics. This was fertile ground for the British military's various "dirty tricks" units to infiltrate and politically direct the violence of Loyalist paramilitaries (see Dillon 1990 and Urban 1992). The British deployed in Northern Ireland some of the lessons learned in their use of counterterror gangs in Kenya and Malaya. Brigadier Frank Kitson, whose books *Low Intensity Operations* (1971) and *Gangs and Counter-Gangs* (1960) became the British army's counterinsurgency manuals, advocated a strategy of establishing unofficial "countergangs" or "pseudogangs" which could be manipulated in British interests without incurring British responsibility for their actions (Faligot 1983).[20] From the beginning the Loyalist paramilitaries were closely associated with Kitson's strategy.

There are many examples in the 1970s of direct input by the British military in the sectarian campaign against Catholics. Units such as the Military Reaction Force, trained by the Special Air Service (SAS, the British equivalent of the U.S. Green Berets), were responsible for many killings, which were usually attributed to Loyalist death squads. By the mid-1970s, British intelligence had already heavily infiltrated the Loyalist paramilitaries at all levels. Many of these agents were former British soldiers, and the expertise and experience they added — not to mention their provision of weapons and intelligence information from the security forces — significantly im-

5.3. Protestant working-class districts are marked by Loyalist paramilitary murals. This one in the lower Shankill district celebrates the Ulster Freedom Fighters. To the left is Divis Tower located in lower Falls Road district, indicating the very close proximity of the two communities. From Rolston (1995).

proved the capabilities of the Loyalist death squads. The most notable of these agents in the early 1970s was Albert Baker, who operated in Belfast. Baker's gang was responsible for the notorious "Romper Room" murders, where Catholics were beaten, tortured, then mutilated before being shot. Baker, who was sentenced to life imprisonment in 1974, admitted his role as a British agent and said the killings "were designed to fit into a British intelligence plan to terrorize the Nationalist community and push off support for the IRA" (*Saoirse* 1991:7). The most recent example is Brian Nelson, discussed below.

In September 1976, a UDA commander wrote in the organization's magazine *Combat*, "There is only one way to control an area or ghetto that harbors terrorists and insurgents and that is to reduce its population to fear by inflicting upon them all the horror of terrorist warfare. Where these means cannot, for whatever reasons be used, the war is lost" (*Irish News*, 26 January 1993, p. 8). That is, in a nutshell, the story of Loyalist death squads in Northern Ireland. In the Catholic ghettos of Belfast and other cities, sectarian assassination is a constant possibility, an everyday reality they have had to learn to live with. Because of ethnic residential segregation, it is possible for Loyalist death squads to mount rapid incursions into Catholic districts to kill residents with the assumption that they will be Catholics (resulting in several dozen Protestants being killed by Loyalist death squads for being in the wrong place at the wrong time).

As noted earlier, more sectarian murders have occurred in north Belfast than anywhere else. More than a third of fatal attacks carried out by the UVF and UFF have taken place there, and in the Catholic ghettos everyone knows someone who has been killed, and there is a good chance you will have seen someone being killed. North Belfast attracts political murders because of the social geography of the area.[21] Like west Belfast, the north side is largely divided along sectarian lines. But whereas the Falls Road is the largest Catholic enclave and stands on its own, the north of the city is a patchwork of green (Catholic-Nationalist) and orange (Protestant-Loyalist) urban village districts. Sectarian murder happens in the heart of the Falls Road, but not as often. In north Belfast there are more sectarian interfaces than anywhere else in the city, and more "peacelines" (six of Belfast's thirteen peacelines are in a one-square-mile area of North Belfast). Loyalist death squads in north Belfast do not have to go far to kill Catholics. Protestants and Catholics at opposite ends of the political spectrum live just a street away from one another. Within minutes, Loyalist killers can be back in the protection of their own areas. Such was the case, for example, of the triple murder at an Oldpark betting shop in 1992. The killers switched cars little over a hundred yards away, leaving a ninety-second run to a Loyalist heartland. When Gerard O'Hara was shot dead in September 1993, his killers, within seconds, had left the New Lodge and were in neighboring Loyalist Tiger's Bay. These people were killed simply because they were Catholics, and it was because of geography—because of where they lived—that they were selected as victims.[22]

Over a twenty-five-year period between 1969 and the paramilitary cease-fires of 1994, Loyalist death squads killed hundreds of innocent Catholics in random sectarian attacks.[23] Loyalists were responsible for the worst atrocities—the bombing of McGurk's bar in Belfast in December 1971, in which fifteen people were killed, and the Dublin and Monaghan car bombs in the Republic of Ireland which left thirty-three dead on 17 May 1974.[24]

The pattern has been to attack Catholics who live in fringe streets along escape routes, but Loyalists have also been confident enough to go into the heart of Nationalist areas. Loyalist death squads have mounted frequent bomb and gun attacks on pubs, sometimes causing multiple deaths. There were over eighty attacks on bars and clubs between 1971 and 1994 by Loyalist death squads. Nearly 160 people were killed in these attacks. Catholics—including Protestants mistaken for Catholics—were also mur-

5.4. Ulster Volunteer Force mural, Dover Place, lower Shankill, Belfast, depicting the "Loyalist skeleton key" at work. From Rolston (1995).

dered at their place of work, or in their homes, or simply walking home at night. Many were shot standing at street corners, and many more were "doorstop murders" — the death squad would come to the door of a house or flat, knock, and then either ask for the victim by name or shoot the first person to answer the door, frequently regardless of their age or gender. Often, the door was simply broken open with a sledgehammer — eventually it earned the nickname "Loyalist skeleton key" — and gunmen would run in and single out victims or open fire randomly on whoever was in the house.

Between 1975 and 1977, the notorious Shankill Butchers struck terror in the Catholic community, roaming the streets of north and west Belfast in a black taxi, seeking victims to be tortured and murdered, sometimes ritualistically, with their selection of knives, axes, and meat cleavers. The gang murdered at least two dozen Catholics, probably more (Dillon 1989).[25] Explaining the random selection of victims, one of the Butchers simply said "We were looking for a 'Taig' " [a Loyalist epithet for Catholics, similar in meaning to "nigger"[26]] (*An Phoblacht/Republican News*, 1 August 1996, p. 17).[27]

In 1974, the Republican movement published the following warning about sectarian attacks by Loyalist assassins:

A Clear Warning to All Residents
(*Republican News*, 30 November 1974)

In a study of the spate of brutal assassinations we have discovered many close similarities in these murders. Many of them fall into clearly definable groups:

(1) Those who are killed opening their doors late at night: This is one of the most regular methods used by these killer squads. We have found out personally that most people open their doors only too readily without first checking on the identity of the caller — THIS IS ABSOLUTELY FATAL.

(2) Those who are murdered on their way to work, or returning from work: These people die because their movements have been fingered by their workmates and then relayed to the assassins.[28] DISCUSS NOTHING WITH YOUR WORKMATES no matter how long you have worked with them. HUGH MARTIN OF ARDOYNE worked with the man who fingered him for 8 years! HE'S DEAD.

(3) Those who accept lifts from strangers: This is very foolish and courting death, as was recently discovered in Portadown. Never accept a lift from someone you do not know.

(4) Those who accept a joint taxi ride: Make sure the cab you hire is from a reputable firm; never travel in a cab that has already got passengers; observe the route taken by the taxi driver, question him and GET OUT OF THE CAB. Never sit beside the driver, sit directly behind him.

(5) Never accept an invitation to a party which may be extended in a pub: Many Catholics have been lured to their deaths by people purporting to be going to a party.

(6) Standing on street corners, especially late at night: This is an all too common occurrence in these areas, and young people are asking for trouble.

(7) Never go out at night alone in areas recognised to be the assassins' murder

ground. Lads have been pulled into cars while walking along a street. MURDER, whether it be from Loyalist groups or the SAS, is rampant on our streets, 350 people have died [up to November 1974]. Every one of us should regard ourselves as a potential victim. By taking that little extra care and time in our daily habits we can prevent death to ourselves and untold misery and heartbreak to our relatives. EXERCISE A LITTLE CARE.

Recognizing the risks and taking precautions like those described above quickly became an accepted, necessary, and "normal" part of everyday life in the Catholic ghettos.

In 1988 the Loyalist paramilitaries were rearmed with South African supplied weapons under the direction of British intelligence. As mentioned above, the latest British military agent to be exposed was Brian Nelson. A native of Belfast, he was a British soldier and active in the UDA's death squads in the early 1970s, and was jailed in 1973 with two other UDA men for kidnapping and torturing a Catholic man, who died after they released him. In the 1980s, after his release from jail, Nelson rejoined the UDA at the behest of British intelligence, working closely with his MI5 handlers. He became UDA director of intelligence and was responsible for selecting targets for and rearming the death squads. He had unlimited access to security forces intelligence documents on Nationalists and Republicans, and organized the largest-ever shipment of Loyalist arms, obtained from South Africa and other countries, with the full backing of his British intelligence handlers who directed the reorganization and rearming of the UDA, until he was arrested again in 1990 (Adams 1986:85–86; Sinn Fein 1994a, 1994b; *Saoirse* 1996, pp. 3–4; Friel 1998b).[29]

The result of the rearming of the Loyalist paramilitaries was a major upsurge in sectarian killings in the first half of the 1990s, with Loyalists for the first time claiming more victims than the IRA/INLA campaign and emerging as the single major source of political violence in Northern Ireland. In the six years before the arrival of the Nelson arms shipment, from January 1982 to December 1987, Loyalist paramilitaries killed 71 people of whom 49 were sectarian (that is, innocent civilians). In the six years following from January 1988 to 1 September 1994, Loyalists killed 229 people of whom 207 were sectarian (Relatives for Justice 1995:3). During this period the death squads continued to attack pubs in Catholic areas, and also began to attack betting offices. On 5 February 1992 members of the UFF killed five Catholics in a gun attack on Sean Graham's bookmakers on Ormeau Road in Belfast. On 14 November 1992, they shot dead three men in an attack on James Murray bookmakers on Oldpark Road, also in Belfast. On 30 October 1993 they killed seven people in an attack on the Rising Sun Bar in Greysteel. The killers shouted "trick or treat" just before they sprayed the bar with gunfire. On 18 June 1994 the UVF was responsible for the last major atrocity prior to the cease-

5.5. The Catholic ghettos are marked by anti–death squad murals, frequently highlighting collusion. Springhill Avenue, Ballymurphy, West Belfast. From Rolston (1995).

fires — the Loughinisland massacre where a death squad shot six people dead in a pub as they watched the Republic of Ireland World Cup game.[30]

British Counterinsurgency and Loyalist Violence

In the literature on political violence, death squads are generally defined as progovernment groups who engage in extrajudicial killings of people they define as enemies of the state, whose members are either directly or indirectly connected with the government and/or security forces. There is usually overlap in membership and various forms of collusion — including the provision of weapons and intelligence — between the death squads and the security forces. It is necessary to state this definition because in the highly politicized context of any discussion of Northern Ireland there are many people — particularly British people and their allies — who completely reject the idea that there are anything like death squads in Northern Ireland, and certainly not like the better-known death squads in Latin America. Generally, it appears that to refer to death squads in Northern Ireland is frequently interpreted as evidence that the speaker is biased against Britain and Ulster Protestants. The fact is that the Loyalist paramilitaries fit the definition to a tee, and the death squads in Northern Ireland bear striking similarities to those found all over the world.

Death squads are one of the main tools employed by oppressive regimes and cultures of terror around the world to intimidate and control people who hold legitimate aspirations for political change. These "countergangs" are drawn from the state's own forces and organizations which support the state's policies (the status quo). While the media has called world attention to the use of such state terror in many contemporary Third World countries, when it comes to Northern Ireland the same perception of collaboration between government and terror groups does not exist. This is because the British government has established a sophisticated system of direct control, through its military and intelligence services (MI5 and MI6), of the Loyalist paramilitaries who direct the war of attrition against the civilian population in Catholic-Nationalist areas, which has been effective in maintaining a respectable distance between the government, at the top, and the people who do the killing, at the bottom.

Relatives for Justice have identified the common forms of collusion in Northern Ireland:

The RUC informed some of the victims that their personal details, contained in official British Intelligence files, were in the hands of Loyalist paramilitaries. Some victims were killed by Loyalist gangs with members of the Security Forces in their ranks. Some were killed by weapons reportedly stolen from members of the Security Forces. Some received death threats from members of the Security Forces before their deaths. Some were killed by weaponry acquired by Loyalist paramilitaries with the assistance of a number of British Intelligence agents, Brian Nelson being the best known of these. (Relatives for Justice 1995:2)

Since the beginning of the war, there has been mounting evidence of state forces' involvement in the Loyalist terror campaign, indicating a substantial degree of collusion between the Loyalist paramilitaries and the security forces and intelligence services. This is typical of death squad activity around the world. Collusion has always been complex, but structured and widespread. It has never been merely the actions of malcontents or "rogue elements" in the security forces. A large number of human rights organizations have consistently documented British state involvement in and management of the Loyalist death squads. For example, Amnesty International, in a statement following the release of people charged with possession of leaked files in October 1990, concluded that it is obvious from all the evidence that collusion remains a fact of life and that the government is not prepared to confront it. In a major report in 1994, it again highlighted mounting evidence of collusion between government forces and groups like the UDA, exposing the Catholic minority to random attack from Loyalist death squads: "Such collusion has existed at the level of the security forces and services, made possible by the apparent complacency, and complicity in this, of government officials. This element of apparent complicity has been seen, for example, in the failure of the authorities to take effective measures to stop collusion, to bring appropriate sanctions against people who colluded, or to deploy resources with equal vigour against both Republican and Loyalist armed groups that pursue campaigns of political murder" (Amnesty International 1994:6). The 1995 Relatives for Justice study of collusion mentioned earlier reported that, of the 168 Loyalist killings between 1990 and 1994, there was evidence of collusion with state forces in 103 (61 percent).

The direct involvement of British intelligence in directing and supplying information to the Loyalist death squads has been repeatedly documented, and hundreds of members of the British army and RUC have been charged with supplying weapons and intelligence about Catholics to the UDA and UVF. Over 3,000 security intelligence files on Nationalists and Republicans—including their personal details and movements— have been passed on to the UDA and UVF since 1969 (Clergy for Justice 1994), and they have used these to plan their attacks. The locally recruited and almost entirely Protestant Ulster Defense Regiment of the British army (now renamed the Royal Irish Rifles) was heavily infiltrated by the UDA and UVF almost from the start, and quickly became intrinsically linked with Loyalist violence. Over 320 members have been convicted of offenses against Catholics, including murder, maimings, kidnap-

5.6. Anti–death squad mural, Oakman Street, Beechmount (Falls Road), Belfast, highlighting overlap in membership and collusion between Loyalist paramilitary groups, the Ulster Defense Regiment and the Royal Ulster Constabulary. From Rolston (1995).

pings, serious assault, and passing information to Loyalist paramilitaries. Hundreds of other members have been purged from the regiment—most of them suspected of having links with Loyalist paramilitary groups (see Sinn Fein 1990).

But the term "collusion," as defined and accepted in Northern Ireland, is restricted to explaining the relationship between individual "bad apples" inside the security forces and Loyalist extremists. It implies that the British government has no responsibility or control over the killing of Irish Catholics. In other countries where similar relationships exist between official state forces and unofficial forces who support the state, and where nothing is done to end such relationships, the governments of those countries are accused of using death squads. But in Ireland, as in other colonies where the British military have allowed and assisted death squads to terrorize the population, successive British governments have always been able to wash their hands of the blood spilled by their agents.

No matter how horrifying Loyalist violence is, it is neither mindless nor pointless: It is a direct result of British state policy and military practice. It is as old as British colonialism in Ireland,[31] and, while the Loyalists have their own agenda, their attacks fit in with British counterinsurgency strategy. The Loyalist death squads have been armed and supplied with information by British military intelligence, and act as unofficial auxiliaries to the British forces. Their objective is to prevent any forward political movement which would undermine the current constitutional status quo. They seek to terrorize and subdue the entire Catholic-Nationalist population by killing uninvolved civilians and by selective assassinations of political opponents of the state, as a way of ending resistance, getting them to accept any settlement that stops the killing, and undermining support for and ultimately defeating the IRA and INLA. As in similar situations in Latin America, uninvolved civilians, families, women, and children are intended targets. The aim is to terrorize as many Catholics as possible and make all perceived opponents of Unionism feel that they could be the next victim. This is why there has always been collusion both at an unofficial or personal level and at an official level.[32]

Shifting the Blame: Psychological Warfare Myths

Two other "big lies" or political myths propagated by the British and Unionist authorities and the media in general are (1) that Loyalist violence is a defensive or retributive "reaction" to the Republican armed struggle to achieve a united Ireland; and (2) that the war in Northern Ireland is a sectarian conflict between Catholics and Protestants, marked by "tit-for-tat" killings, in which the British are a third "neutral" party trying to keep the peace between them. Both of these characterizations fly in the face of the historical and contemporary record. They are propaganda or psychological warfare myths which ultimately emanate from the British government and its military apparatus in Northern Ireland. This is a classic "blaming the victim" tactic (Ryan 1971), the purpose of which is to lay the responsibility for the slaughter of Catholic-Nationalist civilians at the door of the very community which is being targeted. Specifically, it is intended to blame the IRA for all the deaths — particularly the ones done by Loyalists.[33] Those who describe Loyalist death squad killings as reactive and tit-for-tat are working to a British government agenda in failing to confront the truth.

The Loyalist paramilitaries have acknowledged in several newspaper interviews that their actions have been proactive, not reactive (*An Phoblacht/Republican News*, 29 June 1994), and even a cursory knowledge of the actions of Loyalist extremists, from the foundation of the Northern Irish state in 1920 and before, shows that Loyalist violence has resulted whenever Protestants have perceived that Catholics were making political gains. Loyalist violence is reactive, not to the actions of the Republican guerrillas, but to any sign of resistance by or forward political movement for Catholic-Nationalists, and has never operated on a tit-for-tat basis.

With regard to British propaganda and media characterizations of the conflict as "a grim cycle of tit-for-tat sectarian violence," the authorities have made strenuous efforts to encourage the media to portray both sides as being equally involved in sectarian killings, and to not state the religion of the victims of sectarian attacks in order to conceal the fact that they are overwhelmingly Catholic (Burke et al. 1996:11). Popular tactics of disinformation employed by the RUC include:

- professing not to know who or what is behind these killings and treating them as "motiveless murders" when the sectarian motive is obvious;
- deflecting responsibility back on the Catholic-Nationalist community by speculating about particular shootings as perhaps being the result of "local feuds" or "IRA gangland-style executions";
- claiming that the state and RUC do not keep a tally of the ethnic/ religious affiliations of the victims; and
- equating the random sectarian killing of Catholic civilians with IRA attacks on armed members of the Northern Ireland security forces (the RUC and Royal Irish Rifles regiment), because nearly all of them are Protestant.

These tactics are intended to actively misrepresent Loyalist terror and cultivate the impression that Catholics and Protestants are senselessly killing each other in some sort of unfathomable religious or "tribal" vendetta (cf. Kelly 1982:169–171). The truth is that almost all of the sectarian killing in Northern Ireland has been one-sided. Unlike Loyalist ideology, a cornerstone of Republican ideology is antisectarianism, and the IRA do not select targets on the basis of religion. Sectarian killings — that is, killing people simply because of their religion — is the hallmark only of the Loyalist death squads.

In June 1994, a Northern Ireland-based human rights monitoring group slammed "tit-for-tat" reporting in the media. Describing Loyalist killings as attempts "to create fear in the Catholic community," they said there was "a deep sense of frustration within the Nationalist community [created by] the media fixation with 'retaliation' and 'tit-for-tat' murders," and condemned these "inaccurate and dangerous descriptions of the current violence." They noted that in the period from 2 June to 20 June of that year, Loyalists had killed nine people, eight Catholics and a Protestant drinking with Catholic friends. "The reality is that all Catholics in the North of Ireland, and indeed any Protestants who work or socialize with Catholics, are potential targets for Loyalist paramilitaries." They argued that Loyalist death squad killings were "a response to any perceived political progress seen as detrimental to Unionism, and above all, because of a deeply embedded fear and hatred of Catholics inherent in extreme Loyalism," and noted that "the targeting of an individual because of their religion is almost exclusively a Loyalist phenomenon and it is erroneous and dangerous to talk of 'sectarian tit-for-tat' murders" (cited in *An Phoblacht/Republican News*, 30 June 1994, p. 2).

Conclusion

In October 1996, the chief constable of the RUC, Sir Hugh Annesley, reiterated the consistently maintained state explanation for why the security forces' priority is countering Republican rather than Loyalist violence. He claimed Loyalist violence was "reactive," and implied that if the IRA ceased their campaign, the Loyalist paramilitaries would cease theirs. He also complimented the Loyalist paramilitaries for maintaining the cease-fire they declared in 1994 in response to the IRA cease-fire and emergence of the Northern Ireland peace process. But he also commented that "If they were pushed back into violence, and they have been very severely pushed up to now, then one would have to imagine attacks on the Republic of Ireland and throughout Northern Ireland" (Reuter, 22 October 1996). This view basically condones Loyalist violence as an understandable response to provocation. As has always been the case in Northern Ireland, as far as the state is concerned, the provocation has been all one-sided; when Catholic-Nationalists resist Unionist oppression and British state terror, they are provoking their oppressors to kill them.

As far back as 1991, an editorial in the *Irish News* (the major Catholic daily in Northern Ireland) responded to similar comments Annesley made then, arguing that he was wrong:

> there is not a single shred of evidence to support his hypothesis. Sooner or later, the police force, which purports to protect all members of the community, is going to have to recognise that those most at risk in Northern Ireland are innocent Catholic civilians. Mr. Annesley and his colleagues will have to accept that between 1969 and 1989, the first 20 years of the troubles, 896 uninvolved Catholics were killed. Over the same period 575 uninvolved Protestant civilians were killed. When you take into account the fact that there are more Protestants than Catholics, the danger to Catholics shows up as being all the greater. Catholic civilians are in graver danger than members of the Security Forces and yet very few resources are deployed to help protect them.

Security policy in Belfast remains overwhelmingly geared towards combating the IRA — that is, counterinsurgency — rather than "peacekeeping" or protecting people from or preventing sectarian violence. Despite the fact that Loyalist gunmen pose a greater threat, Catholic districts are policed more intensively and aggressively than Protestant districts. British government security policy indicates that it does not regard the protection of Catholic civilians as being very high on its list of priorities.[34]

Republican violence in Northern Ireland must be understood in the context of a reaction to political oppression and continuing state supported violence (Clergy for Justice 1994). What emerges here is something I have stressed before, the basic contradiction in state repression as a means of social and political control. While intended to pacify the resistance of the oppressed, its application more frequently produces the opposite effect. Perhaps the single main finding of my research on popular support for the IRA and INLA (Sluka 1989) was that the major source of support is the defensive role they play in the Catholic working-class ghetto "killing fields" of Belfast and other Northern Irish cities (see also de Baroid 1989). The primary function of the IRA in Northern Ireland has always been community defense and protection of the Catholic minority from state and Loyalist attacks, and the national liberation struggle is secondary to that. Like the phoenix they adopted as their symbol, the Provisional IRA reemerged from the ashes of the Catholic homes and streets burned down by Loyalist mobs and Protestant policemen in August 1969. Hence, Loyalist death squad activity in Northern Ireland is not only brutal and sectarian, it is totally counterproductive. In the complex dialectic between repression and resistance, the Loyalist death squads produce the very conditions for the existence of what they fear most — armed resistance by the oppressed Catholic-Nationalist minority. This is true despite the apparent contradiction that the IRA and INLA are, in fact, unable to adequately protect Catholics from assassination, as the following words of an Ardoyne (north Belfast) woman expresses:

The IRA have been responsible for many things but they weren't responsible . . . for the assassination of over 850 Catholics and the . . . murders of kids and women by plastic bullets. Loyalist paramilitaries always pretend that they only resort to violence when they're provoked by the IRA, but that's nonsense. There was no IRA activity in 1966 when the UVF carried out the Malvern Street murders of two Catholics. Loyalist violence always seems to flare up when they think the British are going to concede something to the "Taigs" or when they think the IRA are on the run. Besides, it suits the Brits to portray us as mad murdering bastards and themselves as the neutral go-between. The truth of the matter is that the Brits are here to back up the Loyalists and their interests. Why else have they allowed them to stockpile thousands of weapons which are used to murder innocent Catholics simply because they are Catholics? Why else do they let Paisley stomp around the country inciting Protestants to hate us? And then they have the gall to turn round and say to the world, "It's the IRA who started the trouble — we have to stamp them out." But it wasn't the IRA who started it all. It was the Brits who made the country what it is, by allowing a Unionist government to do what it wanted to the Catholic population for over 50 years. It was the Brits and those Unionists who forced the Catholics to support the IRA. Let's face it, I know where I live and I know how my area is surrounded by Loyalists. I know about the [lack of] security, and if trouble broke out what the positions would be, because I've lived through it before. We all know who is going to go out and put their necks on the line. It's the IRA (cited in Fairweather et al. 1984:233).

Postscript: Loyalist Terror During the Peace Process

Despite the apparent end of the war, marked by the IRA and Loyalist paramilitary cease-fires in 1994 and the subsequent peace process, Loyalist terror has continued. In 1997, eight Catholics were killed by Loyalist death squads and extremists, including Robert Hamill, who was beaten to death in April. This prompted one *Irish News* columnist, Brian Feeney, to comment that: "The result is the same old story. 1997 was no different from 1966, 1969, 1972, 1975, 1986. In each of those years governments of one kind or another began to address Nationalist grievances. Whenever that happens Unionist leaders start to bleat about reforms and as night follows day murder gangs start to kill Catholics" (cited in *An Phoblacht/ Republican News*, 8 January 1998, p. 2). These deaths were only the surface of an insidious campaign of violence against Catholics that has been ongoing despite the Loyalist "cease-fire" and the peace process. Along with murders and attempted murders of Nationalists, Catholic Churches, homes, schools, and business premises were attacked and firebombed around Northern Ireland.

In the second half of 1997 a new Loyalist death squad, the Loyalist Volunteer Force, shot dead three Catholics. In response, the INLA killed infamous death squad leader Billy "King Rat" Wright, and said the sectarian killings must stop. Loyalists proceeded to kill four more Catholics, all chosen at random in Nationalist areas. The INLA killed another Loyalist death squad leader, again saying the random sectarian killings of Catholics must stop. They did not, and five more Catholics were shot dead and several others seriously wounded. The UFF/UDA admitted responsibility, claiming these random killings were a "measured military response" to Nationalist initiatives. In overview, twelve randomly selected Catholics were shot dead, and in retaliation two Loyalist terror gang leaders were killed by the INLA, with demands that the sectarian offensive against Catholics stop.

In 1998, there was a marked upsurge in ongoing Loyalist violence, from intimidation and petrol bombings to gun attacks against Catholic communities throughout Northern Ireland. That year, up to November, fifteen more Catholics were killed and over a dozen seriously injured in another Loyalist murder campaign. Over this three-year period of "peace" in Northern Ireland, despite the obvious anomalies in basic arithmetic which contradict this claim, the British and Unionist authorities and the media persisted in describing these attacks as several "series of tit-for-tat sectarian killings," using this characterization to effectively rationalize, if not justify, the activities of the Loyalist death squads (MacRuairi 1998).

Thus, the idea of "tit-for-tat sectarian murder cycles" is a political fiction or "myth" (Friel 1998a), representing an attempt to hide the true nature of the indiscriminate assault waged against the Catholic community. The media also frequently failed to report who was responsible when Loyalists killed Protestants, reinforcing the sectarian tit-for-tat theme, and tended strongly to describe all of the deaths during this period as sectarian, including the deaths of the two leading Loyalist terrorists, which were clearly not sectarian. The deaths of those who organize sectarian attacks cannot be objectively equated with the deaths of their victims. The purpose is to push the false propaganda line that the conflict is essentially sectarian, with Nationalists (particularly the IRA and INLA) to blame, and that Britain must maintain its presence to keep the rival "tribes" apart. As Republican journalist Laura Friel concluded (*An Phoblacht/ Republican News*, 15 January 1998, p. 3), sectarian killings of Catholics are not acts of revenge or retaliation, but rather "the bloody expression of a supremacist elite determined to protect its privilege."

Notes

1. For a description of the opposed but dialectically interrelated cultures of terror and resistance in Northern Ireland, see Sluka 1995. The culture of terror includes three domains of pro-state violence against innocent Catholics: (1) that

of the state security forces (which have killed at least 176 Catholic civilians [Sutton 1994:204]); (2) that of the Loyalist paramilitaries; and (3) a continuous low level of everyday forms of racist and sectarian violence when Catholics are basically lynched—beaten up and attacked with knives and clubs, frequently by drunken gangs of Loyalist youths, including marching band members and soccer fans who get drunk after social events and assault Catholics—and the petrol bombing of Catholic homes, schools, and churches. This is particularly true during the Loyalist Orange Order marching season in the summer, when Loyalist hatred becomes exaggerated and inflamed.

2. This number includes 250 Catholic civilians and 160 Protestant civilians.

3. The district commemoration garden lists the names of 130 IRA and Sinn Fein members and over 100 civilians. While the New Lodge has the largest number of deaths, statistically I believe the lower Ormeau Road enclave has the highest proportion of deaths. Of the about 1,000 Catholics who live there, 50 or 5 percent have been killed by Loyalists. If you add another 100 or so who have been injured or attacked in sectarian murder bids, about 15 percent of the district's population have personally been attacked. This is largely due to geography; the district is located in east Belfast, surrounded by Protestant districts, and it is cut off from other Catholic enclaves in west Belfast by the River Lagan. It is an easy target.

4. I have been frequently warned by my Catholic research participants that the Loyalist paramilitaries will have identified me, that I am not safe from them, that it would be dangerous to spend time in Protestant districts where I might be recognized, and that I should always be aware of this threat and be careful. Nonetheless, I have no direct evidence that the Loyalist paramilitaries know me or are concerned about my work. Interestingly, the only direct threat I have received from Loyalists is a phone call to my office in New Zealand. A local caller with a northern Irish accent told me, "You're not as far from Northern Ireland as you think, and you can still be got . . . we know who you are, what you look like, and where you live . . . keep your mouth shut if you know what's good for you." (This incident was at a time when I had been recently interviewed and aspects of my research reported in the media.)

5. Renowned journalist John Taylor (1998) has unveiled what he terms the "hierarchy of death" in the British press when reporting the war: "In the first rank—getting the most coverage—are British people killed in Britain; in the second, the security forces, whether army or RUC; in the third, civilian victims of Republicans; and, in the fourth, garnering very little coverage indeed, the victims of Loyalism" (cited in *An Phoblacht/Republican News*, 10 September 1998, p. 15).

6. A group of Catholic clergy concerned with human rights issues and the abuse of state power in Northern Ireland.

7. An umbrella group representing victims of state-sponsored violence and their relatives. Formed in October 1994, it launched a campaign to force the British government to admit a catalog of human rights abuses. The CRT is composed of eight groups—the United Campaign Against Plastic Bullets, the Casement Accused Relatives Committee, the Cullyhanna Justice Group, Relatives for Justice, the Bloody Sunday Justice Campaign, the Friends of Patrick McLaughlin, the Pat Finucane Center, and the Dublin/Monaghan Bombings Victims Support Group.

8. An independent civil liberties organization formed in 1981 to work to improve the standard of justice in Northern Ireland. See Committee for the Administration of Justice 1992 and 1993.

9. An independent Belfast-based human rights watchdog group.

10. Despite its admitted involvement in sectarian killings, the UDA was not declared an illegal organization in Northern Ireland until August 1992, and it is still legal in Britain.

11. Catholics have maintained that since the early 1970s the British army and RUC have operated a "shoot-to-kill" policy leading to extrajudicial killings, including the execution of prisoners and unarmed "terrorist suspects." See Murray 1990.

12. For Protestant perspectives on Loyalist violence see Bell 1976; Miller 1978; Nelson 1984; Galliher and Degregory 1985; Bruce 1992; and Clayton 1996.

13. The Republican movement says that "British forces" have killed 357 civilians, or "more civilians than the IRA" (*An Phoblacht/Republican News*, 7 November 1996, p. 11).

14. Sutton (1994:202), by including Protestants killed because they were mistaken for Catholics or associated with Catholics, attributes 713 sectarian killings of civilians to Loyalists.

15. The UVF reemerged in 1966 and killed two Catholics in sectarian attacks.

16. Catholics believe that most victims are randomly selected simply because they are Catholics, but it appears that some are deliberately singled out for various reasons — because they are working on building sites in Protestant or mixed areas and make easy targets (or may be perceived as competing for jobs), because they are involved in Irish cultural activities, because they have publicly criticized the authorities and security forces, and so on.

17. To put these deaths in context, bear in mind that Catholics represented only about one-third of the population of Northern Ireland at that time, but suffered nearly three-fifths of the casualties.

18. For the history of anti-Catholic riots and pogroms in Northern Ireland, see O'Brien (1989); Farrell (1980); and Boyd (1969). As Clergy for Justice have noted: "For the past 120 years, there has been an anti-Catholic uprising in the north of Ireland, supported by the British government, on average once every 12 years [a reference to periodic localized attacks and pogroms against Catholics by Protestant mobs and armed gangs of Loyalists]. So the present spate of government killings is not new. People talk about the Red Hand Commandos, UDA, UFF as if they were separate organizations of fanatical Protestants. They are in fact a coolly organized network of one government's killers" (Burke et al. 1996:21–22).

19. Republicans (such as Sinn Fein President Gerry Adams [1986]) and others dispute this interpretation. Their view is that the British army was brought in, not to defend Catholics, but rather to support the Orange State to control them. This is a valid interpretation, but the British army did defend Catholic districts from Loyalist attacks when it first arrived in August 1969.

20. The complexity of the relationship between state forces and death squads is revealed in the observation by Clergy for Justice that "Different types of pseudo gangs have been identified. We have Kitson's Military Reconnaissance Force units, made up of SAS personnel or 'Special Duties Teams,' trained to carry out SAS style covert operations. There are mixed gangs of security personnel and 'turned around insurgents.' There are paramilitary groups carrying out operations inspired by military agents provocateurs who have penetrated their ranks. And there are paramilitary groups actually controlled by security personnel" (Burke et al. 1996:21–22). Most of these types have been employed in Northern Ireland.

21. For analysis of the social geography of political murder in Belfast, see Boal 1974, 1981; Boal et al. 1976; Murray and Boal 1979; and Feldman 1991.

22. One "territorial" aspect of death squad killings of Catholics in north Belfast is their relationship to sectarian tensions resulting from large population shifts. The upheaval of the war helped establish a pattern in north Belfast, primarily along Antrim Road, where Protestants left and Catholics moved in to replace them. They were then attacked by Loyalists who wanted to maintain the "purity" of so-called Protestant areas, and the area came to be known as the "murder mile." Research in the 1970s (e.g., Dillon and Lehane 1973) showed that Catholics were shot in particular areas where they were moving into housing that had never been occupied by Catholics before.

23. Over the years, compelling evidence has emerged that British intelligence was behind the Dublin and Monaghan bombings. A British agent planted in the UDA has admitted driving the car containing the explosives part of the way to Dublin, and Clergy for Justice, among other reputable observers, has stated unequivocally that these bombings "were the work of Loyalists linked to the Security Forces through the RUC Special Branch" (Burke et al. 1996:6). See also Bowyer Bell 1996.

24. After the cease-fires, on 15 August 1998, the Real IRA, a breakaway group from the IRA opposed to its cease-fire, was responsible for the Omagh city bomb which killed twenty-three and injured over two hundred. However, unlike the Loyalist atrocities mentioned in this chapter, these deaths were the result of a military operation gone wrong, and not intentional. This terrible and tragic mistake destroyed the Real IRA, which disbanded shortly afterwards. Certainly, no Loyalist paramilitary group would disband in similar circumstances. Objectively, these accidental civilian casualties cannot and should not be equated with the intentional civilian casualties from Loyalist bombings.

25. See Feldman (1991) for an insightful discussion of the Shankill Butchers as representing the "outer limit" of Loyalist paramilitary killings.

26. Protestant stereotyping of Catholics is similar to the stereotypes of "natives" held in settler colonial societies and constitutes a form of racism little distinguishable from settler racism (Clayton 1996).

27. The Shankill Butchers "had no ideological struggle to wage so they used the strategy which Gusty Spence [best-known figure in the revived UVF] had initiated in 1966: 'If you can't get an IRA man, get a *Taig*' " (Dillon 1989:12).

28. Many working-class Catholics refused to fill out census forms in 1981 and 1991 because they believed that the information would go into their intelligence dossiers (virtually all working-class Catholics have such dossiers), including the route they took to and from work, and that this information could be passed on to Loyalist paramilitaries and used to plan their assassinations.

29. In February 1992, Nelson was convicted of five counts of conspiracy to commit murder. Defense Secretary Tom King pleaded for leniency, and in court a British army officer described him as a hero who was working out of a sense of patriotism, but became "a little too enthusiastic." A senior judge, Basil Kelly, handed down a ten-year prison sentence to Nelson, the minimum he could impose, and described him as a man who had shown "the greatest courage." He served five years, and was released again in February 1996. Catholics interpreted this episode as another obvious sign of, if not formal collusion, at least informal collusion and the "natural" sympathy between British state authorities and Loyalist death squads.

30. Employing the international definition of mass murder as five or more homicides in a single event, Loyalist death squads have, on a number of occasions, been guilty of political mass murder.

31. For example, in the 1790s, Catholics in the north of Ireland suffered at the hands of mobs from the forerunner of the Orange Order — the Peep O'Day Boys. This gang of sectarian supremacists would raid Catholic homes, beat and sometimes kill the occupants, torch the house, destroy the crops, stampede the farm animals, and wreck any industrial implements or machinery. Their aim was to "make the croppies lie down" — that is, to ensure that Catholics posed no political, economic, social, or cultural threat to Protestant hegemony.

32. In 1998, investigative journalist Sean McPhilemy published *The Committee: Political Assassination in Northern Ireland*, which blew the lid off RUC collusion with Loyalist death squads. He revealed the existence of a secret committee of high-ranking RUC and locally recruited British army officers who ran a campaign of political and sectarian assassination against Nationalists in the late 1980s and early 1990s. Central to the committee was an "inner circle" of RUC officers who colluded with senior Unionist politicians and members of the Loyalist death squads in a campaign of political murder by proxy. According to McPhilemy, this inner circle "routinely assisted the Loyalist death squads to assassinate Republicans and Catholics whom the Committee selected for elimination" (cited in *An Phoblacht/Republican News*, 19 March 1998, p. 5).

33. To provide an example of this, in October 1996, following an IRA bomb attack on the British army headquarters in Lisburn which killed a soldier, the media spent a lot of time speculating about whether or not the Loyalists would abandon their cease-fire in retaliation. The reports said things like: "Since 1969, and most particularly in 1989–94, the Loyalist death squads carried out 'defensive' attacks on the IRA that were considered some of the most ruthless of the Northern Ireland conflict" (Reuter-AFP, 9 October 1996). These attacks were *not* attacks on the IRA but rather against innocent Catholic civilians, and they were certainly not "defensive" since the victims represented no threat whatsoever.

34. The Relatives for Justice report (1995) recorded the following complaints made by Catholics against the security forces and their attitude to Loyalist violence; failure to respond to Catholic demands for protection; failure to detect or deter Loyalist murder gangs despite massive security forces' presence and surveillance in Catholic districts; slow and complacent police response after Loyalist attacks; that the security forces flood Catholic areas following Loyalist attacks rather than direct their attention to the areas into which the Loyalists have escaped; incidents when there has been no follow-up operation by the police; that members of the security forces have sometimes insulted and abused the families of the victims and have beaten and insulted mourners at funerals of their murdered relatives; that police forensic teams have been willfully negligent or incompetent in gathering evidence at the scene of murders carried out by Loyalist paramilitaries; and the denial of gun licenses to elected representatives of the Catholic community (Relatives for Justice 1995:1–2).

Bibliography

Adams, Gerry
    1986 *Free Ireland: Towards a Lasting Peace.* Niwat: Roberts Rinehart.
Amnesty International
    1994 *Political Killings in Northern Ireland.* London: Amnesty International.
Bell, Geoffrey
    1976 *The Protestants of Ulster.* London: Pluto Press.

Boal, Frederick
   1981 "Residential Segregation and Mixing in a Situation of Ethnic and National Conflict: Belfast." In *The Contemporary Population of Northern Ireland and
   Population-Related Issues.* P. Compton, ed. Belfast: Institute of Irish Studies.
   1974 "Territoriality in Belfast." In *The Sociology of Community.* C. Bell and H. New-
   by, eds. London: Frank Cass.
Boal, Frederick, C. Russell, and A. Poole
   1976 "Belfast: The Urban Encapsulation of a National Conflict." In *Urban
   Ethnic Conflict.* S. Clark and J. Obler, eds. Chapel Hill, N.C.: Institute for Re-
   search in Social Science.
Bowyer Bell, J.
   1996 *In Dubious Battle: The Dublin and Monaghan Bombings, 1972–1974.* Dublin:
   Poolbeg.
Boyd, Andrew
   1969 *Holy War in Belfast: A History of the Troubles in Northern Ireland.* New York:
   Grove Press.
Bruce, Steve
   1992 *The Red Hand: Protestant Paramilitaries in Northern Ireland.* Oxford: Oxford
   University Press.
Burke, Maurice, Joe McVeigh, Thomas Walsh, and Des Wilson
   1996 *Injustice in Ireland: The Truth About British Repression.* Dublin: Clergy for
   Justice.
Chomsky, Noam
   1969 *American Power and the New Mandarins.* New York: Pantheon.
Clayton, Pamela
   1996 *Enemies and Passing Friends — Settler Ideologies in Twentieth Century Ulster.*
   London: Pluto Press.
Clergy for Justice
   1994 *Putting Violence in Context.* Dublin: Clergy for Justice.
Committee for the Administration of Justice (CAJ)
   1993 *Adding Insult to Injury: Allegations of Harassment and the Use of Lethal Force by
   the Security Forces in Northern Ireland.* Belfast: Committee for the Administration
   of Justice.
   1992 *Inquests and Disputed Killings in Northern Ireland.* Belfast: Committee for the
   Administration of Justice.
Davis, Shelton, and Robert Mathews
   1979 "Anthropology Resource Center: Public Interest Anthropology — Beyond
   the Bureaucratic Ethos." *Practicing Anthropology,* 1:3, p. 5.
de Baroid, Kieran
   1989 *Ballymurphy and the Irish War.* London: Pluto Press.
Dillon, Martin
   1990 *The Dirty War.* London: Arrow Books.
   1989 *The Shankill Butchers: A Case Study of Mass Murder.* London: Hutchinson.
Dillon, Martin, and D. Lehane
   1973 *Political Murder in Northern Ireland.* Harmondsworth: Penguin Books.
Downing, Theodore, and Gilbert Kushner (eds.)
   1988 *Human Rights and Anthropology.* Cambridge: Cultural Survival.
Fairweather, Eileen, Roisin McDonough, and Melanie McFadyean
   1984 *Only the Rivers Run Free — Northern Ireland: The Women's War.* London: Pluto
   Press.

Faligot, Roger
   1983 *Britain's Military Strategy in Ireland: The Kitson Experiment.* London: Zed Books.
Farrell, Michael
   1980 *The Orange State.* Second revised edition. London: Pluto Press.
Feldman, Allen
   1991 *Formations of Violence: The Narrative of the Body and Political Terror in Northern Ireland.* Chicago: University of Chicago Press.
Friel, Laura
   1998a "Myth of Tit-for-Tat." *An Phoblacht/Republican News*, 22 January, p. 3.
   1998b "British Army Ran UDA Death Squads." *An Phoblacht/Republican News*, 2 April, pp. 10–11, 20.
Galliher, John, and Jerry Degregory
   1985 *Violence in Northern Ireland: Understanding Protestant Perspectives.* Dublin: Gill and Macmillan.
Gordon, Edmund
   1991 "Anthropology and Liberation." In *Decolonizing Anthropology: Moving Further Toward an Anthropology of Liberation.* F. Harrison, ed. Washington, D.C.: Association of Black Anthropologists, American Anthropological Association.
Huizer, Gerrit
   1979 "Anthropology and Politics: From Naivete Toward Liberation?" In *The Politics of Anthropology: From Colonialism and Sexism Toward a View from Below.* G. Huizer and B. Mannheim, eds. The Hague: Mouton.
Kelly, Kevin
   1982 *The Longest War: Northern Ireland and the IRA.* London: Zed Books.
Kelters, Seamus, and Chris Thornton
   1993 "Where Death Stalks the Streets." Three-part *Irish News* special investigation, 27–29 January.
Kitson, Frank
   1971 *Low Intensity Operations: Subversion, Insurgency, Peace-Keeping.* Harrisburg, Pa.: Stackpole Books.
   1960 *Gangs and Counter-Gangs.* London: Barrie and Rockcliffe.
Kuhlmann, Annette
   1992 "Collaborative Anthropology Among the Kickapoo Tribe of Oklahoma." *Human Organization*, 51:3, pp. 274–283.
MacRuairi, Marcas
   1998 "Understanding Loyalist Death Squads." *An Phoblacht/Republican News*, 22 January, p. 9.
McPhilemy, Sean
   1988 *The Committee: Political Assassination in Northern Ireland.* New York: Roberts Rinehart.
Messer, Ellen
   1993 "Anthropology and Human Rights." *Annual Review of Anthropology*, 22, pp. 221–249.
Miller, David
   1978 *Queen's Rebels: Ulster Loyalism in Historical Perspective.* Dublin: Gill and Macmillan.
Mills, C. Wright
   1963 "On Knowledge and Power." In *Power, Politics and People: The Collected Essays of C. Wright Mills.* I. Horowitz, ed. New York: Ballantine Books.

Murray, Raymond
1990 *The SAS in Ireland*. Cork: Mercier.
Murray, R., and F. W. Boal
1979 "The Social Ecology of Urban Violence." In *Social Problems and the City: Geographical Perspectives*. D. Herbert and D. Smith, eds. Oxford: Oxford University Press.
Nelson, Sarah
1984 *Ulster's Uncertain Defenders: Loyalists and the Northern Ireland Conflict*. Belfast: Appletree.
O'Brien, Jack
1989 *British Brutality in Ireland*. Cork: Mercier.
O'Duffy, Brendan
1995 "Violence in Northern Ireland 1969–94: Sectarian or Ethno-National?" *Ethnic and Racial Studies*, 18:4, pp. 740–772.
Paine, Robert (ed.)
1985 *Advocacy and Anthropology*. St. John's: Institute of Social and Economic Research, Memorial University of Newfoundland.
Relatives for Justice
1995 *Collusion, 1990–1994: Loyalist Paramilitary Murders in the North of Ireland*. Derry: Relatives for Justice.
1993 *Shoot-to-Kill and Collusion: Violations of Human Rights by State Forces in N. Ireland—A Record of Murders by Loyalist Paramilitaries, 1990–1992*. Derry: Relatives for Justice.
Rolston, Bill
1995 *Drawing Support 2: Murals of War and Peace*. Belfast: Beyond the Pale.
Ryan, William
1971 *Blaming the Victim*. New York: Vintage Books.
Saoirse (*New Zealand Irish Post*)
1996 "Nelson: Steeped in Blood." *Saoirse*, 12:2, pp. 3–4.
1991 "Britain's Death Squads in Ireland." *Saoirse*, 8:1, pp. 6–7.
Silent Too Long
1982 *Silent Too Long: The Association of the Families of Innocent Victims of Loyalist, UDR, RUC and British Army Violence*. Belfast: Silent Too Long.
Sinn Fein
1994a *Collusion—Britain's Links with Loyalist Death Squads. Ireland Information Fact File*. Dublin: Sinn Fein Department of Foreign Affairs.
1994b *British Intelligence, Brian Nelson and the Rearming of the Loyalist Death Squads*. Dublin: Sinn Fein.
1990 *The Ulster Defense Regiment—The Loyalist Militia*. Dublin: Sinn Fein Publicity Department.
Sluka, Jeffrey
1995 "Domination, Resistance and Political Culture in Northern Ireland's Catholic-Nationalist Ghettos." *Critique of Anthropology*, 15:1, pp. 71–102.
1989 *Hearts and Minds, Water and Fish: Popular Support for the IRA and INLA in a Northern Irish Ghetto*. Greenwich, Conn.: JAI Press.
Sutton, Malcolm
1994 *An Index of Deaths from the Conflict in Ireland, 1969–1993*. Belfast: Beyond the Pale.
Taussig, Michael
1984 "Culture of Terror—Space of Death: Roger Casement's Putumayo Re-

port and the Explanation of Torture." *Comparative Studies in Society and History*, 26, pp. 467–97.

Taylor, John

1998 *Body Horror: Photojournalism, Catastrophe and War.* Manchester: Manchester University Press.

Urban, Mark

1992 *Big Boys' Rules: The SAS and the Secret Struggle Against the IRA.* London: Faber and Faber.

van Willigen, John

1993 *Applied Anthropology: An Introduction.* Revised edition. Westport: Bergin and Garvey.

Chapter 6
Ninjas, Nanggalas, Monuments, and Mossad Manuals
An Anthropology of Indonesian State Terror in East Timor

George J. Aditjondro

During the past two decades, the Indonesian state has employed a five-pronged strategy of state terror to subjugate the population of East Timor. This strategy consists of a combination of five tactics, some of which have been applied simultaneously. The first tactic is physical terror, ranging from mass killings, which took place most horribly during the first decade of the Indonesian occupation of East Timor, to a huge repertoire of torture techniques. The mass killings of armed guerrillas and their accompanying women and children, when the armed struggle was the main form of resistance, shifted to mass killings of young Indonesian-educated East Timorese in the towns, as the main resistance was taken over by the urban-based clandestine movement. The second tactic of Indonesian state terror is the depurification of the bodies of the East Timorese women through rape, forced female fertility control, and the widespread promotion of prostitution in East Timor. The third tactic is symbolic violence, whereby the Catholic church and all its icons and personnel have been targeted and an elaborate repertoire of intimidating language has been developed which has accompanied all the psychological torture during the massive military campaigns and interrogation sessions. The fourth form of state terror is the demonization of the enemy by initially labeling the East Timorese freedom fighters as "communists" and lately as "anti-Muslim Catholics." Accompanying all those four tactics has been the demographic dilution of the country's original population by encouraging Indonesians to immigrate to East Timor and East Timorese youth to emigrate to Indonesia.

There are several reasons why the understanding of this five-pronged strategy of state terror is very crucial. The main reason is the common-sense notion that in order to fight the beast, you have to know it first, and know it well. The second and also more practical reason, as pointed out by Sidney Jones, a researcher and advocate against the human rights violations of the Indonesian New Order state, is that East Timor has become a type of laboratory to test different counterinsurgency strategies, which have then been transposed to Indonesia itself, in particular to Aceh (Bentley 1995:165–166).

The third and more theoretical reason is that this type of study has often been avoided by anthropologists, even by those who have sided with the victims of "development" and state terror and have defended those victims through their academic, journalistic, and political work. In the case of East Timor, for instance, two American anthropologists — Shepard Forman and Elizabeth G. Traube — need to be named for their scholarly work and their testimonies before the U.S. Congress and the United Nations. Forman, who did fieldwork in 1973–1974 among the Makassae people, the third largest ethnolinguistic group in East Timor (Forman 1978, 1980), testified before the U.S. House of Representatives Committee on International Relations in June–July 1977 on the enthusiastic response of the Makassae people to the Portuguese offer of political freedom in mid-1974 (Gray 1984:32, 41–43; Dunn 1996:5–6). Traube did fieldwork in 1972–1974 among the Mambai people, the second largest ethnolinguistic group in East Timor (Traube 1980, 1986, 1995). She testified before the UN Decolonization Committee in October 1980 about the Mambas' social structure and values, in explaining why this people chose to fight for independence and describing the effect of the Indonesian occupation on them (Gray 1984:29–30, 46). As Traube wrote in the introduction to her book on Mambai cosmology and rituals: "At the time of this writing, the chances that the East Timorese will be allowed to exercise that right [of self-determination] appear slim. My scholarly activities will not obtain for them that chance. But I hope that, at the least, my work will testify to the capacities of one particular Timorese people to think imaginatively and profoundly about the meaning of collective life" (1986:xxi).

In their earnest attempts to defend the victims of blatant as well as structural oppression, however, anthropologists have rarely taken as their duty to understand the perpetrators of human rights violations, which is more commonly seen as the duty of political scientists and human rights lawyers. This negligence is quite telling about the discipline and the community, since many anthropologists have not shunned studying rituals of non-Westernized societies, which, in the United Nations' human rights standards, are quite barbaric. So, why is it that, with some exceptions (Hilsdon 1995), most anthropologists have avoided studying the barbaric practices of governments whose commandos have reinforced and refined those practices in the elite special forces' training centers in the United States?

This chapter is an attempt to redress that negligence. As an Indonesian applied anthropologist, who has carried out participant observation of Melanesian communities in West Papua (Irian Jaya) and East Timor, I have in the past shied away from studying the military and their unpleasant behavior towards detainees, regardless of whether those victims had or had not been involved in violent armed guerrilla activities toward the military. However, my own involvement in defending the rights of West Papuan and East Timorese peoples has led to several unpleasant encounters with Indonesian security agents, which has allowed me "to get under their helmets," metaphorically speaking.

The fourth reason to understand the strategy of Indonesian state terror in East Timor is to prevent a reproduction of similar state terror in a future independent East Timor, when East Timorese police forces will have to maintain law and order among citizens who have been brought up with terror as their daily bread. Several studies have exposed the dehumanizing effect of torture under repressive political systems, and how that "cancer" has infected — or may infest — postrevolutionary societies (Freire 1972; Memmi 1990; Fanon 1985; Vidal-Naquet 1963). As Freire puts it, when the dominated classes reproduce the dominators' style of life, it is because the dominators live "within" the dominated. The dominated can eject the dominators only by gaining distance from them and objectifying them. Only then can they recognize them as their antithesis (1972:36). Hence the deliberate efforts to come to terms with the violent past of South Africa under Bishop Desmond Tutu's Truth and Reconciliation Commission. In contrast, the current brutal behavior of the Palestinian police — who themselves were often victims of brutal Israeli detention practices (Williams 1995; Bhatia 1996; Cockburn 1997; Hirst 1997) — is the more common course of history, and will hopefully function as an alarm bell for a future independent East Timor.

Finally, to put the East Timorese experience in a more global context, I will try to find some of the sources and parallels of this strategy of Indonesian state terror in the state's overseas links. Here I will describe that apart from the overt military and security links with the main protagonists of the Western bloc, namely the United States and the United Kingdom, the Indonesian state has also maintained more hidden links with Israel, which has exercised a strategy similar to that of Indonesia in East Timor in attempting to quell the Palestinian independence movement for the last fifty years.

With that introduction in mind, let us now move on to the first tactic of

Indonesian state terror in East Timor, namely physical terror, ranging from mass killings to physical torture.

Physical Terror (Political Murder, Torture, and Rape)

The most extreme form of physical terror, mass killings, occurred predominantly during the initial phase of the occupation from late 1975 until late 1979, beginning with the invasion of December 1975. According to U.S. political scientist J. William Liddle, sixty thousand East Timorese men, women, and children — about 10 percent of the population — were killed during the first two months of the war either in the fighting or as a result of war-related deprivations (Liddle 1992:22). The death toll of the Timor war quickly escalated during the following years, with the result that up to 200,000 East Timorese or one-third of the population lost their lives. This act of genocide has been accurately characterized by Noam Chomsky as "perhaps the greatest death toll relative to the population, since the Holocaust" (*An Phoblacht/Republican News*, 1 May 1997, p. 19).

Different statistics have been used by various researchers to emphasize or de-emphasize the demographic effect of the occupation. According to M. Hadi Soesastro, an Indonesian progovernment researcher at the Jakarta-based Center for Strategic and International Studies (CSIS), an annual population growth rate of 0.9 percent (as in 1970–1973) should have resulted in a total population of 667,100 East Timorese in 1980. In fact, the census of that year only recorded a population of 555,350 — a discrepancy of 112,000 people (Soesastro 1991:210).

Soesastro's estimate resembles one by an Indonesian general, Theo Syafei. According to the then commander of the Udayana Army division which covers East Timor, "Around 100,000 were killed from 1974 to 1981." He added, though, that "It was not ABRI [the Indonesian armed forces] who did the killing, but rather, the Portuguese" (*Indonesia Business Weekly*, 19 November 1993). He did not realize, it seems, how amazing it would be for the Portuguese to kill so many East Timorese after deserting their colony in late 1975!

However, despite the difficulties in conducting censuses during the Portuguese and Indonesian colonial eras, and apart from the actual number of East Timorese living abroad, several microstudies have confirmed that the number of lives lost in the villages of the East Timorese interior was indeed extraordinarily high. Despite the difficulties of carrying out a proper census in the midst of a war zone, it is safe to say that the "unassimilated" Timorese, or *gentios*, who lived in the valleys of the Ramelau mountain range in the western part of the country were most drastically affected. According to an Indonesian Jesuit who worked in East Timor in

March 1979, the Maubisse village in the district of Ainaro, which had a population of 9,607 in 1976, had lost 5,021 inhabitants in three years time. The priest himself sometimes had to bury four people a day (Dirdja 1979:23).

The high death toll was paid not only by the non-Christianized highlanders in the western part of the island, but also by thousands of lowlanders in *ponta leste*, the eastern point of the country, who fled with the Fretilin and Falintil guerrillas to Matebian Mountain, which borders the three districts of Manatuto, Lautem, and Viqueque. Faithful to its name, "the abode of death," Matebian became the silent witness when Indonesian counterinsurgency airplanes raided the mountain slopes with their fatal bombs, forcing the surviving guerrilla fighters and villagers down to the lowlands of Baucau and into the resettlement camps in Laga.

Although Indonesia ratified the 1925 Geneva Protocol on Chemical Weapons in 1971 and the Biological Weapons Convention in 1972 (Lowry 1996:34), the Indonesian air force used napalm and defoliants in the aerial bombings over East Timor. The main aim of these bombings, which took place between 1976 and 1980 and were reminiscent of U.S. operations in Vietnam, was not only to destroy the resistance strongholds on Matebian and other mountains, but also to destroy food crops and livestock, thereby denying food to the guerrillas and civilians who joined them for protection from the advancing Indonesian troops (Turner 1992: 114, 172; Aditjondro 1994:40–41; Taylor 1995:240; Gama 1995:100; Lowry 1996: 153; Pinto and Jardine 1997:62–63; *Angkasa*, January 1993, pp. 39–42).

Many other forms of mass executions were carried out by the occupation forces against anybody suspected of being a freedom fighter or of supporting them. Many air raid survivors were forced from the banks of the Quelicai River in the district of Baucau and from the Sarei River banks in Builico in the district of Ainaro, or were thrown to their deaths from helicopters on the rocky mountains between Dili and Aileu, in the Dili Bay, and in the sea around Jaco Island near the eastern tip (Taylor 1991:101; Turner 1992:166; Aditjondro 1994:39–40; Dunn 1996: 282). Others died slowly in overcrowded prison barracks on the island of Atauro, which had housed between 5,000 and 6,800 prisoners, with each barrack occupied by forty to eighty men, women, and children. Some of these barracks were covered with black canvas to turn them into human ovens. According to a former inmate, 387 of the Atauro inmates had died from the bad prison conditions in thirty months time (Aditjondro 1994: 40, 87).

On top of that, many survivors died from the disastrous famine of 1979, which rivaled its Cambodian and Biafran counterparts in severity. According to the U.S. Catholic Relief Service (CRS), the total death rate in 150 settlements rose again at that time to fourteen hundred per month. The large number of deaths among the refugees who came down from the mountains became the subject of a heated debate in the American Congress in 1981. This debate and protests from international humanitarian organizations forced the Indonesian state to open East Timor to the CRS and the International Committee for the Red Cross and Red Crescent (CRC), and to close down the Atauro prison island (Taylor 1991:105; Aditjondro 1994:40, 87).

During the five-year pacification war (1975–1979), the existing health facilities in East Timor could not cope with the flow of internal refugees from the mountains, since these institutions also were not spared from rockets and looting by Indonesian soldiers. According to eyewitnesses, Indonesian soldiers even took the operating theater, X-ray equipment, and air conditioner from the Dili hospital. On top of that, East Timorese medical personnel who were suspected of pro-independence feelings were not free to carry out their humanitarian duties.

Major massacres of East Timorese people have been carried out by the Indonesian army and their East Timorese collaborators since the 1975 invasion, and even long after the 1975–1979 pacification war. After the killing of as many as 2,000 persons in Dili during the first week or so after the invasion, mass killings subsequently occurred in May 1976 in Liquica, Suai Maubara, and Basartete. The next month one of the bloodiest massacres occurred at Lamaknan in the border area, where about 2,000 people — including women and children — were killed in one day. In early August in the area around Zumalai, six villages were burned and hundreds of their inhabitants executed. In the same year massacres were reported near Bobonaro, and at Aileu. In 1977 other massacres occurred in Bobonaro and at Quelicai, and in 1978 in the Matebian area thousands were killed by indiscriminate air attacks on the civilian population (Taylor 1991:71; Dunn 1996:268, 299). After the end of the major pacification war, which had involved the Indonesian army, navy, air force, and police, further massacres still continued in the 1980s and 1990s, involving mainly the Indonesian army and their East Timorese collaborators.

Over time, the nature of the mass killings changed drastically, which indicates the increasing level of desperation of the occupation forces in facing an increasingly militant population. In the Lacluta massacre in 1981, the victims targeted by the Indonesian military were surrendering guerrilla fighters and their wives and children, in a remote village in the countryside. The 1983 Kraras massacre also targeted villagers far away from the capital. In both instances, intensive armed conflicts were still taking place between the occupation forces and the armed front of the resistance. These two massacres differ radically from the massacres of Taci Tolu and Santa Cruz. In the 1983 Taci Tolu massacre, some victims were killed for trying to influence world opinion by contacting an Australian parliamentary delegation. But that happened before East Timor was officially declared an "open province" by the Indonesian government. Eventually, in the 1991 Santa Cruz massacre, the victims were harshly punished for publicly expressing their nationalist feelings in the capital city of East Timor, in front of the UN special rapporteur on torture, Peter Kooijmans, and other foreign observers. The victims were predominantly young people, high school students who hailed from all over East Timor, who mostly had never been involved in the armed struggle. Their only weapons were banners, flags, T-shirts, and support from the international press. Still they were gunned down, stabbed, crushed with stones, and injected with lethal chemicals.

Speaking about mass killings, East Timorese themselves also committed such atrocities — on a much smaller scale — during the civil war from 11 August to mid-September 1975, and when the resistance had to retreat into the mountains after the massive Indonesian invasion on 7 December 1975. This controversial issue is continuously exploited by Indonesian propaganda to justify Indonesian control over the territory, and different — and contradictory — versions of the total death toll of these fratricidal killings have been raised by various Indonesian, Australian, and East Timorese authors. The highest death toll — 50,000 East Timorese, all killed by the radical pro-independence party Fretilin (Frente Revolucionária de Timor Leste Independente) — has been claimed by E. M. Tomodok, the last Indonesian consul in Portuguese Timor (1994:351–353). Another Indonesian source mentioned that 150 former Tropas (Portuguese army) members were killed in Aileu at the order of the Fretilin Central Committee (*Editor*, 28 October 1989, pp. 102–104).

In contrast to those Indonesian sources, two Australian authors — Jill Jolliffe (1978:134–135, 286) and James Dunn (1996:156–158, 257, 269–270) — have raised an important point which was totally ignored by Tomodok and *Editor*, namely atrocities carried out by Fretilin's main political rival, the conservative pro-independence party UDT (União Democrática Timorense), before the Indonesian invasion. Dunn, a former Australian consul in Portuguese Timor, also mentioned the killing of about 150 UDT and Apodeti prisoners by Fretilin, reportedly on 25 December 1975.

Meanwhile, Jose Ramos-Horta, an East Timorese diplomat and former Fretilin secretary for foreign affairs, and Paulino Gama, a former commander of Falantil (Forças Armadas de Libertação Nacional do Timor Leste), which at that time was Fretilin's military wing, also raised their observations about these events. Gama claimed that his troops had freed 250 Timorese prisoners in Aileu and Same, but admitted that others had been executed, without mentioning a number (1995:98–99). Ramos-Horta, in contrast, admitted to between 2,000 and 3,000 casualties of the civil war, from both sides, based on an ICRC survey (Ramos-Horta 1987:55–56, 91).

He failed to mention, however, the killings of Timorese prisoners by his former Fretilin comrades in Aileu and Same.

In the meantime, the two Fretilin leaders who have been named in Indonesian and Australian sources as the persons most responsible for the pre- and postinvasion Fretilin atrocities, namely Fretilin's former president Xavier do Amaral and the party's former secretary general Alarico Fernandes, have never been tried by an Indonesian court for those mass killings after deserting to the Indonesian side. On the contrary, they currently live under military protection in Indonesia. This fact does not match the strong condemnation by the Indonesian government of Fretilin's fratricidal killings. Or, from a different perspective, the protection given by the Indonesian military to the two former top Fretilin leaders seems to fit the military's aim to use those fratricidal killings — partly instigated by Indonesian intelligence agents — to justify the Indonesian state's much more brutal massacres of the East Timorese people.

Blaming the East Timorese for those massacres, however, fits with the overall strategy of the occupation forces to "indigenize" the pacification war as much as possible. Even back in the late 1970s, Indonesian troops already relied on East Timorese scouts, some of whom belonged to the anticommunist pro-independence party UDT or were former Portuguese soldiers, to track down the guerrillas in their hiding places in the mountains (Turner 1992:91–92). This strategy was further institutionalized by the formation of two all-East Timorese battalions, commanded by Indonesian officers.

To conclude this section, it is quite logical — and ethical — to ask the questions: what has motivated the Indonesian occupational forces to exterminate so many East Timorese — up to one third of the entire population — since 1975? What justification did the Indonesian military commanders give to their troops in the battlefield for killing all those human beings?

The answer given by an Indonesian corporal captured by the East Timorese guerrillas during the early decade of the occupation is quite telling. "I came here to kill the Communists," he said (Turner 1992:87–88). In other words, the first decade of the occupation can be seen as a replay of events in Indonesia in 1965–1966, where between 500,000 and one million suspected leftists, mostly landless peasants, were killed by the Indonesian military with the enthusiastic assistance of mostly Muslim mass organizations (Cribb 1990). As in the case of Indonesia, the supposedly anticommunist purge in East Timor also had a *jihad*, or "holy war," connotation attached to it for many Indonesian soldiers (Dunn 1996:260–261).

The Islamic holy war argument, however, certainly does not apply to the Christian ABRI commanders, such as then commander in chief General Maraden Panggabean, a Protestant from North Sumatra, and General Benny Murdani, a Javanese Catholic, who was the actual commander of the 1975 invasion and later succeeded Panggabean as the ABRI commander in chief. For them, I believe, anticommunism may have been a major driving force in the beginning of the twenty-two-year occupation, plus the urge to actually command and carry out a major campaign, integrating all the armed forces (army, navy, and air force) — a dream of all ambitious military officers.

For troops in the field, other motivations were at play. The complete extermination of enemy forces, including their civilians and children, has often been mentioned in Indonesian military literature, treating the enemy as if they are a pest which needs to be eradicated, to prevent the body from future possible infestation. *Tumpas kelor*, or "eradicate to the roots," is a Javanese expression for this mentality, as expressed by Indonesian political scientist Riswandha Imawan (*Forum Keadilan*, 17 July 1995, p. 27). Or, as James Dunn documented in his comprehensive book on the occupation, when an East Timorese asked an Indonesian soldier why he had killed the wife and child of a Fretilin guerrilla during the Lacluta massacre, the reply was: "When you clean the field, don't you kill all the snakes, the small and large alike?" (Dunn 1996:299). Apart from the "communist," "infidel," and "pest control" justifications, the self-preservation instinct and a desire to take revenge for fallen comrades played important roles in justifying mass killings on the actual battlefield.

Underlying all those motives is the overriding fear of many of the older Indonesian officers of what they believe may become the "boomerang" or "domino effect" of the East Timorese independence struggle. A young Indonesian dissident in Germany, who faced the threat of nonrenewal of his passport after being involved in anti-Suharto rallies in Germany, had to face a furious Indonesian army officer who functioned as political attaché in the Indonesian consulate general in Bonn. "Our generation died fighting the Dutch to liberate Indonesia! We would not allow you young kids to splinter it up with all those anti-Indonesian gangs!" so the officer in mufti exclaimed to the young student activist, referring to the East Timorese, West Papuan, and South Moluccan activists in the anti-Suharto demonstration. So, to defend the integrity of the territory of the Indonesian state, which when it was proclaimed on 17 August 1945 did not include East Timor, any human sacrifice of East Timorese people — and Indonesian soldiers who have died in their struggle to defend what they consider to be their country's territorial integrity — is justified. This supports Ruth McVey's thesis that for the relatively young nation-states in Southeast Asia, the territory is more important than the actual inhabitants living within it (1984:11–15).

The 1975–1979 pacification war, despite killing one-third of the population, did not quell the East Timorese people's quest for independence, so thousands of ABRI personnel were maintained in the occupied territory (Aditjondro 1994:88). The usual state terror principle that by killing one person the occupation forces can frighten ten thousand others (Clutterbuck 1986:23) did not work in East Timor. Hence, torture became the second form of physical terror used by the Indonesian state to subdue the people of its unwilling colony.

I refer by the term "torture" to the definition adopted unanimously by the UN on 9 December 1975 in Article 1 of the declaration on the protection of all persons from being subjected to torture and other cruel, inhuman, or degrading treatment or punishment, more popularly known as the Declaration against Torture, namely: "any act by which severe pain or suffering, whether physical or mental, is intentionally inflicted by or at the instigation of a public official on a person for such purposes as obtaining from him [or her] or a third person information or confession, punishing him [or her] for an act he [or she] has committed, or intimidating him [or her] or other persons" (Amnesty International 1984:13). Amnesty International and many other human rights organizations, as well as East Timorese freedom fighters and their supporters, have documented the various forms of torture employed by the occupation forces and their East Timorese collaborators. From these numerous documents, we can deduce some general patterns and typologies.

The most general typology has to encompass physical and psychological torture. I will, however, discuss psychological torture under the section on symbolic violence. Physical torture can, following Johan Galtung, be divided into torture focused on the victim's anatomy and torture focused on the victim's physiology (Windhu 1992:73–75). Both types of physical torture have been developed very elaborately by the Indonesian occupation forces, and more predominantly by the Indonesian army's special forces, known by its most recent acronym, Kopassus (Komando Pasukan Khusus), or, in popular jargon, the Red Berets.

Based on the various arenas where it is committed, one can also distinguish between different forms of public and private torture. The major arenas for public torture during the first decade of the occupation were the public places where mass surrenders of the guerrillas and their accompanying civilians, mostly women and children, occurred. In these places in the remote villages of East Timor, usually far away from Red Cross officials, journalists, and lawyers, the Red Berets refined their knife-throwing skills. Hence, the East Timorese have given the meaning of "knife throwers" or "knife-wielding killers" to the name Nanggala which these counterinsurgency units called themselves (Budiardjo 1991:185).

This knife-throwing practice originated in the 1965–1966 anticommunist purge in Indonesia, when the Red Berets led the mass murder of communist suspects (Cribb 1990).

Urban open spaces are another public torture arena which has become more popular during the second and third decades of the occupation. Torture in these spaces has frequently happened during "riot control" actions by the Indonesian policy and military. Under the guise of controlling the mob and protecting public property, units of the Indonesian army as well as the Mobile Brigade (Brimob) of the Indonesian police regard themselves as free to physically harass demonstrators. They have not limited themselves to dispersing crowds, but have sought to physically punish demonstrators for embarrassing the mighty Indonesian state in front of foreign observers. And because the army is also involved in riot control, in many instances live bullets have been used during these "riot control" exercises, in accordance with the military's policy of "shoot on sight," which in practice means "shoot to kill."

It is not surprising, then, that public protests or demonstrations in East Timor during the last decade have ended with fatal casualties. This happened, for instance, during the visit of U.S. Ambassador John Monjo to Dili in January 1990, when one student was confirmed dead (*The Australian*, 20 January 1990). The most horrible case, though, was the Santa Cruz massacre of 12 November 1991, where "riot control" was completely left to the army, who did not hesitate to use their rifles with live ammunition, and finished off many wounded demonstrators with their bayonets.

More commonly in public torture only a few persons are actually killed to terrorize the rest of the group members. For instance, in a campsite named Mauptili, near Lospalos, thirty villagers were imprisoned in August 1983 and under interrogation named the organizers of the local Fretilin resistance group. The population of the camp was then gathered together by the local army commander, who paraded before them the five leaders named by those interrogated. The terrified population did not yet suspect what would occur. Suddenly, a Nanggala executed all five with his knife. The Indonesian officer forbade the population to cry, and threatened them, saying that if he learned of anyone else continuing to support the resistance, he or she would get the same fate. According to an eyewitness account, the population, quiet and with their heads lowered, was motionless (Taylor 1991:103).

Another important public arena where torture often takes place are fake "escape corridors." Torture victims in East Timor have sometimes been provided with fake opportunities to escape, so that they can be shot to death or killed through slower torture sessions, such as being hung upside down from trees and then beaten and stabbed to death. The bodies can then be buried, or burned before being buried, to reduce the trouble of keeping too many living victims in cramped detention centers. The authorities report that the victims tried to escape while being transported from one detention center to another, were given warning shots, but since they were still dangerous, they had to be shot dead on the spot. The long distance and the lack of formaldehyde to preserve the body then sounds like a rational excuse to bury the body on the spot. The case is then closed, without a coroner's inquest.

Let us now move on from those horrible arenas to the even more terrible private torture arenas. There are three main types of private torture arenas in East Timor: first, the official or regular ABRI buildings; second, private houses and hotels turned into interrogation centers; and third, strangely enough, Catholic church compounds, such as churches and colleges.

Nearly all ABRI units have their own detention and/or interrogation centers in their unit headquarters, although the most official place to carry out interrogations, according to Indonesian law, are the police interrogation cells in the provincial police headquarters, or Mapolwil (Markas Wilayah Polisi). To pay lip service to the law, interrogations of political prisoners often take place physically in the police headquarters, although the main interrogators are not police agents, but plainclothes military men.

The use of private buildings transformed into detention cum interrogation centers seems to be mainly a prerogative of Kopassus. Their main interrogation unit is called SGI, an Indonesian abbreviation for Satuan Tugas Intelligence, or Intelligence Taskforce (Tanter 1994:220, 241–248, 277). Their headquarters is in an unmarked house in the Colmera ward in Dili (Gomes 1995; Pinto and Jardine 1997:148–157, 269). Apart from this main interrogation center, the SGI also keeps three other interrogation centers in Dili, namely Wisma Senapati I, II, and III (McMillan 1992:105; Gomes 1995:107). The term *wisma*, which originates from Sanskrit, simply means "residence." But the names Senapati I, II, and III connote the association of SGI with the headquarters of the Indonesian state's main intelligence organization, Bakin (Badan Koordinasi Intelligence) on Senapati Boulevard in Kebayoran Baru, Jakarta. From this it can be deduced that the domestic origin of the torture techniques applied in East Timor is Bakin.

Apart from those four main private interrogation centers in Dili, in other towns the Red Berets have also turned some private residences and hotels into interrogation centers. For instance, in East Timor's second major town, Baucau, they transformed the best tourist hotel, Hotel Flamboyan, into an interrogation center. After this place was exposed by John Pilger's film *Death of a Nation* in the early 1990s, the Red Berets moved their interrogation center to a red brick house in Baucau, called appropriately *Rumah Merah* ("red house"), where allegedly they tortured and killed the famous Falintil commander, David Alex, in late June 1997.

The practice of turning private buildings into interrogation centers originated in the Red Berets' tendency to work as undercover agents. Ironically, although they daily go around doing their business in mufti, using privately marked cars, most people in the places controlled by them, such as East Timor, West Papua, and Aceh, do recognize these places as interrogation centers, as well as recognize the Red Berets themselves and their vehicles. This practice must have been a long-standing one among the Red Berets, because that was also my observation in West Papua from 1982 to 1987. The strategically located Panorama restaurant on the cliffs overlooking the bay of Jayapura was turned by the Red Berets into a notorious interrogation center, where the late West Papuan anthropologist Arnold C. Ap was interrogated, before his detention was made public by a Jakarta newspaper, *Sinar Harapan*, and he had to be handed over, officially at least, to the police. The young artist was eventually killed by a Red Berets death squad on a lonely beach west of Jayapura on 26 April 1984, after being lured into escaping from the police detention center by West Papuan collaborators.

It is quite ironic that from all these nice houses, hotels, and restaurants the Red Berets have developed, over the twenty-two years of occupation of East Timor (and thirty-five years of occupation of West Papua), a very wide repertoire of private torture techniques. This repertoire usually begins with blindfolding the victim with black cloth, which reduces eye-to-eye contact between the torturer and the victim and thereby increases the anxiety of the victim while reducing the latent humane feelings of the torturer. Slapping the victim with the palm of the hand or beating the victim with the fist are quite normal and mild practices. So are the use of cigarette butts to burn holes in the skin of the victim, or the use of electric shocks administered with special rods.

More violent ways of administering pain are crushing the victim's feet or hands with table or chair legs while a well-built torturer sits on the table or chair; poking the victim's mouth with big bamboo sticks; inflicting pain on the genitals, which includes raping of female victims; and plunging the victim in metal tanks filled with water, which is then charged with electric shocks. Pulling out victims' toenails and fingernails, cutting their flesh with razor knives, and cutting male victims' penises, tongues, and ears are also standard practices of torture in East Timor.

A new indoor torture arena has emerged since 1994, namely Catholic Church buildings — churches, convents, and colleges. Various forms of torture, from beatings to killings and attempts to assassinate Bishop Belo, have occurred in these places, which in the past have been avoided by the occupation forces due to their claim that Indonesia is a religion-respecting nation-state, as emphasized in the Panca Sila state philosophy.

From this litany of torture in East Timor, the question emerges: what aims do the torturers want to achieve? The following motives can be deduced from the information available to the author. For the Red Berets' special intelligence unit (SGI) in particular, torture is carried out for five main reasons. First and foremost, to obtain information about resistance networks in East Timor, Indonesia, and the diaspora, and thereby maintain supremacy of the Kopassus in ABRI, and in turn the supremacy of ABRI over the civilian Foreign Affairs Department in Indonesia's international East Timor diplomacy. Second, to crush the fighting spirit of the freedom fighters. Third, to prohibit the Catholic Church of East Timor from providing any form of support to the independence movement, by forcing parishioners to sign "confessions" which might incriminate Bishop Belo and other priests (especially foreign missionaries whose visas might more easily be revoked) of pro-independence political, sacrilegious, and ordinary criminal acts. Fourth, to protect business interests of the Jakarta oligarchy in East Timor, and fifth, to minimize any negative press coverage of East Timor by the only local daily, *Suara Timor Timur.*

More generally speaking, torture is carried out by Indonesian army units to obtain more specific information about the strength and whereabouts of the resistance guerrilla units, to avenge fellow soldiers killed by the guerrillas, to increase income from "tactical funds" allocated for counterinsurgency activities, which include interrogating suspected nationalists and cracking their spirits, and lately, to obtain additional income from selling photos of torture in progress to the resistance and their overseas supporters. Meanwhile, the Indonesian police also carry out torture to obtain more specific information about criminal (non-political) cases, such as murder, rape, robbery, arson, destruction of public and private property, and to avenge police who have been killed by guerrillas.

Torture practices are also not limited to the Indonesian occupation troops in East Timor. East Timorese military-trained vigilante groups, initially known as ninjas but lately renamed and restructured as Garda Paksi (Youth Guards to Defend Integration), also torture their fellow Timorese. These Timorese paramilitary units have some additional motives for the practice of torture, namely to protect themselves, their friends, and relatives from their fellow Timorese, following their collaboration in the first years of the invasion with the Indonesian troops in hunting the resistance forces in the mountains, and to avenge their relatives killed by Fretilin members during the 1975 civil war and its aftermath.

As mentioned above, a new pattern has emerged in SGI interrogations since the late 1980s, namely the concerted effort to force East Timorese youth activists and parishioners to incriminate Bishop Belo and other priests critical of the occupation. This forced incrimination of religious leaders is consistent with the policy of the Indonesian state to "indigenize" its terror machinery in East Timor. This policy also involves using East Timorese terror squads, dressed as Japanese ninjas, to terrorize their own people in the darkness of the night by raiding the houses of suspects, detaining and beating them, and then handing them over to Indonesian military units. Officially, the Indonesian military has denied any link with these ninja units, but according to East Timorese sources, these ninjas were actually trained by the military and carried out some of the military's dirty work. Major General Prabowo Subianto, President Suharto's son-in-law, and his Red Berets were seen as the protectors of these thugs, who operated openly in East Timor and Indonesia under the label of "pro-integrasi" youth (Broek 1997:20).

Depurification of the Bodies of East Timorese Women

In the previous section I have mentioned rape as one form of private torture. This does not stand by itself, but forms a part of the Indonesian state terror tactic which I call the depurification of the bodies of East Timorese women. I want to elaborate this subject in a separate section, because it involves a much deeper impact than the physical scars from cigarette butts, electric shocks, or bayonet stabs. It is part and parcel of the occupation forces attempts to "depurify" the bodies of the female population of East Timor, which have a profound demographic and cultural effect on the people, by raping, forcing the use of female fertility control methods without consent, and promoting prostitution in the country.

The impunity of the state rapist is a pressing issue in East Timor, as it is in all occupied territories (see Stiglmayer 1994), and the frequent raping of East Timorese women has been widely reported by international media and human rights organizations, as well as by East Timorese women activists themselves. In a typical example reported by Amnesty International in 1995, one woman and her family were tortured for several days by Indonesian soldiers in Baucau who were looking for her twenty-two-year-old son, a freedom fighter. When she denied knowing his whereabouts, she was stripped naked, beaten and kicked, and given electric shocks. Three days after her arrest, one of her nephews and her unmarried sister-in-law were called in for questioning. They too were interrogated under torture; her sister-in-law was also sexually abused (Amnesty International 1995:21).

In July 1996, in their petition to the UN Decolonization Committee in New York, the Free East Timor Japan Coalition raised several examples of

rape and other forms of sexual abuse committed by the Indonesian occupation troops against East Timorese women. Rape by Indonesian soldiers is, they stated, extremely common in East Timor. Two cases that
were included in their report illustrate how rape in East Timor is a systematic tactic used by the occupying forces against the female population.
On the evening of 12 January 1994, a woman from Bua Narak hamlet was
arrested and raped by an army platoon commander because she did not
have a travel permit from her hamlet to Loi Huno. The commander used
her inability to show a travel document as grounds for accusing her of
being a guerrilla. The other case, of rape and murder, on 30 October
1993, was also perpetrated as a reprisal for noncompliance with demands
by the military. The incident began with soldiers going from house to
house in the village and forcing girls to come with them to attend a party
in Wai-Mori village, Beloi. Two girls resisted being forced into the soldiers' truck; one was beaten until she bled, then stripped naked in front
of her family; the other was gang-raped, then stabbed to death.

Other examples of rape given by East Timorese who have testified in
Japan also show a pattern of rape of wives or daughters of men accused of
involvement in the resistance movement. Sometimes the rape takes place
in the presence of the husband, as in the case of the wife of Lucas Bayasa.
In this case the husband became mentally unstable after witnessing his
wife's rape, and the woman herself gave birth to the child of the rapist.
Furthermore, the wives of guerrilla leaders, left behind in the towns and
villages, are frequently forced to live with Indonesians or East Timorese
in the pay of the Indonesian authorities. This is particularly so if their
husbands are in important positions in the resistance movement. This is
both in order to monitor any communication with their husbands in the
bush and to compromise the women in the eyes of the Timorese community as "unfaithful" wives and to isolate them. This practice is, in other
words, part of Indonesian "military strategy" to weaken the unity and
morale of the enemy.

In another example of using women against the resistance movement,
six women in a village in the Los Palos area were abducted by Indonesian
troops in 1990. They were ordered to pass themselves off as supporters of
the guerrillas, with whom they were to make contact for the purpose of
gathering information for the Indonesian troops and leading them to
their hideout. The women were also used as sex slaves by the troops. The
woman who related these happenings said she had been forced to do
these things since 1990 and was still forced to provide sex to the soldiers
who came to her house. The soldiers tell her that if she refuses they will
take it that she is "cooperating with Fretilin."

Another widespread form of sexual abuse at the hands of the military
occupiers is the practice of using Timorese women as so-called "local

wives," on the one hand, and "comfort women," to use the euphemism of the Japanese Imperial Army, on the other. In July 1996 an East Timorese woman, Odilia Victor, was invited to Japan by the Free East Timor Japan Coalition to speak on the issue of sexual abuse of women. She told of the tragic experience of her sister, who was forced to become the local wife of an Indonesian Air Force officer, and of other women used as sex slaves by soldiers. One might think that women in situations like this could simply run away. Victor pointed out that the women who are singled out to work as comfort women usually have a low level of education, making them particularly vulnerable to intimidation, and it is also very difficult to run away because of the extensive presence of plainclothes intelligence agents living in the community, who constantly monitor peoples' movements. Anyone in one's neighborhood might be working for the Indonesian military intelligence agency. Victor said that nowadays many of the noodle vendors on the streets of Dili, for instance, are actually military personnel, and, "If my sister had tried to run away, she would certainly have been caught."

Victor also testified that while blatant cases of sex slavery are more frequent in towns and villages than in Dili, where foreign visitors are more common, in Dili itself there are several houses in Mascarenhas which are run by the military as brothels exclusively for Indonesian troops. These are not ordinary houses of prostitution, and the women are not paid per customer or per service. The women live there, are under constant surveillance by soldiers, and come from nearby neighborhoods. Soldiers simply go to a home, threaten the woman or family, and take her with them.

I believe that it is very important to underline this gender-specific form of torture towards East Timorese women, because it has not been taken up more seriously by Indonesian feminists and human rights activists in general, in contrast to their well-publicized concern for the rape victims of the Japanese occupation troops in Indonesia during World War II, or rape victims of the Serbian soldiers in Bosnia-Herzegovina. They do not realize that Indonesian troops in East Timor have constantly carried out the same type of atrocities. Ironically, this fact has also been emphasized by the deputy commander of the Indonesian invasion of East Timor, retired Major General Dading Kalbuadi, when he stated that "the military in the battle field are always close to the 'triple Ws,' war, wine, and women" (*Jakarta-Jakarta*, 14–20 August 1993, p. 22).

This form of sexual abuse is not simply a matter of sexual imbalance between the influx of male soldiers and the local women folk. It is a weapon of the occupying troops, to subdue the local population. It is also a weapon to destroy the opponent's culture, by biologically depurifying their ethnic constituency (see Seifert 1994:62–64).

Apart from rape, there were other less violent means of intervention by the Indonesian state into East Timorese family life, namely the so-called family planning program — which I prefer to call, more properly, forced female fertility control — and prostitution. The first is an officially sanctioned policy supported by the Indonesian state. The second seems to emerge automatically with the influx of Indonesian immigrants but is indirectly supported by the occupation forces, who have created a market for this profession. With the latest trend in Indonesia's family planning program, injectables, which can prevent pregnancy for up to six months, and implants, which can prevent pregnancy for years, have been widely applied in East Timor. The Catholic Church's strong opposition to this imposed program has received unanimous support even from pro-Indonesian East Timorese leaders. What is at stake is the survival of the East Timorese people in their homeland, especially after losing one third of their population during the 1975–1979 pacification war and in response to the increasing influx of Indonesian immigrants.

Two aspects of family planning policy have been criticized by leaders of East Timorese opinion. The first is the aggressive family planning propaganda by Indonesian civil servants in the villages of East Timor, and the second is the aggressive way contraceptives have been imposed on East Timorese school girls in the towns. By showing family planning films in the village halls to general audiences, they violated strongly held taboos against discussing sex and showing the male and female reproductive organs in public. Allegedly "by mistake," family planning officials in Viqueque inserted a pornographic film among the propaganda films, which further infuriated East Timorese elders (*Suara Timor Timur*, June 1994). Regarding the imposition of contraceptives, Isabela Galhos, an East Timorese student who defected to Canada in 1995, claims that "Every six months, the military goes to all the high schools, seeking out the young girls for compulsory birth control. They came, and closed the door, and just injected us. We didn't know, we didn't have the right to ask. We don't have children anymore. After visiting the schools, the military still goes around to individual villages and houses to inject the women they find. They don't know who we are, so they just inject us again. Some women get injected maybe three times" (Storey 1995:9). Similar allegations have been raised by the Jakarta-based Institute for Policy Research and Advocacy (Elsam) and the New York-based Lawyers Committee for Human Rights. As they state in their 1995 joint report, in 1987 and 1988 in schools in East Timor, female students received (Depo-Provera) injections without clear indication of their function. The government asserts that the injections were routine, but the climate of suspicion and the fact that male students did not receive the same injections led to rumors of contraceptive injections without consent that have never been fully resolved.

Apart from the World Bank, the U.S. government and its Population Council have underwritten the two most popular family planning devices in Indonesia and East Timor, namely Depo-Provera injectables and Norplant implants. Statistically, the use of Depo-Provera in East Timor far exceeds that in the twenty-six provinces of Indonesia. Norplant is produced by the Wyeth-Ayerst Laboratories in the United States, with the approval of the New York-based Population Council. Two-thirds of all Norplant produced has been consumed in Indonesia. The promotion of these two contraceptive techniques has continuously escalated, despite numerous cases of side effects, including strokes (Storey 1995:10; Elsam and LCHR 1995:8–10, 128; *Media Indonesia,* 5 October 1993; *Wawasan,* 6–8 October and 6 November 1993; *Kedaulatan Rakyat,* 9 October 1993; *Kompas,* 12 November 1993; *Republika,* 20 January 1994). Indonesia, East Timor, and other developing countries have been targeted by Norplant even though its use of poor and African-American women as "guinea pigs" was strongly criticized by doctors, women activists, and journalists in the United States in the early 1990s (Jensen 1993:67–70; *Women's Global Network for Reproductive Rights Newsletter,* July–December 1995, p. 15, April–June 1996, pp. 10–11).

In the meantime, while the Indonesian "family planning" machinery has invaded deeper and deeper into the bodies of East Timorese women, prostitution has also began to violate the integrity of Timorese families. Since 1984, an army of prostitutes from Java, Sulawesi, and West Timor has invaded the territory, which in November 1991 had a population of 3,000 prostitutes, including East Timorese ones. In Dili they operated from a brothel near the Comoro airport, in the Area Branca ("white beach") tourist resort, and even in Dili's two luxury hotels, Hotel Mahkota and New Resende Inn. These brothels are not confined to Dili, though, since the prostitutes also operate in all district capitals, mostly under the cover of restaurants, where customers can ask for "raw meat" (*daging mentah*), borrowing from the local Indonesian lingo. Sadly enough, with the limited employment opportunities for young East Timorese women who have become the sole source of family income due to the war, many have been forced into prostitution. East Timorese women also say that many young women were forced to become prostitutes because they lost their virginity to rape by the occupation troops (Shackleton 1995:116; *Fakta,* 1 April 1994, p. 74; *Suara Timor Timur,* 21 July 1994; *The Australian,* 13–14 January 1996).

Symbolic Violence

In general, we can talk about two layers of symbolic violence exerted by the occupation forces toward the East Timorese people. The first is the psychological torture associated with physical violence during the large-scale pacification war and physical torture in the interrogation centers, and the second is all the forms of symbolic violence carried out by the occupation troops to consolidate their power over the people in their occupied colony.

Let me now elaborate what the first layer of symbolic violence encompasses. Since the 1975 invasion, tens of thousands of East Timorese all over the country have had to see their loved ones being killed in horrible ways before their own eyes, without being able to save their lives. This includes the agony of imagining and later knowing what had happened to female relatives—sisters, mothers, or wives—who had fallen into the hands of the Indonesian soldiers, as we have discussed in the previous section.

During the pacification war, when a significant part of the population fled into the hills with the armed resistance, those left behind as well as those fleeing into the mountains had to suffer tremendous pain. Many of those left behind were forced to spy on their relatives and friends and had to report any activities which could be associated with the independence movement. Those fleeing into the mountains, on the other hand, were faced with the agony of having to leave friends and family behind, leaving them prone to arrest, detention, and imprisonment by the occupation forces, without knowing when or whether they would meet them again alive.

Part of the pacification war was the "fence of legs" operation in March to April 1981 all over the central mountain range, which carried its own share of psychological torture. East Timorese living under Indonesian control had to assist—or at least pretend to assist—the occupation forces to kill their own people, who had voluntarily or otherwise joined the resistance. Those fleeing from the advancing Indonesian troops and their East Timorese human shield often had to abandon or see hundreds of abandoned children and babies, who mostly died of starvation because their parents were killed by the Indonesian soldiers, or who were killed by their own parents because they were afraid that they would slow them down, or because their crying would put everyone else's life in danger, or because there was simply no more food to feed them.

After the full-scale pacification war was over, the majority of the East Timorese people had to endure other forms of psychological torture. They were forced to erase the history of their own people from their mind, including the history of their independence movement with all its heroes and heroines, and had to learn the history of the colonial power (Indonesia), while being convinced about the greatness and glory of the new colonialists, and to be grateful to them for "liberating" them from the Portuguese colonialists and the Fretilin "communists." They were also forced to learn the language of the new colonial power and unlearn the language of the previous one, while being convinced that the new colonial power is better than the previous one. As new "citizens" of the Indonesian Republic, they were forced to joyfully exercise all the Indonesian political rituals, such as raising the Indonesian national flag, singing the Indonesian national anthem, reciting the Indonesian state philosophy, *Panca Sila*, and cheerfully joining all Indonesian parades, ceremonies, and parties, because if they did not do that, they could face arrest, interrogation, and physical torture.

Then, when the East Timorese clergy, under the leadership of Bishop Belo, began to take a strong, pro–human rights stance, a new type of psychological torture began. From 1987 to 1994, there were constant reports that detained activists were forced to confess that several priests — including Bishop Belo — suspected of pro-independence activities had been involved in sacrilegious acts, such as destroying Holy Mary statues, or in crimes such as murder or involvement in the independence movement, which might have caused the arrest, detention, torture, or even assassination of those priests.

The East Timorese youth in Indonesia — mainly students — were also not exempted from this kind of psychological torture. Since the occupation of the U.S. Embassy in Jakarta by twenty-nine pro-independence youth activists, other East Timorese youth had to rally against their own compatriots, at the instruction of Red Beret officers. And when Bishop Belo was awarded the 1996 Nobel Peace Prize, they also had to rally against their own bishop, calling him names (traitor, etc.) at the order of the Red Berets, and thereby facing the wrath of their own people.

Let me now talk about the second, less explicit layer of symbolic violence. This type of symbolic violence involves intimidating semantics, the building of "pro-integration" monuments, the prohibition of the Portuguese language, and the destruction and desecration of Catholic icons.

Let me first talk about the semantics of violence. Various new expressions have been created over the years which connote the methods of execution and torture employed by the occupation forces in East Timor. The term "GPK" (Gerakan Pengacau Keamanan or "security disturbance movement"), is used to intimidate East Timorese who refuse to cooperate with the Indonesian state authorities by identifying them as suspects, which singles them out to the Red Berets to interrogate and torture them. As an editorial in a local East Timorese daily stated, "the GPK label is a death verdict without due process." *Mobil tidak apa-apa* ("the car that can do no wrong") is a reference to the Japanese Hino trucks used by the Indonesian forces, since they are allowed to violate the traffic rules with impunity, including running down people on the roads. *Jalan-jalan ke Jakarta* or *jalan-jalan ke Lissabon* ("taking a trip to Jakarta or Lisbon") and

Berangkat studi lanjut ke Jawa ("going for further study in Java") are common euphemisms that mean the person referred to is going to be executed. *Mani laut* ("taking a bath in the sea") refers to the practice of weighting the bodies of suspects with rocks and dumping them from a helicopter into the sea, *piknik ke Builico* ("going for a picnic to Builico") refers to being dumped in the Sarei River ravine near Builico, a notorious execution place, and *dipangil ke Quelicai* ("called to Quelicai") means one is going to be thrown from the cliffs in Quelicai. *Menginap di Hotel Flamboyan* ("spending the night at the Hotel Flamboyan") means one is going to be interrogated by the Red Berets, whose headquarters was located there in the late 1980s. *Di-Santa Cruz-kan* ("Santa Cruz-ified") is an expression some East Timorese mothers use to threaten their children when they are naughty, with the sinister connotations of the Santa Cruz massacre. Finally, *ayam kampung* ("village chickens") is a term used to describe East Timorese prostitutes, to distinguish them from their supposedly more "experienced" Indonesian sisters, who are called *ayam ras* ("specially bred chickens") (Taylor 1991:101; Turner 1992:166; Aditjondro 1994:46; Dunn 1996:282; Pinto and Jardine 1997:147; interviews with East Timorese and Indonesian sources, 1993–1997).

Another form of symbolic violence is the building of monuments to glorify East Timor's "integration" into Indonesia, to remind the population of the strength of the Indonesian armed forces and of "Fretilin atrocities," and finally, to remind them of how good the Indonesian state has been to the Catholic Church of East Timor. An example of the first type of monuments is the Integrasi monument erected in a park in central Dili, showing a young man breaking his shackles of (Portuguese) colonialism, which may be inspired by similar monuments commemorating Indonesia's own struggle for independence from Dutch colonialism (Anderson 1990). Similar monuments have also been built in all the district capitals of East Timor. An example of the second type of monument are the wrecks of the Indonesian army landing ships left stranded on the beach of Dili, right in front of the Indonesian navy headquarters, and also within sight of the popular Turismo Hotel. An example of the third type of monument is the Cathedral of Dili. Called the Church of the Immaculate Conception and hailed as "the largest church in South East Asia," it was dedicated by President Suharto in November 1988, in anticipation of the Pope's visit to the disputed territory a year later (Ryan 1993:86; Pinto and Jardine 1997:105–106).

A more controversial monument is the twenty-seven-meter-high statue of Christ on Cape Fatucama, east of Dili, which was dedicated by President Suharto in mid-October 1996. This statue — the second highest of its kind in the world after the Cristo Rei statue in Rio de Janeiro — was built without consulting Bishop Belo or any other East Timorese clergy. The

East Timorese Catholic community was, however, not happy with the statue, since it blatantly symbolizes Indonesia's political domination over the territory. Its seventeen-meter height symbolizes two important dates which the occupation forces always celebrate in the territory, namely 17 July, the "integration" day, and 17 August, Indonesia's own independence day. Then, the statue stands on a ten-meter globe, raising the entire structure twenty-seven meters high, to symbolize East Timor as Indonesia's twenty-seventh "province" (CCJDP 1993:3).

The other form of symbolic violence, the destruction and desecration of Catholic icons by the Indonesian state apparatus in East Timor, has moved from more war-related destruction, where the damage was caused by rockets and gunfire, to destruction which is carried out mostly by individual members of the military and their civilian collaborators. During the first decade of the occupation, the damage to churches, a seminary, and several colleges had more to do with indiscriminate Indonesian bombing and artillery fire, which violated the 1949 Geneva Convention Relative to the Protection of Civilian Persons in Time of War, one of the few international human rights instruments which has been ratified by Indonesia (Lillich 1986:100). Nevertheless, these acts of destruction were not part of a deliberate strategy to terrorize the East Timorese Catholic Church, because at that time the neocolonial masters of East Timor tried to woo the support of the church, or, at least, dissociate it from the Fretilin-led independence movement, which at that time was strongly branded as a communist movement. The same could not be said about the incidents of destruction and desecration of Catholic icons during the second and third decades of Indonesian occupation of East Timor. Although the stealing of crucifixes from corpses which had been laid to rest in the cemeteries had already been observed during the first days of the invasion, the increasing frequency of similar sacrilegious offenses in the 1980s and 1990s — such as the destruction of statues of the Virgin Mary, the theft of tabernacle keys, the use of rosaries as torture instruments, and spitting and trampling on the Holy Communion — makes it difficult to imagine that this type of symbolic violence took place without the blessings of the Indonesian military commanders.

Demonization of the Enemy

The physical and psychological attacks on the Catholic clergy and religious personnel in East Timor, which were not only carried out by the Indonesian occupation troops inside East Timor, but also engaged parts of the Indonesian media and intellectuals in Indonesia proper, were part of another form of state terror, which is certainly not an Indonesian invention or monopoly. This is the strategy of demonizing the enemy.

Just as Western governments demonized the Eastern bloc states during the Cold War, and then shifted to demonizing the Muslim and/or Arabic states after the Cold War (Said 1981), the Indonesian state has proceeded in similar steps in its campaign to subdue the East Timorese independence movement.

In the preparatory months before the invasion of 7 December 1975, the Indonesian state-controlled media ran a campaign to portray the leading pro-independence party, Fretilin, as a communist party. Relying heavily on the support of Indonesian Muslim and Christian organizations and their media, the campaign to portray the freedom fighters as bloodthirsty baby-and-women-killing terrorists was quite effective in concealing what was really happening in the territory from large sections of the Indonesian population, including the usually more critical students and academics.

Entering the second decade of the occupation, the strategy to demonize the East Timorese resistance as communists did not seem to be very effective anymore. Most of the old Fretilin and Falantil leaders had died, been captured, joined church and other nongovernmental organizations, or even become Indonesian collaborators. In the meantime, a new generation of young East Timorese had emerged to carry on the freedom struggle from the towns and cities in East Timor and Indonesia, while the Catholic Church of East Timor — under the inspiring leadership of its young bishop, Carlos Felipe Ximenes Belo — had also become a strong voice for the oppressed Timorese.

As we can observe from the reports of torture and desecration, this is when the church became the main target of demonization. Together with their brothers and sisters in Flores and West Timor, a new image of violent and fundamentalist East Timorese Catholics, who were very jealous of keeping their numerical dominance in East Timor and the Indonesian province of East Nusa Tenggara (NTT), began to emerge in the Indonesian state-controlled news media. And when East Timorese mobs eventually attacked and destroyed two mosques in East Timor in September 1995, which resulted in an exodus of tens of thousands of Indonesian Muslim business immigrants to Java and Sulawesi, the picture was complete. Belo became the main target of demonstrations and verbal attacks by Muslim organizations and politicians in Java (Walters 1995).

This campaign to demonize the Timorese resistance as a mob of intolerant Catholics further culminated when the young Salesian priest was nominated for the 1996 Nobel Peace Prize together with his compatriot, Jose Ramos-Horta, the main international spokesperson of the resistance. This time many more Islamic intellectuals, ministers, and generals publicly attacked him. The result was contrary to what the occupation forces had expected; nearly the entire East Timorese population, including the armed guerrillas in the mountains, rallied behind the bishop and were even ready to die and be tortured for defending their spiritual leader, in the absence of their political leader, Xanana Gusmao, who was still languishing in the Cipinang jail in Jakarta, among dozens of other political prisoners. Here history has repeated itself; just as the Dili cathedral, which was Suharto's "bribe" to his colonial subjects, had become a focal point for Timorese nationalism, the Christ statue has provided the Timorese people with another public space and focal point to express their nationalistic feelings.

Demographic Dilution

As has been practiced by numerous regimes in history from the seventeenth-century English monarchy to twentieth-century China (Brain 1972: 50–52), the Indonesian state has also tried to quell East Timorese nationalism by tampering with the population balance in the colony. For the past fifteen years, after the carpet bombing ended, the Indonesian state has tried to stimulate a population influx from Indonesia into the territory. It is impossible to obtain conclusive statistics on how many Indonesians have settled in the territory so far. But from studying the growth of several religious groups, the frequency and number of passengers of Indonesian ships visiting the territory, the improvement of roads, and the frequency of busses and trucks on these roads, one can make some informed guesses. By 1993, of the officially recorded population of 811,656, my informed guess allows for at least 200,000 Indonesian immigrants in East Timor. But according to Rui Gomes, a former staff member of the Indonesian regional planning board (Bappeda) in Dili, there are already 400,000 Indonesian immigrants who have settled in the territory. This nearly fifty-fifty ratio between East Timorese and Indonesians is also reflected in some major towns in East Timor, such as Dili (de Sousa Saldanha 1994:355).

This tactic of demographic dilution has, however, failed to quell the East Timorese freedom movement. Within East Timor, Indonesian Muslim immigrants have become the target of public dissent, including physical attacks by East Timorese youth. On the other hand, East Timorese youth studying in the various universities in Indonesia have spread their gospel of independence and shown their courage to stand up against a brutal, military-capitalistic regime, right inside the lion's den. This courage has infected fellow young Indonesian activists. In fact, several ad hoc as well as more permanent coalitions have been formed between the clandestine East Timorese youth movement in Java and the Indonesian pro-democracy movement (ASIET 1996). A similar pattern was repeated in Indonesia as twenty years earlier in Portugal, where African students such as Augustinho Neto, Amilcar Cabral, and Samora Machel educated their young Portuguese peers about the evils of Portuguese colonialism.

Indonesian State Terror in Its International Context

Indonesia's strategy of state terror in East Timor is not unique. It has parallels in many other places around the world, such as Northern Ireland, Puerto Rico, and Israel's Occupied Territories, to name just a few. These parallels beg the question whether the Indonesian state has developed its terror strategy from interacting with other states. The Indonesian military's close cooperation with the U.S. military, including U.S. Special Forces, has been open knowledge for the last fifty years. Until the overthrow of President Sukarno in 1965–1966, the relations between the Indonesian and U.S. militaries were quite minimal. But after the installation of General Suharto as Indonesia's second president, military cooperation between the two states flourished, and ranged from supply of American military hardware to imitation of the American military's civic action and counterinsurgency strategies (Simpson III 1983:188–194).

Compared to the military cooperation between Indonesia and the United States, similar links between Indonesia and the United Kingdom are more complicated, because they also involve the top brass of Tel Aviv, which has no official diplomatic representation in Jakarta. Since Suharto came to power, the Israeli secret service, Mossad, has been allowed to operate under the cover of the British MI6 residence in Jakarta. This operation was initiated directly under the command of Major General Meir Amit, then Mossad head (Melman and Raviv 1989:174; Ostrovsky and Hoy 1991:67; Ramadhan 1994:250–251). This covert cooperation between the Indonesian and Israeli militaries was not limited to information gathering and exchange. When General Benny Murdani, the former commander of the East Timor invasion, became the head of Indonesia's main intelligence body, BAKIN, the Indonesian military began to forge a much closer cooperation with the Israeli Defense Forces and their military-industrial complex. That was when ABRI bought Israeli Uzi submachine guns and U.S.-made Skyhawk fighter planes through under-the-counter channels (Leifer 1985:156; Ramos-Horta 1987:147, 148; Melman and Raviv 1989:367–368; Ostrovsky and Hoy 1991: 125–126). Since then, this military cooperation has moved from shadowy arms deals to an open admiration of Israeli military prowess. For instance, during the forty-second anniversary of the Red Berets on 16 April 1994, guests attending the three-hour ceremony were surprised to find in their handbags a long translation of a chapter taken from a book on the history of the Israeli army, extolling the virtues of a typical Israeli commando (*Indonesia Business Weekly*, 29 April 1994, p. 13).

Hence, it would be fair to assume that Indonesia's state terror strategy was also partly derived from Mossad manuals and operatives. In fact, several elements of Indonesian state terror in East Timor parallel Israel's state terror in the Occupied Territories. These parallels not only involve various torture techniques (O'Brien 1991), but also more sophisticated demographic dilution techniques, developed to counter the danger of a Jewish state facing a Palestinian majority in Israel and the Occupied Territories (Melman and Raviv 1989:194).

Finally, there is an interesting parallel between Indonesian state terror and Angolan state terror in Africa. In the early 1990s, the MPLA-led government in Angola also used "riot police" units to terrorize their own people into submission and into avoiding any contact with the rival UNITA party. These riot police units which are "licensed to kill" are, interestingly, also called ninjas, as are the pro-Indonesian paramilitary groups of East Timorese backed by the Indonesian Red Berets (Maier 1996). It is not clear yet to me whether this is a case of independent innovation or diffusion, considering the fact that both East Timor and Angola are Lusophone countries with a lot of CIA connections.

Conclusion

In spite of the five-pronged strategy of state terror employed by the Indonesian state to subjugate the population of its unwilling colony, the East Timorese resistance has not withered and has even grown stronger with the international recognition drawn to their cause by the award of the 1996 Nobel Peace Prize to Bishop Belo, the spiritual father of the East Timorese independence movement, and the East Timorese diplomat in exile Jose Manuel Ramos-Horta.

Nevertheless, I believe that East Timorese leaders need to be alert to the danger of internalization of the violence exerted on the East Timorese people by their current rulers, so that this repressive system, based on violence, terror, and intolerance, will not be reproduced in the future by an independent East Timorese state. It was Nietzsche who warned, "Have a care when fighting monsters, lest you become a monster yourself."

Bibliography

Aditjondro, George J.
  1994 *In the Shadow of Mount Ramelau: The Impact of the Occupation of East Timor.* Leiden: INDOC (Indonesian Documentation and Information Center).
Amnesty International
  1995 *Human Rights Are Women's Rights.* London: Amnesty International.
  1984 *Torture in the Eighties.* London: Amnesty International.

Anderson, Benedict R.
    1990 *Language and Power: Exploring Political Cultures in Indonesia.* Ithaca: Cornell University Press.
ASIET (Action in Solidarity with Indonesia and East Timor)
    1996 *Fighting Together: Indonesians and East Timorese Join the Struggle.* Sydney: ASIET.
Bentley, G. Carter
    1995 "Dimensions of Domination in East Timor Colloquy." In *East Timor at the Crossroads: The Forging of a Nation.* P. Carey and G. Carter Bentley, eds. New York: Social Science Research Council and Cassell.
Bhatia, Shyam
    1996 "Arafat Drops Pretence at Democracy." *Guardian Weekly,* 11 August.
Brain, Robert
    1972 *Into the Primitive Environment.* Englewood Cliffs, N.J.: Prentice-Hall.
Broek, Martin
    1997 *Indonesia: Arms Trade to a Military Regime.* Amsterdam: ENAAT.
Budiardjo, Carmel
    1991 "Indonesia: Mass Extermination and the Consolidation of Authoritarian Power." In *Western State Terrorism.* Alexander George, ed. Cambridge: Polity Press.
Carey, Peter, and G. Carter Bentley (eds.)
    1995 *East Timor at the Crossroads: The Forging of a Nation.* New York: Social Science Research Council and Cassell.
CCJDP (Catholic Commission for Justice, Development and Peace)
    1993 *The Church and East Timor: A Collection of Documents by National and International Catholic Church Agencies.* Melbourne: CCJDP.
Clutterbuck, Richard (ed.)
    1986 *The Future of Political Violence: Destabilization, Disorder and Terrorism.* London: Macmillan.
Cockburn, Patrick
    1997 "Corruption of the Palestinian State." *Independent,* international edition, 18–24 June.
Cribb, Robert (ed.)
    1990 *The Indonesian Killings, 1965–1966: Studies from Java and Bali.* Clayton: Monash University Center for Southeast Asian Studies.
de Sousa Saldanha, Joao Mariano
    1994 *The Political Economy of East Timor Development.* Jakarta: Pustaka Sinar Harapan.
Dirdja, Alex
    1979 "Timor Timur: Beberapa Pengalaman Dan Pemikiran." *InterNos,* 23:2, April–June 1979, pp. 22–23.
Dunn, James S.
    1996 *Timor: A People Betrayed.* Sydney: Allen and Unwin.
Elsam and LCHR
    1995 *In the Name of Development: Human Rights and the World Bank in Indonesia.* New York: Institute for Policy Research and Advocacy (Elsam) and the Lawyers Committee for Human Rights.
Fanon, Frantz
    1985 *The Wretched of the Earth.* Harmondsworth: Penguin Books. (First published in French in 1961).
Forman, Shepard
    1980 "Descent, Alliance and Exchange Ideology Among the Makassae of East

Timor." In *The Flow of Life: Essays on Eastern Indonesia.* James Fox, ed. Cambridge: Harvard University Press.
    1978 "East Timor: Exchange and Political Hierarchy at the Time of the European Discoveries." In *Economic Exchange and Social Interaction in Southeast Asia.* K. Hutterer, ed. Ann Arbor: Center for South and Southeast Asian Studies.
Freire, Paulo
    1972 *Cultural Action for Freedom.* Harmondsworth: Penguin Books.
Gama, Paulino (Mauk Muruk)
    1995 "The War in the Hills, 1975–85: A Fretilin Commander Remembers." In *East Timor at the Crossroads: The Forging of a Nation.* Peter Carey and G. Carter Bentley, eds. New York: Social Science Research Council and Cassell.
Gomes, Donaciano
    1995 "The East Timor Intifada: Testimony of a Student Activist." In *East Timor at the Crossroads: The Forging of a Nation.* Peter Carey and G. Carter Bentley, eds. New York: Social Science Research Council and Cassell.
Gray, Andrew
    1984 "The People of East Timor and Their Struggle for Survival." In *East Timor: The Struggle Continues.* Torben Retboll, ed. Copenhagen: IWGIA (International Work Group for Indigenous Affairs).
Hilsdon, Anne-Marie
    1995 *Madonnas and Martyrs: Militarism and Violence in the Philippines.* Sydney: Allen and Unwin.
Hirst, David
    1997 "Arafat's Bold Revolution Turning Sour." *Canberra Times,* 26 April.
Jensen, Carl (ed.)
    1993 *Censored! The News That Didn't Make the News — and Why.* Chapel Hill, N.C.: Shelburne Press.
Jolliffe, Jill
    1978 *East Timor: Nationalism and Colonialism.* St. Lucia: University of Queensland Press.
Leifer, Michael
    1985 "The Islamic Factor in Indonesia's Foreign Policy: A Case Study of Functional Ambiguity." In *Islam in Foreign Policy.* A. Dawisha, ed. Cambridge: Cambridge University Press.
Liddle, R. William
    1992 *Pemilu-Pemilu Orde Baru: Pasang Surut Kekuasaan Politik.* Jakarta: LP3ES.
Lillich, Richard B.
    1986 *International Human Rights Instruments.* Buffalo, N.Y.: William S. Hein.
Lowry, Robert
    1996 *The Armed Forces of Indonesia.* Sydney: Allen and Unwin.
Maier, Karl
    1996 *Angola: Promises and Lies.* London: Serif.
McMillan, Andrew
    1992 *Death in Dili.* Sydney: Hodder and Stoughton.
McVey, Ruth
    1984 "Separatism and the Paradoxes of the Nation-state in Perspective." In *Armed Separatism in Southeast Asia.* Lim Joo-Jock and Vani S., eds. Singapore: ISEAS.
Melman, Yossi, and Dan Raviv
    1989 *The Imperfect Spies: The History of Israeli Intelligence.* London: Sidgwick and Jackson.

Memmi, Albert
    1990 *The Colonizer and the Colonized*. London: Earthscan Publications.
O'Brien, William V.
    1991 *Law and Morality in Israel's War with the PLO*. New York: Routledge.
Ostrovsky, Victor, and Claire Hoy
    1991 *By Way of Deception: An Insider's Devastating Expose of the Mossad*. London:
    Arrow Books.
Pinto, Constancio, and Matthew Jardine
    1997 *East Timor's Unfinished Struggle: Inside the Timorese Resistance*. Boston: South
    End Press.
Ramadhan, K. H.
    1994 *Soemitro — Dari Pangdam Mulawarman Sampai Pangkopkamtib*. Jakarta: Pus-
    taka Sinar Harapan.
Ramos-Horta, Jose
    1987 *Funu: The Unfinished Saga of East Timor*. Trenton: Red Sea Press.
Ryan, Paul
    1993 *Timor: A Traveler's Guide*. Darwin: Self-published.
Said, Edward
    1981 *Covering Islam: How the Media and the Experts Determine How We See the Rest of
    the World*. New York: Pantheon Books.
Seifert, Ruth
    1994 "War and Rape: A Preliminary Analysis." In *Mass Rape: The War Against
    Women in Bosnia-Herzegovina*. Alexandra Stiglmayer, ed. Lincoln: University of
    Nebraska Press.
Shackleton, Shirley
    1995 "Planting a Tree in Balibo: A Journey to East Timor." In *East Timor at the
    Crossroads: The Forging of a Nation*. Peter Carey and G. Carter Bentley, eds. New
    York: Social Science Research Council and Cassell.
Simpson III, Charles M.
    1983 *Inside the Green Berets: The First Thirty Years — A History of the U.S. Army Special
    Forces*. Novato: Presidio Press.
Soesastro, M. Hadi
    1991 "East Timor, Questions of Economic Viability." In *Unity in Diversity: Re-
    gional Economic Development in Indonesia Since 1970*. H. Hill, ed. Singapore: Ox-
    ford University Press.
Stiglmayer, Alexandra (ed.)
    1994 *Mass Rape: The War Against Women in Bosnia-Herzegovina*. Lincoln: Univer-
    sity of Nebraska Press.
Storey, Sarah
    1995 "Coercive Birth Control and Settler Infusion: The Indonesian Prophy-
    lactic Against East Timorese Self-Determination." East Timor email bulletin
    board (reg.easttimor@conf.igc.apc.org), 7 May.
Tanter, Richard
    1994 "The Totalitarian Ambition: Intelligence and Security Agencies in Indo-
    nesia." In *State and Civil Society in Indonesia*. Arief Budiman, ed. Clayton: Mo-
    nash University, Center for Southeast Asian Studies.
Taylor, John G.
    1995 "Chronology." In *East Timor at the Crossroads: The Forging of a Nation*. Peter
    Carey and G. Carter Bentley, eds. New York: Social Science Research Council
    and Cassell.
    1991 *Indonesia's Forgotten War: The Hidden History of East Timor*. London: Zed Books.

Tomodok, E. M.
   1994 *Hari-hari Akhir Timor Portugis.* Jakarta: PT Pustaka Jaya.
Traube, Elizabeth G.
   1995 "Mambai Perspectives on Colonialism and Decolonization." In *East Timor at the Crossroads: The Forging of a Nation.* Peter Carey and G. Carter Bentley, eds. New York: Social Science Research Council and Cassell.
   1986 *Cosmology and Social Life: Ritual Exchange Among the Mambai of East Timor.* Chicago: University of Chicago Press.
   1980 "Mambai Rituals of Black and White." In *The Flow of Life: Essays on Eastern Indonesia.* James Fox, ed. Cambridge: Harvard University Press.
Turner, Michele (ed.)
   1992 *Telling East Timor: Personal Testimonies, 1942–1992.* Sydney: New South Wales University Press.
Vidal-Naquet, Pierre
   1963 *Torture: Cancer of Democracy—France and Algeria, 1954–62.* Harmondsworth: Penguin Books.
Walters, Patrick
   1995 "Muslims Back Hard Line on East Timor." *Weekend Australian,* 23–24 September.
Williams, Ian
   1995 "Palestinian Professor Pours Scorn on Arafat." *Weekend Australian,* 20–21 May.
Windhu, I. Marsana
   1992 *Kekuasaan Dan Kekerasan Menurut Johan Galtung.* Yogyakarta: Kanisius.

Chapter 7
Murdered or Martyred?
Popular Evaluations of Violent Death
in the Muslim Separatist Movement
in the Philippines

Thomas M. McKenna

Two emphases are discernible in recent approaches to the anthropology of terror. On the one hand there may be found studies of the semantics of political violence focused on those who trade in terror and the gruesomely explicit messages they send and receive through the media of bombings, assassinations, detentions, and torture (see, for example, Feldman 1991; Suarez-Orozco 1992; Zulaika 1988). On the other we find primary attention paid to the irrationality and meaninglessness of political terror as experienced by its civilian victims (see especially Nordstrom 1992). That emphasis on incomprehensibility is heightened in those accounts in which citizen victims of terror are incapable even of distinguishing its agents—unable, for example, to establish whether it was government soldiers or insurgents who attacked the village or assassinated a neighbor (Nordstrom 1992; Warren 1993). Stated differently, many anthropological treatments of terror have tended to focus either on the perceptions, actions, and intentions of those employing political violence or on terror's crushing consequences—its devastation of lives, communities, and systems of meaning. These two emphases, while obviously complementary, appear separated by considerable analytical distance, especially insofar as most ethnographers of terror have not explicitly studied the fighters and noncombatant victims of dirty wars in tandem.[1] In this chapter I examine one dimension of that analytical space—the creative and strategic efforts of ordinary citizens to make sense of extraordinary political violence. I argue that explicit focus on the unauthorized expressions and actions of ordinary noncombatants in dirty wars offers one solution to a vexing problem facing anthropological studies of political terror: that of finding an appropriate analytical stance from which to examine ethnographic situations of political terror — one that avoids both the disturbing bias of intense partisanship and the disappointing aridity of ironic detachment.

Armed Separatism and State Terror in the Muslim Philippines

Between 1972 and 1980, a ferocious war raged throughout the southern Philippines between Muslim separatist rebels and the Philippine military. At least 50,000 people were killed in the fighting, which also created one million internal refugees and caused more than 100,000 Philippine Muslims to flee by boat to Malaysia. Separatist fighters, numbering as many as 30,000 armed insurgents, fought the Philippine armed forces to a stalemate, obliging the Philippine government to negotiate a cease-fire and peace treaty in 1977. For the past sixteen years an uneasy and fragile cease-fire has obtained — one periodically broken by armed clashes between the military and separatist fighters who remain under arms in remote camps. A recent peace agreement between the Philippine government and one of the rebel factions represents the first real progress toward a genuine settlement of the conflict, but most commentators are not optimistic about its ultimate outcome.

There are approximately three million Muslims in the Philippines, the only majority Christian country in Southeast Asia. Though they represent only a small percentage of the Philippine population (about 5 percent), Muslims are geographically concentrated in the south of the country, and are distinguished from Christian Filipinos not only by their profession of Islam but also by their evasion of three hundred years of Spanish colonial domination. Although Spanish colonizers had consolidated their hold on the northern tier of the Philippine archipelago by 1600, they never accomplished the complete subjugation of the Muslim south. Philippine Muslims are also separated from one another in this archipelagic nation by very significant linguistic and geographic distances. They are divided into three major and ten minor ethnolinguistic groups and dispersed across the southern islands. The modern movement for Muslim separatism originated among a small set of Philippine Muslim students and intellectuals in the late 1960s. It gained popular support after the eruption of sectarian violence in the southern Philippines in 1970 and emerged as an armed secessionist front in response to the declaration of martial law by Philippine President Ferdinand Marcos in 1972.

I first conducted research in the Muslim Philippines in 1985 and 1986, with return trips in 1988 and 1995. My investigations have centered on

Campo Muslim, a poor urban community in Cotabato City, the principal city of the region of Cotabato on the southern island of Mindanao. Campo Muslim, a community composed primarily of political and economic refugees from the countryside, has served as a base from which to examine the causes and consequences of the armed separatist struggle as well as efforts to continue the movement in unarmed form by mobilizing the urban Muslim population for mass actions. The accounts presented here of evaluations by community residents of extraordinary political violence are primarily drawn from my first period of fieldwork.

The ordinary Muslims[2] of Cotabato have been the victims of a great deal of brutal violence since 1972, almost all of it at the hands of the Philippine military. Much of that violence has taken the form of direct military reprisals for civilian support of the rebels and has made chilling sense to Muslims. Other incidents they find far more difficult to understand, and still others appear entirely senseless to them. On the day before I first arrived in Cotabato city in 1985, a hand grenade was thrown into a crowd celebrating a Muslim holiday in the central city plaza, wounding several celebrants. Shortly before I ended my first research period sixteen months later, a government soldier drinking with his comrades in a second-story beer hall at the edge of the Muslim quarter of the city pulled the pin on a grenade and tossed it (reportedly without looking) into the street below, killing a young Muslim girl and wounding her brother. No coherent intended message was evident in those incidents. For ordinary Muslims, the medium was the message; grenades kill indiscriminately, thoughtlessly. Those who possess them and the effectively unrestricted power to use them (overwhelmingly but not exclusively government soldiers) are to be feared. While these incidents were perceived by Cotabato Muslims as examples of state terror, similarly deadly incidents were, as shall be seen, not clearly acts of state terror, nor could they be said with any certainty to be acts of political violence at all.

For the purposes of my argument it is necessary, for the time being, to shift attention away from civilians as *victims* to civilians as *witnesses* of terror. While analyses of ordinary victims of state terror often portray them as suspended precariously between two contending forces in "wars they did not start and do not control" (Nordstrom 1992:261), it is nonetheless true that in many of those cases civilian victims are strongly identified with the antistate forces. This is not to say that those so identified are in perfect ideological agreement with (or are even fully aware of) the formal goals of insurgent leaders. It is merely to point out that in many instances, ordinary civilians have friends and relatives among rank-and-file insurgents and are likely to share significant interests, attitudes, and objectives with them (primary among them the desire to defend themselves from state aggression). As supporters (even if not in the formal sense), civilians who identify themselves with insurgents attempt to discern the meaning of the violence applied against those who fight in their name.

Nearly every household in Campo Muslim had a family member or close relative among the Muslim insurgents at the height of the armed rebellion (1972–1980) and many lost loved ones fighting for the cause. The Muslim separatist rebellion was much more a nationalist struggle than an Islamic one, and such Islamic notions as *jihad* (righteous struggle in defense of the faith) were not strongly emphasized in the formal ideology of the rebel leadership. Nevertheless, ordinary Muslims, both rank-and-file fighters and civilians, relied on the idea of jihad to understand the struggle. In unofficial rebel songs fighters referred to themselves as both *paninindeg a inged* (fighting for the community) and *jihad pi sabilillah* (fighting in the path of Allah). For rank-and-file rebels, struggle in defense of Islam was coincident with armed defense of cultural tradition, property, livelihood, and life. As one young Islamic activist, too young to have fought in the rebellion, related to me: "During the rebellion there was no true jihad; it was more nationalistic. But the rebels were true mujahideen because of their sincerity. They defended Muslims, and those who died doing so received divine reward." Throughout the Muslim Philippines, those considered to have martyred themselves defending Islam and their communities were referred to as *sabil.*

The term *sabil* and its usage in reference to Philippine Muslim martyrs merits examination. Martyrdom has been a particularly important motif in Islam, and the term most commonly used in the Islamic world to refer to a Muslim martyr (one who has died in the service of Islam) is *shahid.* Martyrdom has played a signficant role in Philippine Islam as well but is not typically referenced by the Arabic term *shahid* or any of its variants. Instead, *sabil* is used (in various forms) to speak both of martyrs and of those who have pledged to fight to the death to defend Islam (broadly defined). *Sabil* is also of Arabic origin and is almost certainly a variant of Arabic *sabr*, meaning literally to restrain or bind, but also denoting endurance and steadfastness when used in reference to holy war (jihad) (Houtsma 1987). The Arabic *sabr* has both an active sense, that of performing difficult tasks, and a passive one, the suffering of injury and death, and this duel sense is also seen in its Philippine Muslim variant *sabil*, which refers both to those who have pledged themselves to fight steadfastly as well as to those who suffer death in a just cause.

While none of the rebel fighters I spoke with had specifically sworn an oath to fight to the death in the Muslim separatist rebellion, the term *sabil* strongly suggested such a pledge, at least an implicit one. That is because *sabil* is a term powerfully charged with associations to an earlier liberation struggle—armed resistance to Spanish and American colonizers of the Philippine south—and specifically to its most dramatic embodiment, ritual suicide. Most widely known by the designation given it by the Spaniards — *juramentado* (lit., one who has sworn an oath) — the practice of personal jihad was referred to by Philippine Muslims as *pagsabil* (Kiefer 1972). In the last decades of the nineteenth century, the Spanish colonizers of the northern Philippines finally succeeded in occupying (though not completely controlling) the territory of most of the major Islam polities of the south. The main (and most disquieting) form of resistance to the Spanish occupiers became the *pagsabil*, or ritual suicide. In its most common form, an individual Muslim male would undergo a ritual preparation (including the learning of special magic to help him fight bravely), then proceed to an area frequented by Spanish soldiers and attempt to kill as many of them as possible with his sword before he himself was killed. In some cases, large groups of men would engage in suicidal attacks against far superior forces. The goal of the *pagsabil* was twofold, to kill enemy soldiers and to be killed by them, thereby achieving the blessings of martyrdom, including immediate entrance into paradise.

The practice of *pagsabil* continued into the first decade of the American colonial period (beginning in 1899) but eventually diminished as American colonizers consolidated territorial control to a far greater extent than the Spaniards and also convinced Philippine Muslims that, unlike the Spaniards, they were not intent on forcibly converting them to Christianity.[3] I did not hear of a single instance of *pagsabil* during the Muslim separatist rebellion. The term *sabil*, however, continued in very wide use and carried the accreted meanings of the ritual suicides of the colonial period; a *sabil* had fought to the death (or was willing to do so) to defend the Philippine Muslim community from non-Muslim military occupiers.

I heard numerous martyrdom narratives related by Campo Muslim residents. The one that follows is typical: "the son of Bapa Adza and his companion were both brave fighters. They were captured with documents by the military in the city at a checkpoint near the Quirino Bridge. The soliders placed them in handcuffs and manacles, then tortured them. When left alone, the two young men used their *kamal* (magical powers) to remove their restraints but were too injured and weak from torture to escape. So they killed their guards, seized their guns and held off the military at the checkpoint until finally subdued by tear gas and crushed by an armored personnel carrier." This account demonstrates two common themes in martyrdom narratives. First, most of them are set in the city. The city was an exceedingly dangerous locale for rebel fighters because it was fully controlled by the Philippine military, which patrolled the streets and manned numerous checkpoints. A number of rebels were caught and killed by the military in a similar fashion, and Muslim urban communities often suffered reprisals after such incidents for suspicion of harboring rebels. Second, this story takes note of the supernatural powers possessed by rebel fighters, who made use of charms, amulets, and esoteric knowledge to acquire magical abilities and protect themselves from blades and bullets. Ultimately, however, magical protection only allowed rebels to fight harder for the cause, and their deaths proved only that their time had come to sacrifice themselves. Although impervious to bullets because of their strong supernatural protection, these two fighters eventually succumbed to tear gas and tank treads.

While stories such as this one of the martyrdom of rank-and-file fighters were universally acknowledged by Cotabato Muslims, I found others that were imperfectly shared. The first and most frequently told martyrdom narrative I heard in Cotabato was that of Datu Ali, the first commander of the Cotabato rebel forces. By May 1974, Muslim rebels were launching coordinated assaults throughout the province and were reported to be preparing an attack on Philippine military headquarters in Cotabato City. On the eve of the rumored attack, Datu Ali was assassinated and rebel offensives throughout the province faltered. The story told to me on numerous occasions by ordinary Muslim civilians was that Datu Ali was martyred on the eve of a great battle to liberate Cotabato City, and if he hadn't been killed by a government assassin, Philippine Muslims would today be free and independent of Philippine government control.

I was thoroughly surprised to discover much later that this account of Datu Ali's death was not shared by any of the rebel commanders (or former rebel commanders) I interviewed. They reported that Ali was ambushed and killed as the result of an internal power struggle within the rebel leadership. His death was not a martyrdom but murder, an instance of ordinary political violence in Cotabato. Neither did I obtain evidence for any organized effort by rebel leaders to mislead Muslim civilians about the events of Datu Ali's death. Datu Ali was a popular, almost legendary, figure among poor Muslims before his death. He was the son of a commoner family and had been a social bandit of sorts before the rebellion. At the time of his killing the city was swollen with Muslim war refugees, and military assaults on civilians were at their peak. Many poor Muslims saw Datu Ali as the potential savior of the Muslims of Cotabato City and believed he was martyred for his efforts. Some told me that Cotabato City was secretly referred to as Datu Ali City in his honor.

By far the most interesting discrepancy in martyrdom accounts, however, has to do with a special manifestation of divine mercy shown to rebel martyrs, as illustrated in the following narrative: "Previously, when the fighters were killed, their bodies did not smell bad or decompose, even for one entire week. The bodies exuded a pleasant fragrance. They had the scent of flowers. They were martyrs who fought and died for Allah." This observation of divine mercy shown to martyrs is not unique to the Muslim Philippines. I have been told essentially identical stories by Afghans about the magical preservation of the corpses of martyred mujahideen during the war against the Soviets. In Cotabato, however, these perceptions had a distinct perodicity. At one point in the rebellion this mercy ceased, and rebel corpses decomposed just as those of government soldiers. The previous quote continues: "Later, if the rebels fought the soldiers or paramilitaries they would all smell bad; because now it was all just for politics." That perceptual shift on the part of Muslim civilians demarcated the period of 1978 to 1980, a period of the armed rebellion marked by the urbanization of the war, political infighting between rebel factions, and general confusion and disillusionment. Rebel actions had come to resemble "normal" political violence rather than jihad, the fallen were murder victims, not martyrs, and as a result divine mercy had been withdrawn.

From 1978 to 1980, what had always been a dirty war became an extraordinarily messy one as well. Already by 1977 there were numbers of rebel defectors in the city who had surrendered to the government for promises of cash payments which often never materialized. Those more larcenous among the defectors had taken up extortion and kidnapping to earn money. Kidnappings of members of wealthy families became a regular occurrence in the city, often instigated by powerful Christian Filipinos who had hired defectors to carry them out. Poor Muslims, however, suffered most regularly from the extortions of the defectors, some of whom developed protection rackets to extort money from Muslim street vendors. In late 1977 a cease-fire was arranged between the military and rebel forces. Rebel units moved down from the hills into camps close to the city. Some units disbanded and former fighters entered the city, joining the rebel defectors already there.

Within four months the cease-fire collapsed and rebel camps were attacked by the military. From then on, the war took a form that, while less intense, was far more injurious for urban noncombatants. From 1978 to 1980, fighting centered more than ever before on the city, making the streets of the Muslim districts especially hazardous as urban assassins and guerrillas took over the conduct of the war. The military had developed special intelligence units composed mostly of recruited rebel defectors. These operated as death squads, targeting active rebels in the city who had been identified by informers. Urban squads of active rebels, often acting on their own initiative, carried out assassinations of informants and death squad members and conducted bombings of government offices, military installations, and beer halls frequented by soldiers.[4]

The rise in urban violence was not limited to war-related killings. Old feuds were reactivated as private antagonists began to settle long-deferred private scores, and crime-related homicides also increased as military control was eased somewhat in the city. As the result of the flood of high-powered arms into the region in the previous decade and the willingness of penurious government soldiers to sell weapons and ammunition to the highest bidder, the assailants in every sort of violent action possessed greatly enhanced arsenals and commonly attacked their targets on city streets using automatic weapons or hand grenades.[5] The victims left in their wake were as often accidental as intended.

One response of Muslim civilians to this escalation of chaotic urban terror was to deny the signs of martyrdom to rebel fighters. While a belief in the magical preservation of the corpses of slain rebels continued to be expressed by rebel commanders and sanctioned by Islamic clerics, ordinary Muslims refused to recognize the divine evidence of participation in a righteous struggle. Despite rebel leaders' assertions of the integrity of both the armed struggle and the bodies of recently slain fighters, Muslim subordinates observed only deterioration. Where rebel leaders saw martyrs, civilians discerned murder victims. That withdrawal of blessing was an expression of their assessment, based on shared experience, that the extraordinary political struggle against external occupiers had degenerated into a particularly deadly form of the all-too-ordinary violence associated with "normal" political activity. Unsurprisingly, the Muslim nationalist cause saw its lowest levels of support during this period. Substantial popular backing was only recovered some years later in a reconstituted form through the strenuous efforts of a coalition of Muslim clerics and politicians to build a broad-based political movement for Muslim autonomy.

Incomprehensible Terror and the Meaning of Violent Death

Two observations may be made in respect to the escalation of urban terror and the responses made to it by the ordinary Muslim noncombatants who were so often its victims. First, the chaotic nature of the extraordinary violence witnessed and experienced by ordinary Muslims, while unusually pronounced in Cotabato City in the years between 1978 and 1980, resembles circumstances found in numerous weak states[6] in the postcolonial world and raises a methodological problem for those attempting to discern "state" terror. The urban terror of 1978–1980 was largely incomprehensible to ordinary Muslim noncombatants because they were unable easily to distinguish sides in the urban war, especially as it was oftentimes fought between Muslim separatist rebels and former rebels who had defected to the Philippine government. Equally difficult, however, was differentiating between civilian victims of political (usually state) terror and the (often unintended) victims of privately motivated malice. In the years after 1978 (as before the declaration of martial law in 1972 and continuing to the present), assassinations, grudge killings, extortions, and kidnappings were carried out routinely and with impunity in Cotabato, often by the agents of powerful individuals, many of whom held some governmental position.[7] If apprehended by local authorities, a well-connected suspect in such a case would rarely spend long in custody. The escape rate at the Cotabato City jail for those charged with serious crimes approached 100 percent. Those witnessing the intended and unintended consequences of this privately motivated violence usually had no clear means of distinguishing it from political terror, nor did this ethnographer.[8]

One especially dreadful form of urban terror may serve to illustrate the point. Between 1978 and 1982 there were at least three separate incidents of grenades exploding in crowded movie theaters, killing and injuring patrons. When I arrived in 1985, city residents still talked about these incidents and many remained hesitant to attend theaters. In each case, a hand grenade had apparently been propped under an empty theater seat with its pin pulled. Lowering the seat caused the grenade to be released, roll a short ways, and explode.

There were numerous theories offered suggesting potential perpetrators but no solid evidence ever surfaced to identify those responsible for these acts of terror. The local newspaper blamed Muslim separatist "terrorists." Yet it was difficult to understand why Muslim separatist rebels would direct such an attack on a theater audience that, on average, would be composed equally of Muslims and Christians.[9] Many Muslims saw the attacks as the work of Philippine army operatives attempting to discredit the Muslim separatist movement. They pointed to the timing of some of the attacks, which tended to coincide with critical points in official negotiations between the government and rebel leaders to settle the separatist rebellion. Equally plausible, however, was the possibility that these attacks were parts of privately motivated schemes to extort money from the relatively wealthy families that owned local movie theaters. City residents had no way of knowing the intentions behind these acts of terror. Once again, the medium — hand grenades — provided the only clear message. Those terribly indiscriminating weapons of war had been turned cruelly on noncombatants in the very place that served as a refuge for so many ordinary citizens from the heat, din, dirt, and violence of the streets of Cotabato City.

A second observation concerns the responses of Muslim noncombatants to urban terror and reconnects considerations of civilians as both victims of terror and witnesses to terror. As long as separatist rebels protected — or were viewed as attempting to protect — ordinary Muslims from state terror in the form of Philippine army depredations and reprisals, martyrdom (and its attendant blessings) was bestowed on slain rebel fighters, even when not warranted by the available facts. Early in the war, the assassinated Datu Ali was viewed by ordinary Muslims as a martyr despite clear evidence that he was murdered as the result of political infighting within the rebel ranks. Datu Ali received his martyrdom because he (and by extension those under his command) was perceived to have been fighting not only on their behalf, but in their defense.

With the urbanization of the war, however, rebels not only were unable to protect Muslim civilians but could indirectly cause them harm through gun battles in city streets. Not only was it hard for civilians to discern sides in the urban fighting, it was also extremely difficult to identify the perpetrators or even the motivations behind actions that harmed noncombatants. Grudge murders were virtually impossible to distinguish from political assassinations, armed clashes between hired gunmen resembled street battles between government units and rebel fighters. Most of the urban violence had thus begun to take familiar forms from the pre-rebellion era, but with a sinister new twist: the weapons employed were far more injurious to civilians. The chaos and incomprehensibility of the extraordinary urban violence left ordinary Muslims stunned and often unable to assign meaning to victimizations (as in the case of the theater bombings). But chaos did not produce a paralysis of either imagination or action. The denial of martyrdom was a strategic response to the escalation of urban assaults of all kinds. The marked increase of civilian victims in dubious incidents of violence meant there were to be no more martyrs at all.

Conclusion

One obvious imperative of an ethnography of terror is to counter the objectification of victims of terror by providing analytical alternatives to sense-deadening reportage from such media sites of terror as Rwanda or Bosnia or Chechnya — reports that add insult to obscenity in their presentation of victims as interchangeable assemblages of anguished faces, afflicted bodies, or desecrated corpses. Such a task, however, is even more difficult than one might imagine, given the evident methodological and ethical problems of conducting ethnographic research concerned with extreme violence, brutality, and suffering. There is, in addition, the problem of the appropriate analytical stance for the ethnographic study of situations of terror. How does one, for example, negotiate a course between an overly identified, partisan perspective and a coldly detached outlook toward a particular case of violent social conflict? Tacking too far in either direction invites serious analytical difficulties.

As professional chroniclers of undesirables and outsiders, it would be most surprising if ethnographers did not in the main identify with the aspirations of those who struggle for liberation from state terror and domination. All the same, ardent identification with a particular liberation movement runs the great risk of succumbing to what Sherry Ortner has termed "the impulse to sanitize the internal politics of the dominated" (1995:179), leading to an inadequate analysis of such movements. There is a sense in which ordinary noncombatants do often stand "between two armies" (Stoll 1993) and may possess significantly different intentions and perceptions than those who claim to be fighting in their name.[10] Exclusive attention to the official politics of resistance to state terror ignores the internal political complexities of such movements, especially the often camouflaged conflicts between local-level concerns of civilian supporters and the "national" interests of movement leaders (see McKenna 1996). A separate problem is that, with the current analytical fascination with free-floating signifiers, practitioners of an anthropology of liberation face the charge of "essentializing": employing such terms as "state," "rebel," "peasant" — even "victim" — too uncritically and assuming that they refer to some concrete, categorical reality.

An alternative (though not necessarily antagonistic) stance is to seek interpretive distance, usually by approaching situations of terror as cultural texts, exploring the grammars of political violence and the construction of cultures of terror. In such analyses, an ironic detachment is cultivated which, while not precluding the expression of sympathies, places the analyst far above the fray and usually well beyond the direct consideration of issues of political liberation.

Such efforts at distancing, however, bring their own analytical problems. For one, analyses of cultures as texts, punctuated as they often are by literary allusions and displays of arid cleverness, can seem especially frivolous when applied to the study of terror — an area of research marked by the most deadly immediacy and materiality. At the extreme, such an approach may leach the humanity out of an ethnographic case of political violence, resulting in the objectification of one's research subjects equivalent in its own way to that achieved on the nightly news (see Jenkins 1992).

The complications associated with this distancing might seem worthwhile if such treatments produced consistently incisive analyses of situations of terror. Unhappily, though, the extreme hesitancy to "essentialize" has tended to produce analyses of a type described by Terry Eagleton as one "so endlessly qualified that it disappears up its own subtlety" (1994:28). While it is prudent to approach all social categorizations with caution, overnuanced analyses of political violence carry their own analytical distortions and produce mostly indeterminacy.

I do not presume to know the location of the happy medium for ethnographers of situations of terror, should one indeed exist. The case from Cotabato does, however, suggest a way to avoid some of the more obvious obstacles to effective analysis. First, as also evidenced in other studies (see, for example, Sluka 1989 and 1995; Warren 1993), conventional, community-based, ethnographic research provides greater opportunity for obtaining local-level interpretations and perceptions of extraordinary violence, which may differ from the authorized views of antistate forces. Recording the ways in which community residents speak to one another about the violence visited upon them in both its extraordinary and everyday versions is almost always a problem-laden task in ethnograpic situations marked by unspeakable horrors, forcible silencings, and self-censorship. Yet ethnographic approaches focused on victims as both creative and strategic actors repay those efforts with analytical insights. The imaginative narratives of martyrdom told by Cotabato Muslims not only expressed their understandings of the terror they were experiencing but also provided a means to "transform experience into agency" (Rebel 1989:362). By bestowing martyrdom upon Datu Ali early in the war, ordinary Muslims expressed their preference for a leader from the masses and their requirement for relief from the oppressive military occupation of their communities. By denying martyrdom to rebel fighters in the later stages of the armed rebellion, civilians expressed their withdrawal of active political support for those who fought in their name because their violence had become far too injurious to Muslims but also far too ordinary in its political intentions.

In examining the cultural construction of terror, it is also critical to focus on unauthorized narratives of terror as not only imaginative but instrumental expressions. Those who study situations of terror as cultural texts are intent to point out that "the creative force of human emotion . . . empowers people in political action" (Aretxaga 1993:24). But in investigating the grammar of terror and its emotional force for those both applying and resisting it, one must be careful not to neglect either the other sorts of cultural and material forces associated with terror or the complex motivations, actions, and reactions of those engulfed in it. Equal attention needs to be paid on the one hand to the quotidian aims and survival strategies that influence the perceptions and actions of individuals and on the other to the profound cultural and material constraints that may place them in double binds and impel them against their will down political blind alleys.

The imaginative narratives of ordinary Muslim noncombatants in Cotabato were not only refusals of official reality but also charters for action, in that divine decisions to withdraw the signs of martyrdom sanctioned popular choices to withhold particular types of political support to the separatist movement. The insight this ethnographic case provides for an anthropology of terror is that, in attempting to uncover the meanings hidden in grammars of terror mostly constructed by the official forces of terror and resistance, we must be careful to give full credence to the softly voiced expressions and unauthorized efforts of those attempting to liberate themselves day by day from the grip of armed coercion.

Notes

1. There are important exceptions to this tendency (see, for example, Sluka 1989 and 1995). Contributors to this volume are also working to bridge this gap (see especially the chapters by Mahmood and Pettigrew in this volume).

2. I use the phrase "ordinary Muslims" in three intermingled senses to refer to three overlapping categories of persons. "Ordinary Muslims" refers first to those Cotabato Muslims (the great majority) who comprise the subordinate (or "lower") classes — those who occupy similarly disadvantaged positions in the regional system of resource distribution. In respect to relations of production almost all may be classified as peasants, low-skilled wage-workers, or petty producers or service providers in the urban informal economy. Second, "ordinary Muslims" refers to those Cotabato Muslims who are not political elites. In its third sense, "ordinary Muslims" refers to those Cotabato Muslims who do not possess a highly objectified Islamic consciousness. A detailed discussion of the ethnoreligious consciousness of ordinary Muslims in Cotabato may be found in McKenna (1998).

3. Although the Islamic and anticolonial character of the juramentado is stressed in most accounts (see, e.g., Majul 1973; Gowing 1983), it is important to note that very similar traditions of ritual suicide (referred to generally as *amok*) were found throughout the Malay world and predated both Islam and European colonialism in the region (Reid 1988:125).

4. On 9 September 1978, the Cotabato City weekly newspaper reported 200 casualties throughout the region of Cotabato in the previous month as the result of "an increase in violence." The dead and wounded included 18 government soldiers, 52 "terrorists," and 130 civilians.

5. Prior to 1972, the most typical weapon used in urban grudge killings was a homemade "zipgun" or single-shot .22-caliber pistol.

6. Joel Migdal defines a weak state as one with relatively low capabilities to "penetrate society, regulate social relationships, extract resources, and appropriate or use resources in determined ways" (1988:4).

7. In the summer of 1995, in Manila as well as in Cotabato City, newspapers reported an epidemic of kidnappings and extortions of wealthy individuals, most of them said to be carried out by individuals connected either with local police forces or the Philippine military.

8. To be sure, the line between political and privately motivated violence is not sharp, especially as motives for working violence may overlap. These are terms of convenience used to differentiate two ideal-typical motivations for employing violent means to achieve desired ends. Nevertheless, the privately motivated kidnappings, assassinations, and grudge killings ordered or carried out by agents of the Philippine state are, in theory, distinguishable from the activities of paramilitary death squads in that their principal motives are private economic gain or

personal revenge rather than political advantage. For a fascinating discussion of the private armed forces possessed by public officials in the Philippines see Mc-Coy (1993).

9. Muslims made up just under half of the population of Cotabato City in 1985, and movies were a relatively inexpensive form of entertainment much enjoyed by urban Muslims.

10. At the same time, and as I have noted above, ordinary noncombatants in dirty wars most often do not see themselves as suspended at some midpoint between contending state and antistate forces. More commonly, they identify themselves with one or another side (usually the antistate forces) and are victimized far more by one of the forces in the conflict. Civilian support for liberation forces of various kinds is often, in fact, predicated on those forces defending civilians from state-sponsored aggression (see, for example, McKenna 1996 and 1998; Sluka 1989 and 1995).

Bibliography

Aretxaga, Begoña
    1993 "Striking with Hunger: Cultural Meanings of Political Violence in Northern Ireland." In *The Violence Within: Cultural and Political Opposition in Divided Nations*. Kay Warren, ed. Boulder, Colo.: Westview Press.
Eagleton, Terry
    1994 "Goodbye to the Enlightenment." *Guardian Weekly*, March 6, p. 28.
Feldman, Allen
    1991 *Formations of Violence: The Narrative of the Body and Political Terror in Northern Ireland*. Chicago: University of Chicago Press.
Gowing, Peter Gordon
    1983 *Mandate in Moroland: The American Government of Muslim Filipinos, 1899–1920*. Quezon City: New Day Publishers.
Houtsma, M. Th.
    1987 *E. J. Brill's First Encyclopedia of Islam, 1913–1936*. Leiden: E. J. Brill.
Jenkins, Richard
    1992 "Doing Violence to the Subject." *Current Anthropology*, 33, pp. 233–235.
Kiefer, Thomas M.
    1972 *The Tausug: Violence and Law in a Philippine Muslim Society*. New York: Holt, Rinehart and Winston.
Majul, Cesar Adib
    1973 *Muslims in the Philippines*. Manila: St. Mary's Publishing.
McCoy, Alfred W.
    1993 " 'An Anarchy of Families': The Historiography of State and Family in the Philippines." In *An Anarchy of Families: State and Family in the Philippines*. Alfred McCoy, ed. Madison: Center for Southeast Asian Studies, University of Wisconsin.
McKenna, Thomas M.
    1998 *Muslim Rulers and Rebels: Everyday Politics and Armed Separatism in the Southern Philippines*. Berkeley: University of California Press.
    1996 " 'Fighting for the Homeland': National Ideas and Rank-and-File Experience in the Muslim Separatist Movement in the Philippines." *Critique of Anthropology*, 16:3, pp. 229–255.

Migdal, Joel S.
1988 *Strong Societies and Weak States: State-Society Relations and State Capabilities in the Third World.* Princeton: Princeton University Press.
Nordstrom, Carolyn
1992 "The Backyard Front." In *The Paths to Domination, Resistance, and Terror.* Carolyn Nordstrom and JoAnn Martin, eds. Berkeley: University of California Press.
Ortner, Sherry B.
1995 "Resistance and the Problem of Ethnographic Refusal." *Comparative Studies in Society and History,* 37, pp. 173–193.
Rebel, Hermann
1989 "Cultural Hegemony and Class Experience: A Critical Reading of Recent Ethnological-Historical Approaches." (Parts I and II). *American Ethnologist,* 16: 1–2, pp. 117–136 and 350–365.
Reid, Anthony
1988 *Southeast Asia in the Age of Commerce: 1450–1680. Volume One: The Lands Below the Winds.* New Haven: Yale University Press.
Sluka, Jeffrey A.
1995 "Domination, Resistance and Political Culture in Northern Ireland's Catholic-Nationalist Ghettos." *Critique of Anthropology,* 15:1, pp. 71–102.
1989 *Hearts and Minds, Water and Fish: Support for the IRA and INLA in a Northern Irish Ghetto.* London: JAI Press.
Stoll, David
1993 *Between Two Armies in the Ixil Towns of Guatemala.* New York: Columbia University Press.
Suarez-Orozco, Marcelo
1992 "A Grammar of Terror: Psychocultural Responses to State Terrorism in Dirty War and Post–Dirty War Argentina." In *The Paths to Domination, Resistance, and Terror.* Carolyn Nordstrom and JoAnn Martin, eds. Berkeley: University of California Press.
Warren, Kay B.
1993 "Interpreting *La Violencia* in Guatemala: Shapes of Mayan Silence and Resistance." In *The Violence Within: Cultural and Political Opposition in Divided Nations.* Kay Warren, ed. Boulder, Colo.: Westview Press.
Zulaika, Joseba
1988 *Basque Violence: Metaphor and Sacrament.* Reno: University of Nevada Press.

Chapter 8
Parents and Their Children in Situations of Terror
Disappearances and Special Police Activity in Punjab

Joyce Pettigrew

> When evildoing comes like falling rain, nobody calls out "stop!"
> When crimes begin to pile up they become invisible.
> When sufferings become unendurable the cries are no longer heard.
> (Brecht 1976:247)

In 1984 Indian government forces attacked the precincts of the Darbar Sahib (Golden Temple) complex causing immense loss of human life and damage to the buildings therein. Code-named Operation Bluestar, this attack had been planned for some months beforehand and was timed for an important day in the Sikh calendar when thousands of pilgrims would be expected to be present as well as many people on an outing with their families. Exact casualties have never been known. This attack was followed swiftly by army combing operations in the villages of the Punjab (Operation Woodrose) when many young people disappeared. The army operation did not attack solely individual human beings in their finiteness. Nor were the buildings that were destroyed and damaged mere buildings. They were the collective belongings of all Sikhs as a people, symbolic of their temporal and spiritual sovereignty and of a political tradition which holds that political power has no authority if not based on justice nor can such justice survive without political sovereignty. The violent events of June–September 1984, together with the massacre of Sikhs in India's major cities in November 1984, and the daily terror families subsequently experienced in Punjab's villages were factors in the rise of resistance in the

Punjab. A *Sarbat Khalsa* (general congregation of the Sikh people) was convened in Amritsar in January 1986 which passed a resolution favoring an independent Sikh state (Khalistan), and on 29 April 1986 the Declaration Document of Khalistan was signed and presented to the world. With this development the Indian state's legitimacy had been contested and a counterstate proposed. Such action was deemed traitorous.

The Context for Counterinsurgency Operations in the Rural Punjab

Indian Punjab is adjacent to Pakistan. It produces most of India's wheat. Its inhabitants, predominantly Sikh, have shown their commitment to India in all of its wars and participated actively in its institutional life. Particularly ruralite Sikhs have high positions in the defense forces, civil administration, police, and foreign service. Politically and economically incorporated into India, the Sikhs are also culturally allied through language, literature, and architecture to the Muslim Punjab. Moreover, in the Punjab region the pragmatic concerns of patronage, friendship, and kinship ties rather than state loyalty were a major impact on political alliances. Boundary-making in this region was a comparatively recent event. India and Pakistan became states only in 1947. With this development the region between Delhi and the banks of the Indus River lost its character as frontier territory spanning the divide between the fertile plains of Hindustan and the arid lands of central Asia. The Sikh part of the Punjab became a borderland between the Islamic lands of West Asia and Hindu civilization. In these circumstances the state, as an institution, was fragile. Hence, as support for armed resistance to the Indian state grew in the Sikh rural areas, there was sufficient reason for the Indian state to respond with overwhelming force. Illegal detention, disappearance, false encounter (a fictitious armed engagement as a cover up for police killing of a detainee) became daily events. Such disappearances and illegal detentions continue to occur.

The special units of police which operated in the rural areas did not do so on behalf of class or elite interests. They operated on behalf of the counterinsurgency policy of the Indian state, their purpose being to detach the civilian population from close contact with the guerrillas by generating sufficient fear within that population. Wickham-Crowley (1990:225–230) shows with reference to Latin American data that when there is "a large overlap between the civilian population and the combatants," government terror against the civilian population is "common" and "massive." This was also true of rural Punjab.

The initial aim of security policy was to silence the countryside. As Taussig (1992:27) reminds us, "the point about silencing and the fear behind silencing is not to erase memory. Far from it. The point is to drive the memory deep within the fastness of the individual so as to create more fear and uncertainty." A lesson was being taught to the villagers that while the guerrillas were in their midst, no peace would be possible. Raids and operations within the rural areas were not aimed at active fighters alone but at their civilian population base, the intent being to create distance between the guerrillas and a population angry that it could not be protected. Hence terror was directed against entire areas and their populations. In that regard special units of police operated all over the Punjab but were particularly concentrated in the border districts and in areas where a particular guerrilla leader had massive popular support. Counterinsurgency activity provoked premature outbreaks of fighting so that those associated with the independence movement in whatever ca-pacity could be identified. Special units then went in to eliminate them. There was a joint purpose.

In the post-1984 years young people became fighers because of their ideological commitment to the Sikh nation. Subsequently they joined the resistance movement because of indiscriminate repression affecting both themselves and their families. A further wave joined because guerrillas, in the words of Stoll speaking of the Ixil of Guatemala (1993:30), "were ineffective in defending their supporters." Largely this was so because they were unable or unwilling, unlike the Basques (see Laitin 1995:25), to "police defectors" from within their own ranks. In these circumstances the state was able to create successfully a situation where guerrilla units could not be distinguished from police units by the rural population. Those who were recruited to the special units infiltrated the various guerrilla groups, masquerading as militants, and were an intrinsic part of the overall counterinsurgency effort. Bonds between fighter and farmer were broken as these counterinsurgents involved themselves in land dis-putes and factional rivalries, thereby heightening the traditional divi-sions within rural society. Their actions in this respect caused confusion as to who were the real militants.

Once there was adequate chaos and disorder, the issue of criminal violence and political violence became blurred. Disorder has its own rules wherein, as Taussig puts in (1992:17), "the arbitrariness of power is practiced as an exquisitely fine art of social control." Those with influ-ence in the villages who were sympathetic to the militant movement, but law abiding and moderate, were subject to robbery, kidnapping, and murder from 1989 on. Responsibility for these attacks would be claimed by an organization claiming to be militant. So, as with other movemens of armed resistance, guerrilla networks were not just destroyed by military measures but also by "spreading around responsibility for the killing" (Stoll 1993:303). One source commented, "The really top guerrillas were under intelligence directives and especially if they were on the wrong tracks (extortion, killing, rape) would be given protection. There were Central Reserve Police Force (CRPF) cordons around where they stayed to keep away the Punjab police."

Locally prominent individuals who had had an initial feeling of solidarity with those fighting for an independent state of Khalistan were shaken by what they took to be the corruption within militant ranks. Any families of standing in the villages left, or they saw to it that their children left, for there was no future for them there. Most could not leave. They had to live without defenses. Those who could afford to sell their land went abroad but, as in the ghetto in Rome where a settled population similarly faced an onslaught of sudden, overwhelming force, "people with more limited means forced themselves to be optimistic about staying" (Stille 1992:189).

Retired army personnel, particularly, appeared to be targeted because of their associational linkages, and many ex-servicemen were kidnapped or had their property raided. Some abandoned their property. Ex-servicemen numbered 600,000 in Punjab and along with serving army personnel were under state surveillance. For various historical reasons they had always been identified with the Sikh nation. Some had mutinied in 1984 and subsequently became members of guerrilla units.[1] Others, on their retirement, had supported political organizations with guerrilla connections.

Special Police Activity in the Rural Areas

Special police operations were a part of overall counterinsurgency policy. Extralegal groups operating on behalf of the state engaged in the abduction of the following categories of person: political activists; persons suspected of having association with them; lawyers[2] who defend families whose human rights have been violated; journalists who write about such violations; and human rights workers who record their complaints. However, the largest body of those held comes from a wide range of persons uninvolved with political activity. Once abducted, they are detained in unofficial interrogation centers which include schools, houses, forest bungalows owned by the Public Works Department (PWD), and a variety of official police buildings belonging to the Central Investigative Agency (CIA) of the Punjab police, the Central Reserve Police Force, and the Border Security Force (BSF). Informants and more recently some written reports[3] have suggested, additionally, that Hindu temples provide facilities for the cremation of political prisoners.

According to my own data political prisoners are taken into custody by a wide range of bodies.[4] The detention is unacknowledged by the security forces. The arrest is denied. No arrest report is indeed filed nor any charge sheet prepared. The person is not produced in court but is held incommunicado. Once in custody, arrested persons therefore can be, and are, subjected to threats and torture. When their families go to the local police station to report their disappearance they are asked for money. The initial act of abduction sets in train a process of illegal custody and torture which often culminates in an extrajudicial execution. It renders the political and judicial process irrelevant. If the arrested person can be of use he is taken around as a spotter.[5] Should young men cooperate as informants or as "cats" (those who masquerade as guerrillas), they can postpone, though not avoid, death.[6] The body is rarely handed back to the family (though in some cases families have retrieved bodies from the railroad tracks and from the canals). It is cremated as that of an unidentified person.

Persons can be picked up and detained in a range of situations: by men in unmarked cars or jeeps, but also in raids, in CRPF or commando operations, in police-army combing operations, or as a consequence of counterinsurgency operations that have been conducted in specific areas. The identity of the abduction group varies. It may be composed of low-ranking police constables accompanied by former militants who have been brought over, by those designated as "cats," or it may comprise police in mixed groups. It may be a single unit of either the BSF, the CPRF, or the CIA. Whatever their composition, the gunmen concerned subsequently prove to be unidentifiable. However, their activities have identifiable effects on families: the disappearance,[7] torture, and frequent extrajudicial killing of their sons either in cross fire[8] or in an encounter. Such activites have been documented by international human rights bodies and the United Nations.[9] They have rarely been documented by anthropology which, as Nagengast (1994:112) notes, "has not been in the forefront of the study of collective violence, terrorism and especially violence in state societies . . . because its methods and theory depend on months and years in the field until recently defined as a relatively small self contained community that did not include the state."

According to a village informant with much experience of police activity (the father of Harjit Singh, whose case was taken up by Amnesty International and is discussed on p. 214):

Those directly responsible for kidnappings, interrogations, disappearances, and actual eliminations are not merely the various units of commandos belonging to the police and army. There exist certain hit squads. They are sometimes dressed in khaki uniform and turban [of the Punjab police] though they can be in plain clothes. Whichever district police officer needs them, is free to use them. Some police are indeed members of these units. However, they are not under the control, direction, or otherwise responsible to, the district police chiefs.[10] They have no identification by way of rank or number and in kidnappings and other operations usually operate in mixed groups comprised of the Punjab police, CRPF, BSF, and commando units. They have access to and can command use of the various police stations and indeed of any building such as schools and even Hindu temples. They can command use of any vehicle. They operate from cars which either have Chandigarh number plates or which have no number plates.

That such a category of police with special duties exists in Punjab has never exactly been concealed from Punjab's population. In the early years of the insurgency these were more under the control of the district police chiefs. For example, the *Punjabi Tribune* of 10 October 1989 gives on page 10 a picture of a policeman assigned for undercover work and to whom special protection has been given. The authority letter, signed by the then senior superintendent of police (SSP) of Kapurthala, says the following: "the bearer of this authority letter has been assigned with some special task and as such he may please be rendered every sort of facilities required by him and if something adverse against him comes to your notice, the undersigned may be consulted before taking any action against him."

What most distinguishes members of special police units from ordinary police is that they are permitted to function outside their normal areas of jurisdiction and are directly responsible only to their superiors, whoever they may be, and that on the authority of these superiors they can command use of facilities and of cooperation whether it be military or paramilitary. Thus raids on homes in any one district might not be conducted by the local district police but by police from other districts, put together in a special unit. They are operational units with great mobility who do no routine police work and who also live in special accommodations, that is, not police accommodations.

Routine Policing, Special Police, and Counterinsurgency

Routine policing involves day and night searches, vehicle checks, surprise sealing of areas, area searches,[11] raids on active hideouts, guarding of key installations and key crossing points where canal and road meet. Normal policing also can involve cooperation with the army, who man checkpoints on link roads, and with the CRPF in combined operations. In these respects, therefore, it is meaningless to differentiate either the police and CRPF from the plainclothes units which families so fear, for they provide the infrastructure enabling the latter to operate. Hence legal and illegal force cannot be distinguished. In many ways ordinary policing has effects for families similar to those of the abduction squads — innocent travellers may be picked up on suspicion after a bomb blast or at a checkpoint. They are never seen again, even though they have not been targeted.

Innocent persons were otherwise targeted for elimination because militants came to them for food and shelter.[12] Moreover, ordinary police accompanied these special police units to give directions as to the whereabouts of houses and persons and thereby aided them in the discharge of their duties. The CRPF guarded the entire area when these units were on operations and on occasion were used as a reserve. Where specific information was obtained as to the whereabouts of certain militants, the services of a CRPF battallion would be enlisted. When, for reasons of wider intelligence policy, attacks on trains and buses were planned, cover was provided by the CRPF. Likewise when these units operated on the border they used the facilities of the BSF, though the latter did not enter villages.

One suspects, in the case of special police units, that their activities were under some form of central control, as only central forces were informed about their operations and that, too, minutes before they were about to occur. According to one informant it was military intelligence which gathered the information on which much of the counterinsurgency activity and special police operations were based. This one would expect. In all counterinsurgency activity, intelligence networks from the police, army, and paramilitary structures collude to achieve a single policy against which nonviolent forms of struggle and individual combat actions taken by guerrillas are meaningless.

Punjab's police, being a community police linked to the rural population by kinship, affinal, and friendship ties, was totally porous. It is certainly significant that so long as suspects were in local police custody, information leaked out to their families as to their whereabouts through these networks. However, precisely because of their location within the community, certain policemen of rural background, usually those low in status and initially low in rank but high in local area knowledge, would be coopted into abduction squads. Some were subsequently promoted to the rank of SSP or superintendent of police (SP). In that capacity they would be responsible for recruiting a network for special operations. According to one source, "they were carefully selected for their loyalty from cats and Punjab's constables and their operations done under the protection of the CRPF. Those who had to be blackmailed to give their support were never rewarded. The director general of police's [DGP's] policy toward those bought for special operations was protect, support, use, and then kill."

Summing up, it may be said that the government uses those recruited into special units in different ways. Undoubtedly factional and family animosities within the villages are exploited by the state as a way of hindering the development of new loyalties. In its fight against terrorism police interfered in marital disputes[13] and land disputes[14] in the villages, supporting, and hence compromising, one party. False complaints would be registered by one party to a dispute, supported by the state, to the effect that his opponent had links with terrorists. The individual nature of the many quarrels over land between and within families were eclipsed by the widespread use of such quarrels by the police. Disputes spiralled out of control as the police, as instruments of state, used all such conflicts to advance their mission against terrorism. Incidents were processed and converted into a terrorist framework. Police officers could then claim the resulting rewards. In this they were given protection by superior officers and rarely held accountable. In the midst of situations such as these, innocents with no connection to militancy found themselves in desperate trouble.

Villagers' Responses

The collective and ideological response to any form of attack on one's person, community, or family, as influenced by Sikh historical and cultural tradition is one of defiance. However, responses to such violence in the villages have taken on a range of forms. If resistance was common, so also was flight abroad, movement from the village into the town, and becoming an informer. Defiant responses to the state were by no means universal, nor necessarily meaningful, to either small farmers' families in the villages or richer landlords. Except for committed guerrillas, defiance was possible only when there was a measure of protection. The committed became martyrs, and their deaths were commemorated yearly. They belong to the Sikh nation. However, many young people killed have not been engaged in armed combat. They have been ordinary boys who have disappeared on an errand for their parents, visiting relatives, or while working in their fields, or who have been picked up from their own or their in-laws' home. The fears that parents developed for their children in such a situation may be said to be reasonable in the light of their childrens' vulnerability. They were not simply individual fears. Such pain and suffering, as Das (1994:139) notes, is "actively created and distributed by the social order itself."

Disappearances occurred primarily in the under-thirty age group. Some villages had lost more than forty young men. Sursinghwala in Amritsar district had lost seventy young men. Buttar Kalan, in Gurdaspur district, lost twenty. Each village has not kept a separate account of its losses. Erring on the conservative side, but keeping in mind the material emerging from Patti and Tarn Taran, it is highly probable that most villages in the Amritsar district would have lost on average ten young men. Earlier figures also support the notion of a high civilian death toll, according to information given by a journalist once involved with the *Punjabi Tribune* and also with various official contacts in Delhi. In 1991 he had compiled a list of some of Punjab's detention and interrogation centers, giving figures of estimated killings by police and paramilitary forces at these centers for the eighteen months prior to August 1991. The total for this period alone was 9,580.

It is precisely because the state did not expect to inculcate fear easily that it resorted to measures which kept parents in an almost perpetual state of anxiety. A son's disappearance often occurred after the family home had been robbed innumerable times, their tube well and crops destroyed, his education interrupted, and his parents taken to the police station. It was just as likely to occur without warning. Family harassment was an important element in control of the civilian population. To this end a boy would be released from custody, often temporarily, with the marks of torture visibly apparent on him. Duncan Forrest, an eminent pediatric surgeon, notes that "Tortures of whatever form are communications and are intended to leave their meanings within the victims in the permanent damage both to their bodies and to their minds" (1996:119). I would add that they are also intended to leave a meaning with their families. Women were frequently picked up in place of their husband or son. As Zulaika and Douglass (1996:194) note, "Each victim implies the victimization of an entire family." Sudden, precipitate disappearance was the worst terror parents experienced. An SSP who had once been in charge of Amritsar and Tarn Taran police districts admitted in an article ("After bullets and encounters try civic action," *The Tribune*, 13 October 1992) that "the worst fear which gripped the people was elimination of the boys by the police in encounters. Third degree methods used by the police during interrogation is another fear which haunts the people. Another sensitive issue pertains to those who are bailed out. The police whisks them away."

That low-ranking ex-servicemen, widows with little education, and farmers with not much land would dare to question the circumstances of their childrens' treatment by various police authorities perhaps explains the need of these authorities to create fear and terror. Arrested young people are moved around Punjab's CIA centers but rarely kept in any one of them for long. Many of the arrested were housed in bungalows, clinics, and schools and some in CRPF stations. They cannot therefore be contacted by relatives, the aim being to prevent or reduce any form of intervention, judicial or parental, in the interrogation process. They are kept on the move until the order comes to eliminate them. One militant from Amritsar district spoke of a pattern whereby people picked up in Faridkot district would be killed in Amritsar district, and vice versa. Likewise, Stanley (1996:1) reports for El Salvador that "families of victims sometimes found their loved ones' heads and bodies had been dumped in separate departments of the country." All deaths conducted by special police squads have such a national scope.

Any notice that was paid to police power has to be placed in the context of village social relations. Epstein's point (1992:22) is a pertinent one, namely, that it is essential to explore not only the kinds of situation that elicit or provoke a given emotional response but also the sorts of social relations of the parties involved in a particular situation." Special reference has to be made in this respect to the factionalism within villages and to their lack of corporate identity. Villagers have little possibility of building up trust amongst themselves on the basis of their membership in a local unit. Some are involved in state institutions, specifically the army police and civil service, and have loyalties developed from this type of association. Additionally, one's neighbor might be willing to give false information on one's family in the course of reactivating old enmities. For these reasons, during the period of state repression after 1984, the village became a setting for fear. There were no sure ways of distinguishing friends from enemies. Parents' fears for their children were magnified by the separateness of the family inside the village. Immediate kin might be distant. If sympathetic, they and friends were the sole hiding places for fugitive youngsters. Young people who had been picked up innumerable times by the police and badly tortured might be enrolled by their parents in colleges outside the Punjab, if they had the qualifications and their parents the resources. However, the police would continue to raid the family home and pick up brothers and aged parents in their place.

Villages in Punjab were units significant for revenue purposes alone and were never units of symbolic attachment for their inhabitants. Hence the state could increasingly and successfully treat them as ghettos against which they would plan attacks, in which they would target arrests and killings, descending on these settlements in large numbers.[15]

Emotional displays of fear from any member of a village family on such occasions were rare. There were several reasons for this. First, such emotions can rarely be vocalized since Sikh national identity finds expression, ideologically, through resistance to Delhi. Hence any emotional articulation of fear would not have been acceptable. Moreover, any such expression would have been regarded as indulgent, since so many other parents had similar experiences. Additionally, in rural Sikh culture, the expression of fear is associated with shame. For these three reasons, fear surfaces in ways that are respectable. For example, indicators of parental anxiety emerge in parents' concrete actions when their children disappear. Anxieties surface in telegrams[16] to the president and prime minister of India, the governor of Punjab, and, in some cases, international human rights bodies. Parents' procedural responses to tragedy continue when they are told, eventually, that their son was killed in cross fire, in custody, or in an encounter, usually false. Postmortem reports and affidavits[17] requiring the signatures of a doctor and a lawyer are obtained and letters are sent to influential MPs and judges.[18] Hearings are demanded with the senior superintendent of police and the deputy commissioner of the district concerned. In this procedural process the family is sustained by relatives and, in cases where they have had to abandon their land and home due to police harassment, by the Sikh religious structure. During 1996 the number of cases taken out in court against the Punjab police, the State of Punjab, and specific members of the Central Investigative Agency increased.

Families were without a traditional framework into which they could place their fears and have them explained. Although they were conscious of a religious framework to use to combat fear, they had none to describe the fear that they felt on a daily basis. The fears generated by the threat of sudden disappearance happening in the most mundane of places — at a bus stop, or at a road junction, for example — were of a different order from the tension and anxiety created by family and factional feuds. The latter had a certain time span to them. They did not always necessitate constant vigilance. And even in the midst of village enmities there was a time in each day when one could go to the tube well or sit in one's fruit orchard, drinking tea or country liquor as the sun set. Parents were unaccustomed to the clandestine terror of the contemporary situation, for the activities of the abduction squads could impinge on those who had no direct political involvement. Potentially all young *amritdhari* (baptized) Sikhs were a target.

This situation created fear within the lives of their families, a fear that appeared well justified given the torture practiced in custody, of which medical reports are now emerging (see Forrest 1995). If their son was picked up by plainclothes police, subsequently declared eliminated in cross fire, but then seen alive, as happened in one prominent case — that of Harjit Singh — the pressure and tension of events left a family with no peace and did indeed strike mortal fear. For as one ordinary policeman told Harjit Singh's father, "once you have been shown as eliminated [by forces acting on the instructions of the intelligence services] we [the police] are actually powerless." The following pages of this chapter show in some detail what these conditions of terror have meant for one particular family, the family of Harjit Singh.

Terror and the Family of Harjit Singh

Due to a campaign waged in all countries of western Europe by Amnesty International, Harjit Singh's case received and continues to receive a great deal of attention. I interviewed his father, Kashmir Singh, on 14 and 15 May 1994. Kashmir Singh had been aided in his search for his son by information from friends or sympathizers inside the Punjab police. He also had relatives abroad who had connections with Sikh Human Rights Internet, a body which reports cases to Amnesty International. Additionally, he himself was the son of a freedom fighter. All of these particular points may make this case atypical, in some respects. Yet in so many other ways it is very reflective of the situation parents are in regarding their children. It shows the relentless pressure that is placed on families by the various types of police unit. It illustrates the persistence and resilience of parents in searching for their children. Moreover, Harjit Singh's family is typical of the sort of family from which revolt has come, namely the small and middle farmers whose occupation is supplemented by employment in state institutions, in this case, the Punjab State Electricity Board.

In this particular case a few more resources and protection were available and were channeled into finding out about the son's disappearance. However, all families do what they think is appropriate, in the circumstances, for their children. Poor widows run from pillar to post securing affidavits and sending telegrams about the untoward deaths of their sons in police custody. They can take matters no further. Former army personnel who have lost their sons report their cases to respected army generals. Although their service for India might have involved them in the loss of their life, they now find themselves very cavalierly and disreputably treated. These parents are every bit as heroic as their children, and they are persistent in their pursuit of justice, unknowing of whether their sons merely are illegally detained or in fact have been killed. Indeed, it is because of this multitude of small people refusing to be silenced that the police extend their terror to the families, often silencing them as well. For all parents, their children were good people, so they must fight for them, fearful of what might happen to them and unafraid for themselves. All, equally, have no protection in their villages and have to travel unprotected on the roads. Since Kashmir Singh began court proceedings against the police, state terror has extended to his family: two attempts have been made on his own life, and one of his grandsons was abducted.

Harjit Singh, aged twenty-two, son of Kashmir Singh, was abducted by a number of plainclothes police on 29 April 1992. The reasons for his abduction partially lay in a family vendetta inside the village, yet they were also political. The abduction was organized by a police officer and accomplished by those recruited by him to penetrate local militant networks. These recruits had led him to innumerable militants, as a result of which he had won promotion. The officer concerned had no interest in Harjit Singh, but kidnapping him did not contradict two aspects of state policy. The primary purpose of that policy, as stated, was the pacification of the rural areas. Since there was general sympathy for, and in this area active

support of, the militant movement, the routes taken to achieve that pacification were those of general terror and discreditation. Overall, such abductions, as well as raids, facilitated the expansion of an atmosphere of
terror which was useful in bringing the different parts of Amritsar district
to heel. Baba Bakala was an area in which militants had once offered the
police protection for payment. Now the situation was reversed, and militants had to pay police for their protection. Several militants became
informers and several of these in Harjit's village became part of a group
indulging in rape and extortion, creating the confusion, disorder, and discreditation of the militant cause earlier mentioned. In their fight against
militancy, high-ranking police officials protected the officers who organized abductions such as Harjit's.

Harjit Singh's abduction was witnessed by several people, some of whom
informed his family. His father was told to go to the office of the then
deputy superintendent of police (DSP) of Baba Bakala (subsequently DSP
of Majitha and SP HQ of Amritsar) and that he would find his son at Beas
police station. He traveled there and met the police officer in charge, who
did not produce his son. After making further inquiries, he and a friend
were directed to Gaggarbhana police station on the second of May. There
the police admitted that Harjit Singh had been in their custody, and an
assistant subinspector said he had been sent to Mehta. He asked Kashmir
Singh for a large sum of money to secure his release. On 6 May his father
contacted a relative in England and on 7 May Amnesty International was
informed of his abduction. On 8 May it was confirmed that he was in Mal
Mandi, the CIA's interrogation center in Amritsar. On 12 May, the SP in
charge of Mal Mandi told his father he would need to contact higher
authorities about his son. On 13 May Kashmir Singh read in the newspaper that his son had been killed in cross fire on 12 May. However, as
noted in a 1995 judicial report which was the culmination of a three-year
magisterial inquiry,[19] neither was the postmortem produced, "nor have
any of the witnesses who identified the dead body of Harjit Singh at the
time of the post mortem examination . . . been examined." There was no
doctor to confirm the postmortem report or cremation certificate and no
independent witnesses to identify the body.[20]

Kashmir Singh requested a meeting with the SSP of Majitha, Amritsar
district, but he refused, telling Kashmir Singh he should meet the DSP of
Ajnala. He did so, the latter passing him on to the police officer in charge
of Lopoke police station, and saying Harjit Singh had been killed there.
Kashmir Singh asked the police for his son's clothes and watch, and
requested he be shown his son's dead body. The policeman replied that
he was not compelled to give him anything. Meanwhile, Kashmir Singh
had received information in confidence from a Criminal Investigation

Department (CID) officer that his son was still there in the Lopoke police station. The same day he was moved. On 25 June, while parked outside the CIA building in Kapurthala, his father saw Harjit waving to him from a passing vehicle. He followed it for as long as he could. Subsequently on 9 August a close friend saw him in a CRP jeep. On 13 August a childhood friend who was an official for an agricultural cooperative (and who was himself later eliminated by the police) gained access to Rasulpur jail, Amritsar district, with the help of a police constable who was a friend. He spoke to Harjit. On hearing this, Harjit's father then went to Chandigarh to secure a habeas corpus injunction. A warrant officer was appointed by the high court to search for Harjit Singh on 16 August and a judicial inquiry was ordered to be completed within three months. On 17 October the warrant officer, one R. L. Bhattia, went to Rasulpur. He did not find Harjit Singh there. The police informed him that he had been shifted to the CIA center in Mal Mandi. There, on 19 October, Harjit Singh was seen at a window by his father, who identified him in the presence of the warrant officer. In other words, he was found alive after he had been declared dead five months previously. His father then made a report in the High Court of Punjab, the substance of which was that they were denied entry for a considerable period of time,[21] and when entry was achieved Harjit Singh had been removed once again.

From Mal Mandi, Kashmir Singh and the warrant officer went to see the then SSP of Majitha, PS Gill, an officer with a military background. According to Kashmir Singh, Gill told him, "because of your activities your son will never be able to return home alive." This statement is not exceptional. Those who involved the judicial authorities in what the police considered were its own affairs became the object of particular ire. He went to see the relatives of the policemen concerned as well as the sister-in-law of the police chief but was warned to stay out of police matters. In a letter to the prime minister his lawyer wrote that, subsequent to 17 October, Kashmir Singh had sighted his son four times.[22] Meanwhile, in the village the police spoiled his newly cut wheat field and threatened the life of his grandson.

The intimidation and threats that Kashmir Singh and his family experienced were also extended to his lawyer. On one occasion police surrounded his house, threatening to take the life of his child. Courtroom gossip also had it that he had been given inducements to leave the case. As a result, when Kashmir Singh reported the aforementioned events to him, he refused to record his statement. The police also came to the house of the warrant officer, issuing him, too, with a warning against making any statement, as a result of which, on 21 October, he reported the matter to the advocate general. The police, in the person of Darshan

Singh Mann, DSP of Baba Bakala, approached the bench and said that Kashmir Singh was mad, dreaming that he just saw his son wherever he went. Mr. Bhattia submitted his report on the twenty-first, and on the basis of that the judge insisted that the police present Harjit in court. Darshan Singh Mann submitted affidavits that he had been caught on 11 October and killed on the twelfth. On 31 October the SSP of Majitha submitted his affidavit and confirmed Mann's reports. They brought along with them a postmortem report.

The team of five lawyers representing Harjit's case in court was headed by a Hindu lawyer, Ranjan Lakhanpal, the son of an old freedom fighter against the British. He questioned the judge why Amnesty International should lie about an abduction. The judge, Mrs. H. K. Sandhu, reserved judgment on 10 December 1992, and on the sixteenth she ordered an investigation into the whereabouts of Harjit Singh and that it be held on 24 January 1993 at Amritsar District Sessions Court. On that date there were hundreds of police around the court and Kashmir Singh claimed that he feared for the lives of his witnesses and of his own family. He filed a new petition to have the inquiry done in Chandigarh. This was granted. However, from 27 January 1993 until the present there have been innumerable dates when witnesses could not obey summonses to attend the court, either because they had been murdered or because of intimidation.[23] On several occasions the various parties presented themselves before the court but the judge was not present. At other times there were adjournments of hearings because the relevant police and government officials were not present.[24] The family of Harjit Singh continues to be harrassed. On 12–13 May 1994 two plainclothes police visited the school of the four-year-old son of Harjit Singh. They reportedly demanded to take him away, but the teacher refused (Amnesty International 1995a:3). On 2 August 1994 the judge conducting the case was promoted. Since that date there have been fourteen hearings scheduled but only six have taken place (Amnesty International, ibid.). The young son of his second lawyer was killed "in an accident" in 1995.

As Harjit Singh's father took the case into the international forum, Darshan Singh Mann demanded a 200,000 rupee bribe from his erstwhile village informers to keep Harjit Singh in some form of custody. Harjit had been moved from place to place, maintaining his usefulness primarily as a spotter. He had eventually ended up in Mal Mandi, where the officer in charge was responsible to central authorities. To this day, high-ranking officials in the police force continue to protect their colleagues and put a blanket over happenings, happenings which occurred because two structures are entangled: local village structures relating to family feuds and vendettas and factional alignments, and the more bureaucratically organized killing of the state.

Conclusion

Through the experience of one Sikh family I have sought to describe the context in which a large number of families fear for the safety of their children at the hands of abduction squads in present-day Sikh Punjab. Perhaps because of inadequate support structures in the village or through lack of associational ties, not all parents can respond in as persistent a fashion as Kashmir Singh. Generally, where support of some kind is forthcoming from the army or from the judiciary or from friends in the police force, the fight for justice is sustained. A family's awareness of what can happen to their children causes anxiety and in some cases trauma. However, when the untoward does happen they show little fear in searching for the whereabouts of their children or in attempting to secure their release from custody, even when they themselves are threatened.

However, resistance is a matter of character, ultimately. There are many doctors who, under pressure, allow their names to be used in postmortem reports that the police have concocted. There are doctors who will not admit into hospital those who are severely injured as a result of police interrogation.[25] There are lawyers who have made no protest against the repressive legislation introduced since 1984. The Harjit Singh case shows how difficult it has been for the courts to function in an atmosphere in which their personnel are subject to intimidation. Unsurprisingly, therefore, when mothers and sisters have been held in custody by the police, their ultimate fate unknown, not all fathers and brothers have been able to cope with the threat of what might happen to them and to remain underground to fight. As one old lady from Sabrawan village, Amritsar district, told me, referring to the many abductions of young girls by the police, "In every village and each house there is sadness."[26] Hence, to protect their sisters or indeed some other family member, some young militants and their sympathizers have compromised and become informers.

It is standard police practice to use young men who come from guerrilla strongholds such as Baba Bakala as spotters. In fact, until his last sighting, Harjit Singh was being taken around the villages and used by the police in their identification of those with militant views. In these circumstances, the pressure put on young boys with no previous criminal conviction is overwhelming. In other instances, the relatives of the youngsters have been held hostage while the boy concerned was projected in the media, made popular, given arms, and left in place for awhile to collect information. He would be paid about 5,000 rupees per month and his relatives kept in custody as security. No harm would come to him as long as he remained useful both as an informer and as a fake militant. Villagers understood the behavior of young boys who found themselves in this position though they considered it a matter of shame. However, they themselves remained with the guerrillas only so long as the latter were able to give families in the rural areas a measure of protection. Once the security forces gained the upper hand, any open support fell away. Families refused shelter even to the wives and children of dead guerrilla fighters, fearing their own elimination. Thus the mother of a noted guerrilla fighter told me "if the police give us trouble there is nothing we can do and there is nowhere we can go." It was in this sort of environment that the wife and child of another well-known guerrilla, Sital Singh Matthewal, were killed by the police. To this day, persons are hesitant to deliver either messages or money to the families of known guerrilla fighters.

Kashmir Singh's persistence in pursuing his case through threat and pressure of a very substantial nature do not betoken fear of the state, though they show considerable fear about what is happening to his son. He is not unique in that. Particularly ex-servicemen who have suffered harassment and torture at the hands of special units, or whose children have been killed by them, would have been interested in pursuing their cases. That they have not been able to take their cases further, on their own, is due to lack of financial resources or legal encouragement. In all cases, the careful, legalistic responses to state terror that the families concerned prepare indicate that they see the issue of their children as being one related to justice.[27] In fact, the fear that they feel for their children is inexpressible. I believe that it must be seen in the light of what is happening to the family in contemporary Punjab. There is a three-pronged attack on its identity: through rape, which ruins the line by bringing bad blood into the family for generations to come; through the physical elimination of its young men or by reducing them to impotency; and through the destruction of its existing material prosperity—its land, houses, and agricultural implements. Against such a concerted onslaught only an effective resistance of a collective nature can offer a measure of protection. Fear for their children results in individual parental resistance. Perhaps they believe, as did Primo Levi (1988), that "the aims of life are the best defence against death."

Anderson and Simon (1987:42) accurately describe the current situation: "The structure of terror is in place and operational." Cases of illegal custody, torture, and extrajudicial killing occurred throughout 1995 and 1996.[28] According to human rights lawyers fresh complaints of abuse were also made during 1997 and 1998. Moreover, officers accused of brutal attacks against civilians have not been dismissed. They have merely been transferred, and that, too, only for a time, and only because they have no personal connection to present ruling authorities. Guerrilla violence may have stopped, but only because of superior state violence. In fact there has been no settlement.

Notes

The fieldwork on which this chapter is based was made possible by a grant from the Harry Frank Guggenheim Foundation, New York. I am grateful for this support, which enabled me to go to East Punjab in the autumn of 1992 and the winter of 1993 to witness at first hand the effects of state policy in the rural areas of the province. The chapter's sources are the many parents in the districts of Amritsar, Faridkot, and Bathinda who came to me to record that their children were missing. Subsequently, interviews were conducted in London with Kashmir Singh, father of Harjit Singh, and with two persons from Punjab who wish to remain unidentified who knew the militant struggle well. I am also obliged to those who arranged that I see the relevant court documents referred to in this chapter.

1. Certain high-ranking military officials attempted to explain the mutiny of the Sikh and Punjab regiments in a letter to the president of India in which they show how the observation of religious faith and military duty have been intertwined among the Sikhs. The text of the letter is contained in Nayar and Singh (1984: 160–163).

2. Four lawyers have been killed so far and twenty-nine threatened with police abduction. Two of these had questioned the constitutional validity and legality of the state practice of distributing prize money to police and brought a public interest petition. As their counsel noted, "the practice of putting prize money on the heads of suspects had led to the detestable pursuit of first apprehending subjects and making an illegal arrest, then putting a reward on their heads. Once the reward was decided they were simply taken out of illegal centres and shot dead and the money claimed. No scrutiny was done and no criterion adopted on how the reward is fixed, who decides it and on what material" (*The Tribune*, 21 May 1994).

3. In September 1995, Jaswant Singh Khalra of the human rights wing of the Shiromani Akali Dal alleged that 2,000 families awaited the return of their family members in the Amritsar district alone. Four hundred unclaimed bodies had been brought to the Patti municipality cremation grounds; seven hundred unclaimed bodies to the Tarn Taran municipality cremation grounds; and 2,000 bodies were cremated and unclaimed a the Durgiana Mandir Amritsar. An attendant at the cremation grounds in Patti commented on the fact that "unclaimed bodies have continuously been burnt here. Previously it used to happen once in a while. In the last 4 to 5 years it has been common. They only cremate. No one cares to take away the remains" (from video documentary *"Disappearance" in Punjab* by Ram Narayan Kumar, 1996).

4. Amnesty International (December 1993) lists the names of eighty people who have disappeared in Punjab since 1990 and simply reports them as being picked up by "armed police," or by "police in plain clothes" and "police wearing khaki turbans."

5. The term is used to describe someone who, while in police custody, identifies from public places those espousing the militant cause. Police customarily used young men who came from centers of guerrilla activity as spotters. After a youth was captured it would be announced in the newspapers that he had been killed. In fact he was kept alive so long as he was useful.

6. Civil Writ Petition no. 13195 of 1996, Sardul Singh vs. State of Punjab and others.

7. Disappearance is being increasingly used as a technique of terror. According

to a report for the Independent Commission on International Humanitarian Issues, the key element in the definition of "disappearance" is the involvement of the authorities.

8. Normally when cross fire is mentioned in press reports it refers to the occasion when "a militant is taken for recovery of weapons by the security forces. The party comes under fire of the militants and in the cross fire providentially everyone escapes except the escorted militant" (letter to the prime minister by the Movement Against State Repression, the Punjab Human Rights Organization, and the Punjab Union of Civil Liberties, 15 January 1992).

9. For example, *India: Country Reports on Human Rights Practices for 1994*, issued by the U.S. State Department in 1995, makes reference on its first page to the political killings and extrajudicial executions by police in Punjab and remarks that "problems with the absence of police arrest records is particularly common in Punjab, where a number of disappearances were reported" (ibid:4). Likewise, the Economic and Social Council of the United Nations (E/CN.4/1995/96:45) notes that "The majority of the 224 cases of disappearances (in Punjab and Kashmir) reported to its Working Group occurred between 1983 and 1994" and "were primarily attributable to the police authorities, the army and paramilitary groups acting in conjunction with, or with the acquiescence of, the armed forces." Important official testimony to these sorts of events is also present in the U.S. State Department report of 19 January 1993: in Punjab there were credible reports that police, in particular, continued to engage in faked encounter killings. In the typical scenario, police take into custody suspected militants or militant supporters without filing an arrest report. If the detainee dies during interrogation or is executed, officials deny that he was ever in custody and claim he died during an armed encounter with police or security forces. Afterwards the bodies reportedly are sometimes moved to distant police districts for disposal, making identification and investigation more difficult.

10. This is well illustrated by the case of one Param Satinderjit Singh, a student at Guru Nanak Dev University, Amristar, who was detained by police in May 1992. The then SSP of Amritsar is quoted as saying in a report by Human Rights Watch and Physicians for Human Rights (1994:51) that he "had been detained, but not by his police but by police belonging to some other district who were operating in the area without permission."

11. Human Rights Watch (May 1996) reports that in Kashmir most extrajudicial killings occur after "cordon and search operations during which all the men of a neighbourhood or village are called to assemble for an identification parade in front of hooded informers." In Punjab, by contrast, the frontline work is not done by the army, and killings were the work of special units of police or of the CIA.

12. Civil Writ Petition 12330 of 1995, in the High Court of Punjab and Haryana at Chandigarh. Swaran Singh of Mohalla Rara, Jagraon, District Ludhiana vs. State of Punjab. Criminal Writ Petition 499 of 1994, in the same court of Budh Singh of Sunam, District Sangrur vs. Senior Superintendent of Police Sangrur.

13. See the case of Sarbjit Singh vs. State of Punjab and others. Criminal Miscellaneous Petition of 1996, High Court of Punjab and Haryana.

14. Jaspal Kaur wife of Avtar Singh of village Railon, near Bassi Pathana, District Fatehgarh Sahib vs. State of Punjab and others. Civil Writ Petition of 1996 in the Punjab and Haryana High Court. This is a horrifying case of illegal detention, rape, and torture for failure to relinquish three lakh rupees to another party and put twenty-one and a half acres in his name.

15. One example is the counterinsurgency operations—flood, provoke, destroy—that occurred in the Jagraon area of Ludhiana district in November–December 1992. In two operations the area was encircled by units coming from Kishanpura, Aliwal, Boparai, Bassian/Raikot, Hatur Khas, Dhudike, and Kokari Kalan.

16. One telegram, from the principal, Khalsa Senior Secondary School, Kharar, addressed to the honourable president and prime minister of India and the governor of Punjab, requests an inquiry into the arrest of his only son, saying, "His liquidation in cold blood is apprehended."

17. An affidavit dating from June 1992, one among many for that month, of Avtar Singh, aged twenty, states that his brother's penis was punctured with needles and electric wires attached to it. He became impotent. His family secured his release on bail but the police killed him in his fields in Ghuman village, Gurdaspur district.

18. One ex-serviceman wrote several letters to the governor of Punjab, to Mrs. H. K. Sandhu, additional judge of the Punjab and Haryana High Court (date of letter 26 March 1991) and to his previous army commanders, regarding the death in cross fire of his son. None replied. He gave me a printed list containing the names of twelve prominent Indian MPs to whom he had sent letters. He received replies from only two. He also gave me a transcript of a hearing with the then SSP of Faridkot (Swaran Singh) on 21 September 1991 held in the presence of the deputy commissioner of the district.

19. Enquiry Report of 11 September 1995, Kashmir Singh vs. State of Punjab.

20. Amnesty International (1996:6) registered its great concern at the "absence of censure in the enquiry report of the police . . . who failed to identify the body before cremating it thereby removing any further possibility of identification."

21. Report of the warrant officer, as contained in evidence Kashmir Singh vs. State of Punjab 21 October 1992. In the High Court of Punjab and Haryana at Chandigarh CR. WD no. 651 of 1992.

22. Letter dated 27 August to the prime minister of India by Ranjan Lakhanpal, advocate, High Court of Punjab and Haryana.

23. Amnesty International (1995b:7) quotes from a civil writ petition of a Chandigarh lawyer, Navkiran Singh, which says: "It is noticed that some intelligence officials of the Punjab State are on permanent duty at the High Court premises. They enter the registry of the High Court and keep on collecting information of cases being filed against the state of Punjab especially writs of habeas corpus in which warrant officers are appointed. By the time the poor petitioner takes the warrant officer to the suspected place of confinement of the detenu, the police officer receives the wireless message that the warrant officer is on the way and the detenu is shifted elsewhere."

24. In an urgent action circular of 11 February 1994 Amnesty International makes the following comment on the case: "This lack of progress appears to be largely due to the delaying tactics by the police and the recent absences of the judge hearing the case, most recently on 9 February 1994 . . . Although some of the delay in legal proceedings has been due to Harjit Singh's lawyer (he twice failed to appear in court on time), the principle cause has been the failure of senior police personnel to appear before the court. On 16 April 1993 the Superintendent of Police did not appear. He sent his deputy and so the hearing was postponed. The next hearing on 27 April was again postponed as the judge wanted KPS Gill, the Director General of Police, to appear in court. The next two hearings on 13 and 28 May were postponed as no government or police represen-

tatives were present. The judge hearing the case has been on leave on three recent occasions (19 November 1993, 21 December 1993 and 9 February 1994) when the hearing came to court." Thus the magisterial inquiry into Harjit Singh's case, which was supposed to take three months, in fact took three years. The major cause of the delay in judicial proceedings was the lack of cooperation from high-ranking police officials as a result of which several hearings were postponed.

25. In some cases the local civil hospital has advised the CIA not to admit the injured into hospital to avoid proof of injuries. In this connection see the case of Modan Singh of village Shahpur, Bhiwanigarh, Sangrur. Criminal Miscellaneous Petition of 1996.

26. An increasing number of rape cases are coming to light as individual women take their cases to the courts. One mother registered a case against the police on behalf of her daughter who had been picked up and taken to the police station while her brothers aged twenty-three and thirty were in illegal custody. Her husband was also tortured and he lost his mental balance. Gurdev Kaur, wife of Bhag Singh, village Rangian, District Ropar, vs. State of Punjab, Director General of Police and others. Criminal Writ Petition, 1995.

27. Seeking justice is the main motivation behind many cases now being brought to court which go back as far as 1991. A case in point is that of Swaran Singh vs. the State of Punjab. Civil Writ Petition 12330, 1995. This was a case where an entire family of six, including their three-month-old child, was wiped out in a police raid due to a militant hiding in an outhouse on the farm.

28. Criminal Miscellaneous Petition of 19 August 1996. Modan Singh vs. State of Punjab and others. Charanjit Kaur, widow of the late S. Gamdur Singh, Bhai Ke Pishor, District Sangrur vs. State of Punjab, Civil Writ Petition of 1995. Ranjit Kaur, widow of S. Piara Singh Kirpal Singh Wala Mahil Kalan, Barnala, vs. State of Punjab, Civil Writ Petition 1995. It is significant that in all these cases the writ petition is primarily against the State of Punjab indicating that it is the state that families see as being primarily responsible and hence accountable for what has happened to their family members.

Bibliography

Amnesty International (India)
   1996 *Harit Singh: In Continuing Pursuit of Justice.* London: Amnesty International.
   1995a *Harjit Singh: A Case Study in Disappearance and Impunity.* London: Amnesty International.
   1995b *Determining the Fate of the Disappeared in Punjab.* London: Amnesty International.
   1994 *Harjit Singh.* Urgent Action Circular, 11 February.
   1993 *An Unnatural Fate: "Disappearances" and Impunity in the Indian States of Jammu and Kashmir and Punjab.* London: Amnesty International.
Anderson, K., and J.-M. Simon
   1987 "Permanent Counterinsurgency in Guatemala." *Telos*, 73, pp. 9–46.
Brecht, Bertolt
   1976 *Poems, 1913–1956.* London: Eyre Methuen.
Das, Veena
   1994 "Moral Orientations to Suffering." In *Health and Social Change in International Perspective.* L. Chen et al., eds. Boston: Harvard School of Public Health.

Enquiry Report
   1995 *Kashmir Singh vs. State of Punjab, 11.9.1995.* Chandigarh: Amar Dutt, Sessions Judge.
Epstein, A. L.
   1992 *In the Midst of Life.* Berkeley: University of California Press.
Forrest, D.
   1996 *A Glimpse of Hell.* D. Forrest, ed. London: Cassell.
   1995 "Patterns of Abuse in Sikh Asylum Seekers." *The Lancet,* 345, 28 January, pp. 225–226.
Human Rights Watch and Physicians for Human Rights
   1994 *Dead Silence: The Legacy of Human Rights Abuses in Punjab.* New York: Human Rights Watch.
Human Rights Watch (Asia)
   1996 *India's Secret Army in Kashmir.* New York: Human Rights Watch.
Independent Commission on International Humanitarian Issues (ICIHI)
   1986 *Disappeared: Technique of Terror.* London: Zed Books.
Laitin, D. D.
   1995 "National Revivals and Violence." *European Journal of Sociology,* 36, pp. 3–43.
Levi, Primo
   1988 *The Drowned and the Saved.* London: Abacus Sphere.
Nagengast, Carole
   1994 "Violence, Terror, and the Crisis of the State." *Annual Review of Anthropology,* 23, pp. 109–136.
Nayar, K., and K. Singh
   1984 *Tragedy of Punjab.* Delhi: Vision Books.
Stanley, W.
   1996 *The Protection Racket State.* Philadelphia: Temple University Press.
Stille, A.
   1992 *Benevolence and Betrayal.* London: Jonathan Cape.
Stoll, David
   1993 *Between Two Armies in the Ixil Towns of Guatemala.* New York: Columbia University Press.
Taussig, Michael
   1992 *The Nervous System.* London: Routledge.
U.S. State Department
   1995 *India: Country Reports on Human Rights Practices for 1994.* Washington, D.C.: U.S. State Department.
   1993 *India: Country Report on Human Rights.* Washington, D.C.: Unclassified State Department Document 018642/17.
Wickham-Crowley, T. P.
   1990 "Terror and Guerrilla Warfare in Latin America, 1956–1970." *Comparative Studies in Society and History,* 32, pp. 201–237.
Zulaika, Joseba, and William Douglass
   1996 *Terror and Taboo: The Follies, Fables, and Faces of Terrorism.* London: Routledge.

Conclusion
Death Squads and Wider Complicities
Dilemmas for the Anthropology of Violence

Kay B. Warren

Given that by United Nations mandate states are endowed with sovereignty and, thus, legitimately exercise coercion on many fronts (Falk 1997), scholars are confronted with decisive choices in the study of state violence. State terrorism and death squads — the subject of this collection of essays — can be envisioned as aberrations (arising from fascist, totalitarian, and authoritarian regimes), as temporary state extremism in response to armed opposition to state authority, or as routine forms of social control gone awry.[1] The initial decision among these analytical framings channels subsequent lines of questioning and explanation. In this concluding essay, I highlight these and other difficult choices faced by anthropologists who find themselves forced by the circumstances of their field research to study violent states. As will become clear, these dilemmas are issues not only for the anthropologists who work on violence but also for anthropology as a whole.

From Northern Ireland and Spain to India, the Philippines, Indonesia, Guatemala, Argentina, and beyond, it seems inevitable that government-supported "death squads" will erupt during counterinsurgency efforts, whether or not these are formally declared wars. This technique of organized violence, often viewed as spontaneous, and routinely disavowed by state authorities, is not incidental to these conflicts but rather intrinsic to internal warfare. The essays in this volume illustrate the global patterning of violence across strikingly different states and cultural formations. They also illustrate the many reasons anthropologists still find cultural issues critical to the understanding of conflict.

Death squads operate at the margins, engaging in torture, kidnap, rape, and assassination outside the rule of law. In some cases, such as the "shoot to kill" policy in Northern Ireland, the goal was to kill known IRA terrorists whom authorities were unable to catch in the act and prosecute. In other cases, death squads specialize in what the police and armed forces may officially appear to eschew: the extrajudicial killings of dissenters, the disappearances of local leaders, students, and journalists, and the retaliatory abuse of activists' families, including the rape of wives and daughters to humiliate parents and to pollute family lines. In this instance, the intent is to engage in preemptive violence and intimidate the public. Here death squads supplement the work of official counterinsurgency forces. At other times, militaries organize localized death squad activities for community surveillance in the name of self-defense. Naturally there are many variations within this formation of violence, responding to the particular situations in which the organizations and combatants' objectives emerge. Many of this volume's case studies document the blurring of state terrorism (through the deployment of armed forces against insurgents and civilian communities) and the operation of clandestine death squads (allegedly organized by extremists on their own).

In these circumstances, the dangerous labeling of civilians as subversives, insurgents, and guerrilla supporters often lies beyond the control of those "caught between two fires." As Joyce Pettigrew notes in her essay, patterned violence forms a core component of technologies of terror designed as much to drive civilian populations into submissiveness as to root out armed opposition. Although intimidation rarely succeeds in choking off dissent, it may limit the breadth of armed resistance as civilians find insurgents unable to offer effective protection in the face of the state's superior forces.[2]

Paramilitary death squads are most often composed of former members of the army, police, and intelligence organizations. They operate with impunity, that is, without legal accountability, while they benefit from the direct or indirect logistical support of state institutions, even as authorities disclaim any connection. Characteristically they leave evidence of their activities in the form of tortured bodies or bloody survivors, as messages that convey the brute power of the state. An alternative tactic involves the arbitrary kidnapping of civilians so that they "disappear" off the face of the earth to unknown fates. This switch in tactics is less incidental than cynical when it becomes a political response to human rights monitoring, international public pressure, and future accountability to judicial processes. Without bodies as evidence, states can continue repression in ways that allow "plausible deniability" (Schirmer 1998). For Argentina's dirty war, Antonius Robben adds to this calculus of rationales the military's projection of uncontrollable revenge by its victims. Public trials and the execution of guerrillas, the high command fantasized, would result in reprisals against military courts, executioners, and their families. In fact, the absence of corpses created by the tactic of clandestine murders became a focal point of civilian grief, debates about exhumations of mass graves, and attempts to keep the spirit of the disappeared alive through political action.

Counterinsurgency violence that seeks to extinguish political opposition would seem to be an unstable solution to social conflict. Nevertheless, states from a spectrum of ideological positions have persisted in categorically labeling wide ranges of their civilians as dangerous and undeserving of full rights. Nationalisms have been crafted by political elites not only to create imagined communities but additionally to rationalize forms of repression much wider in scope than any immediate uprising.[3]

The question of whether state-sponsored terrorism inhibits the development of opposition movements is an open one that calls for an ethnographic consideration of the character of repression and the range of movements stifled and generated by internal violence. For instance, in her essay, Cynthia Mahmood shows how a rape by Hindu security forces in Kashmir was experienced as irreversible family humiliation by a Muslim Kashmiri father, who in this instance felt compelled to kill his own daughter and then to avenge her terrible dishonor and death by destroying his home and attempting to join separatist guerrillas. Kashmiri rebels fighting for autonomy from India are pictured as learning the meaning of their struggle through these riveting yet excruciating narratives of outrage which, moreover, depict the spontaneous transfer of radicalized moral duties across generations and families to younger male combatants. One wonders if the highly gendered nationalist discourse that this wartime situation evoked had the effect of undercutting debates over women's roles and gender politics that developed in other Islamic societies.[4]

Mahmood notes "the nonstrategic and nonpolitical quality of the lived experience of state violence, which often prompts a similarly nonstrategic and nonpolitical resistance." Thus, the clash of formal ideologies (of nationalism versus anticolonialism) captures only one of many dimensions of conflict lived in worlds of intimate meanings. On all sides, state-focused stories of resistance and complicity transform themselves into something more complex and personal through the interplay of diverse identities and social situations.[5]

Beyond rebel organizations, violence spurs the families of its victims to create groups such as the Mothers of the Plaza de Mayo in Argentina and the multipurpose widows' association CONAVIGUA[6] in Guatemala to protest against repression. It generates solidarity networks and human rights organizations, such as Amnesty International and Human Rights Watch, that promote a global discourse of human rights and cope with governments that use a variety of strategies to avoid monitoring (Sikkink

1996). Violence also generates transnational networks—of opposition movements and of national governments—which communicate across regimes about the techniques of state terrorism, tactics for resistance and subversion, and negotiating possibilities during peace processes. Despite these instances of organizing, it is apparent that polarized violence undercuts the formation of groups with alternative social agendas and sometimes results in the radical depoliticization of the general public (Corradi et al. 1992). The ethnographic task is to demonstrate the culturally rooted dynamic interplay of politicization and depoliticization in these social spaces.

Anthropological Representations of Death Squads

Once social scientists recognize death squads as part of a wider phenomenon, rather than as the isolated acts of extremists outside anyone's control, they are faced with important dilemmas in the conceptualization of this violence. What stands beyond the compelling task of documenting and condemning incidents of state terror, as international human rights organizations have done to raise international awareness? How can we bring an anthropological perspective to these issues while at the same time attempting to rethink political anthropology itself?

Anthropological researchers face the immediate challenge of representing the relation of militarized forces to civilian populations. It is clear from the study of death squads that the police and army are not bounded institutions set apart from society. Rather, the state, armed forces, paramilitaries, insurgents, and civil society form interpenetrating social fields. Civilians fill the ranks of armed forces on all sides and, as recruits, experience state-centered resocialization to fight these wars. The general population, whatever its sympathies, often finds no feasible exit from the conflict between insurgents and the state. Individuals become complicit by informing on the activities and putative alliances of their neighbors. Whether coerced, offered in exchange for personal gain, or solicited to enhance one's power at the expense of others, these complicities involve betrayals that splinter family and community. The aggravation of existing divisions becomes an enduring cost of this mode of conflict as trust among family members and neighbors erodes in the face of secretive alliances. For anthropology, the issue is how we represent the particularities of interpenetrating yet fragmenting social fields to reveal the interplay of existential dilemmas and power structures in chaotic situations.[7]

In the face of state violence, anticolonial opposition movements pose particular challenges for anthropologists. In instances where cultural minorities or grassroots movements are repressed by overwhelming state power, it has been difficult for anthropologists not to sympathize with those who denounce and resist injustice. For some researchers, the fact of war justifies counterviolence, whatever form it takes. For others, the issue is how repression potentially recreates a sense of common pupose and "homogenizes" resistance across ethnic, geographic, and class lines, as Frank Afflitto argues in his Guatemalan essay.

For still other analysts, resistance to repression involves a painful blurring of motives and allegiances over time, with individuals betraying their established loyalties rather than bridging them, sometimes voluntarily or in other circumstances to put off their own death sentences. A special angst is evident in Cynthia Mahmood's and Joyce Pettigrew's essays, which trace the contradictions and ironies — the mimesis of state violence — in the anticolonial separatism of the Sikhs and Kashmiris in India. As Sherry Ortner reminds us (1995), anthropologists are called upon to contextualize and historicize (rather than ignore) the contradictory impulses of such social movements. A return to richer ethnographic portrayals has become necessary to counteract the earlier tendency to idealize opposition movements by focusing on their activities as exemplars of resistance.[8]

The self-consciousness of the writers in this volume stems from the fact that beyond the horror of state violence and the fact that there is no neutral subject position from which to narrate these histories, there also appear to be no uncomplicated sympathetic position for ethnographers. That counternationalisms can generate their own authoritarianism, death squads, and corruption — mirroring state power as they critique it — and that grassroots insurgents may lose rather than gain civilian support over time create special challenges for anthropological writing in politically charged situations. Another compelling issue is the criminalization of former combatants *on all sides* where peace processes have not coped with the extreme social fragmentation that accompanies protracted violence.

A second closely related dilemma is the conceptualization of "the state" as something other than a distant monolithic antagonist. Across the introduction and essays in this volume there is an unresolved tension between the critique of great powers (specifically the West) and the critique of state power in all political systems. It is clear that classical authoritarian military dictatorships do not have a monopoly over state terrorism and state-condoned violence. As Begoña Aretxaga insightfully argues in her essay, democracies such as Spain have a terrible time distancing themselves from their authoritarian (and, one might add, colonizing) pasts, despite changes in political philosophy. This is especially the case when they leave older policing and bureaucratic structures intact.

In widening the search for indicators of authoritarianism, one can explore the limits of democratization and the particular and often ironic ties democratic states have with their authoritarian pasts. One can deconstruct state bureaucracies ethnographically or show the political stakes involved in endowing the state with unitary powers and a fetishized life of its own.[9] One can focus on the state's definition of its enemies (or its definition of natural limits to democratic inclusion) and study these manifestations of power as impersonal hegemonic processes or as a contingent mimetic process that reflects the internalization of state violence projected on the dangerous "other."[10]

Along this second line of analysis, Aretxaga's essay illustrates the production of political fantasy by state officials for their own consumption, which plays a crucial role in mediating perceptions of internal enemies and rationalizing state violence against Basque radical nationalists living in exile in France. Here, as in the case of Argentina, surreal political fantasies inform the actions of diverse interests and become central, if often neglected, aspects of state violence and its legacies. These arresting images create "a surplus of meaning" that generates "its own fantastic realism which justifies the organized copy of terrorism to combat terrorism" (Aretxaga, this volume; see also Zulaika and Douglass 1996).

Perhaps the triumphalist discourse of democratic modernity — especially the post–Cold War end-of-history variant of this discourse — has inhibited closer examinations of violence in democratic societies. Stanley Tambiah (1996) argues that chronic paramilitary violence may become more common than we would expect. In practice, democracy channels intense competition for power through electoral politics, which is often accompanied by occult violence. Thus, in India, groups frequently provoke communal riots at election time for their own political ends. Echoing these patterns, elections in Guatemala and Colombia bring waves of assassinations of candidates for local and national office. Although these riots and cyclic killings are condemned, electoral violence becomes an anticipated event in these political landscapes. The underside of democracy includes spaces of violence that are integral aspects of state politics even as they are, in effect, public secrets.

A third dilemma facing anthropologists is the interrelation of national violence to wider global issues. Whom do we hold accountable for violence? As Jeffrey Sluka argues in the introductory essay, should we regard political violence primarily as the result of Western capitalist political and economic interventions in the national affairs of other countries? To address this issue, one would have to consider international influences such as the global circulation of capital, the highly unstable world economy, and neoliberal economic policies promulgated as part of democratic modernity that create and tolerate growing gaps between prosperous and impoverished citizens. One consequence has been a proliferation of private armies and policing. Michel-Rolph Trouillot (1999) suggests that we examine the "state effects" created by the contemporary forces of globalization that have reshaped national economies, political life, and sites of cultural struggle while leaving intact the fiction of autonomous, equivalent state entities. One would have to add other issues such as colonial histories of domination that rigidified and exploited the social hierarchies that underwrite present day antagonisms. Still another issue would be the global arms industry, centered in the West but increasingly decentralized in practice, that actively markets guns and surveillance equipment for profit, with little concern for the consequences. Additional international influences would include government policies that secretly support counterinsurgency activities and fund training for military officers from other countries, as has been the case with the U.S. School of the Americas, a training center for Latin American military officers who have been implicated in many human rights abuses. Such centers are part of the U.S. Cold War history of developing counterinsurgency techniques in one part of the world and subsequently exporting them to other regions.[11] Elsewhere, counterinsurgency techniques have drawn on earlier colonial modes of control. As Jeffrey Sluka's essay notes, former colonial powers such as Britain have reimported strategies first developed in Kenya and Malaya and applied them in Northern Ireland to secretly foster Protestant Loyalist paramilitaries and their violent opposition to Irish nationalism.

Alternatively, should analysts focus on national accountability, on the national institutions and political actors who, for their own reasons and interests, seek to foster authoritarian, militarized solutions to social conflicts? Or should researchers concentrate effort on the interplay of local and national formations of violence, showing the intimate interplay of transcommunity organized violence with community conflicts?[12]

To neglect any of these arenas, or to locate the moral or causal explanation of death squads in particular international arenas so that it displaces other considerations, would appear to be a serious misreading of a complex political field of actors and institutions.

There is no simple path through these dilemmas as anthropology attempts to do justice to state violence and the politics of inclusion and exclusion.[13] Each of these groupings of issues presents specific challenges for anthropologists working in situations of state-organized violence. This is especially so in a discipline which has not, in contrast to more policy-driven political science, tended to focus on state stability as the normative locus for social scientific analysis.

Violence, Democratic Transitions, and Peace Processes

It is important to add a hopeful note to the study of death squads: the possibility of peace processes that force a reexamination of the structures and legacies of political violence. The 1990s witnessed instances of seemingly intractable civil war that have ended in negotiated peace. In Guatemala, El Salvador, South Africa, and Northern Ireland, post–Cold War transitions have focused on demobilization, the creation of truth and reconciliation commissions, the resettlement of civilian refugees displaced by violence, and debates over economic and political reforms. These issues echo the concerns of earlier transitions to democracy for countries such as Argentina, Brazil, and Nicaragua. Sometimes with UN assistance — and the collaborative involvement of U.S., European, and regional volunteers — the process has involved the disarming of insurgents and the downsizing of armies, reassessments of the divison of labor between military and civilian police forces, the development of job training programs for ex-combatants, and concern for the lingering effects of war on civilian populations.[14]

In formal terms, peace processes have been promoted as an opportunity to displace authoritarianism with the wider political participation characteristic of democratic regimes. The return to civilian rule has repeatedly involved the reincorporation into the political party system of those who earlier sought to destroy the state — an inconceivable option for warring protagonists at the height of conflict. This remains one of the most important lessons of peace when it is defined as a nonviolent transition to a more inclusive political order. As twentieth-century conflicts have taught us, antagonists are rarely immutably at war with each other. (This was also the lesson of Marshall Sahlin's [1961] classic argument about the political dynamics of segmentary lineages.) That current enemies may become political allies or effectively work within the same system seems politically remote because it is constructed so as a political fact by a variety of political interests.[15] Anthropologically, one must ask how these constructions are made believable or called into question by parties with distinctive stakes in maintaining or changing the status quo.

Another continuing lesson is that peace processes are inherently contingent and political. There has been great interest in documenting atrocities to determine accountability for killings and disappearances when wartime court systems had been unable or unwilling to perform their duties. For instance, the South African Truth and Reconciliation Commission (TRC) offers amnesty to those who detail their complicity with state terrorism under apartheid. This has allowed rare moments of insight into the operation of death squads within the paramilitary police, the organization of assassination campaigns, and the incitement of others to violence. The intimate interconnection with authoritarian regimes, armies, and death squads in this and other "dirty wars" has been revealed through formal court proceedings. One can only hope these revelations will make it all the more difficult to reestablish these symbiotic structures in the future.

Inevitably the fairness of the process has been questioned in South Africa as major figures, who were known to have used brutality to support apartheid or who used violence to settle disputes between factions of the opposition, appear to have escaped the process unscathed. Justice, it would seem, has its own politics.[16] That civilians who hoped for reparations as a consequence of their testimonies of harm and personal loss may be left with unfulfilled expectations illustrates the personal stakes in these transitions. For many, being heard and recognized after being forced to suffer in silence has been a liberating experience. Yet recent research on the public face of the TRC and its special women's commissions highlights the ways in which the process has emphasized women's nonpolitical roles as wives and mothers and discouraged women leaders from contributing their experiences, especially when they might involve testimonies of male sexual violence against women comrades in the ANC (Kim 1998).

Guatemala chose another path in the negotiations between the army, government, and URNG guerrillas that resulted in the December 1996 peace accords and amnesty for combatants.[17] The Commission for Historical Clarification, which at its inception in 1997 was deluged with 50,000 cases of human rights abuses, was given the responsibility to document acts of violence but not to name names for court proceedings. While many agree that this is important work in a country where the military committed many excesses it has long denied, most now worry about the lack of pressure for perpetrators to detail their own crimes and reveal the full scope of extrajudicial violence. Many suspect that the militarized surveillance of civilians and the operation of death squads will be formally dismantled only to emerge elsewhere in the government (Schirmer 1998–99). As Jaime Malamud-Goti (1996) has argued for Argentina, civilian complicity with state violence and perceptions that justice is arbitrary and, therefore, lacking in legitimacy haunt peace processes. This is all the more so in cases where the judicial infrastructure is weak and subject to outside pressure.

One of the most serious problems that Guatemala currently faces is the rise in everyday criminality that shadowed the war in the 1980s and appeared to grow to a crescendo with the declaration of peace. During the counterinsurgency war, it was unsafe to travel and people kept to their homes at night. With the end of the war and the successful conclusion to the peace negotiations after eight years of uncertainty, darkness continued to be dangerous.

Delincuencia, or diffuse violence in daily life, has become an overwhelming experience in the countryside and in major cities. Buses, the major mode of transportation in the countryside, are intercepted, passengers are robbed and sometimes killed on the spot. Now, rather than the soldiers and guerrillas who extorted war taxes from civilians during the war, gangs of highway robbers prey on bus passengers throughout the highlands. Commerce that involves carrying substantial sums of money, a result of inadequate local access to banks, subjects civilians to great danger. On the highways around Quetzaltenango, Guatemala's second city, organized gangs have murdered drivers for their cars. A tour bus of U.S. college students was stopped in 1998, the passengers robbed, and two women raped. Communal lynchings of petty criminals have become commonplace in an environment where the police and courts are widely perceived as unwilling to pursue criminals. Stories of extortion circulate, with a shift in targets from the elites of the past to small-town salaried workers and NGO administrators. Grassroots human rights activists continue to be tortured and killed with apparent impunity. A unique focus on death squads (or any other particular form of violence) would distract analysts from the heterogeneous scope of emerging patterns of violence — in this case, half-organized and half-spontaneous.

The urgent issue is the future of ex-combatants who earned their living violently and after 1996 found themselves decommissioned with the mobilization of guerrilla forces, the downsizing of the army and police forces, and the disbanding of civil patrols that monitored rural communities in the highlands.[18] Moreover, an estimated 20 percent of the national population was displaced during the 1978–1985 counterinsurgency war (Manz 1988). The return of refugees from camps in Mexico only to find their lands occupied has left people with few resources and marginal employment often far from their home communities. Others fled rural communities for urban anonymity during the war. Even when aggregate statistics showed that the national economy was growing in 1997, however, rural wages were stagnant in the face of rising prices for many basic commodities (MINUGUA 1998). Clearly, the peace process has created its own tensions which have been magnified by growing economic insecurity.

Another difficult legacy of the war has been the *patrullas de autodefensa civil*, the civil self-defense patrols, which were expanded by the Ríos Montt regime in 1982 with the goal of consolidating the military domination of rural communities and separating civilians from the leftist insurgents in the highlands. During the worst offensive of the counterinsurgency war in 1980–1983, an estimated 26,000–35,000 people were killed, 440 villages destroyed, and over a million people displaced from their homes as refugees (Manz 1988; Ball et al. 1998; Schirmer 1998; Commission for Historical Clarification 1999). The Guatemala Commission for Historical Clarification (1999) estimates that civil patrols committed 18 percent of the human rights violations and acts of violence during the war period as a whole. Much of the active warfare focused on the predominantly Mayan western highlands that border southern Mexico. By 1983, a million Mayan men from twelve to seventy years of age were forced to patrol their own rural communities in twenty-four-hour shifts one day a week or every two weeks, depending on the size of their community. Their charge was to search for guerrillas and monitor their neighbors as potential leftist sympathizers or insurgents and report their findings to the army through locally appointed military commissioners. Three years later there were still 600,000 active civil patrollers although no guerrilla presence was apparent in most areas (Americas Watch 1989). It was only in anticipation of the signing of the final peace accords that patrols throughout the highlands were disbanded.

Through groups like Americas Watch (1982, 1984, 1986, and 1989) and the Kennedy Center for Human Rights (Jay 1993), the human rights community described the threats and abuses that accompanied the forced recruitment of peasants into civil patrols and argued that paramilitary service was unconstitutional forced labor. They documented repression directed at organizations such as CERJ,[19] locally founded in 1988 to encourage communities to oppose civil patrolling. Human rights reports focused on the failure of the criminal justice system to respond to the torture and killings of civilians and the resulting impunity enjoyed by the military and civil patrollers.

Even after the 1985 election of Vinicio Cerezo, the first civilian president in twenty years, the government and military formed a unified, evasive front in interviews and press releases. Their position — which verged on a parody of plausible deniability — was that patrols were local groups spontaneously created to protect towns from insurgents. Abolishing the patrols would violate the constitutional guarantee of freedom of association. Authorities completely denied institutional responsibility for abuses and portrayed patrols as innocent of any accusations or, alternatively, as practicing violence intrinsic to rural life. The founder of CERJ was denounced as a guerrilla leader or communist collaborator (as, in this view, were the leaders of all other human rights groups) (Schirmer 1998; Americas Watch 1989). Thus, transitions to democracy do not necessarily marginalize militaries. In Guatemala, Schirmer finds that civilian rule gave national governments greater legitimacy in international forums and allowed the military to reposition itself as a force for national development and the guarantor of national security by monitoring civilians to insure domestic stability. In short, the counterinsurgency technologies of control survived the formal redemocratization of the country (Schirmer 1996, 1998, 1998–99).

The question for anthropologists has always been how to portray the civil patrols whose members were both victims and victimizers. While predominantly civilian, patrols were often headed by local military commissioners who found ways to make their unpaid service lucrative. The army is known to have used patrols in mass killings in resistant villages (Ball et al. 1998). In some communities, the patrol members became their own violent enforcers in local affairs, assassinating political enemies or reporting economic competitors and old enemies to the army as insurgents (Davis 1988; Carmack 1988a; Paul and Demarest 1988; Carlsen 1997). Their names were added to the lists of suspects to be rounded up in military raids or disappeared by counterinsurgent shock troops. David Stoll (1993) found that communities in the Ixil region proactively adopted patrols as a strategy of active neutrality. That is, their participation sought to discourage guerrilla involvement in their communities and to convey a message of loyalty to the state so as not to be abused by army sweeps.[20] In other communities, people minimized their service and disbanded patrols as soon as it was politically feasible (Carmack 1988b). In instances where the militarization of civilian life displaced local leaders with another chain of command, parents worried over their sons' loss of respect for the moral authority of community leaders and their families.

One of Guatemala's foremost Mayan writers in exile, Victor Montejo, wrote of his own brush with death at the 1982 massacre of San José Tzalalá, Jacaltenango, where he worked as the school teacher. While in a Mexican refugee camp, Montejo compiled a book of *testimonios* gathered from fellow refugees of the horror of civil patrols, military sweeps, and torture centers. This autoethnography includes accounts of atrocities from an ex-soldier, former civil patrollers, and civilians who escaped torture centers (1987, 1993, forthcoming, and with Akab' 1992). As I have argued elsewhere (Warren 1998), the partial truths in these fragmentary accounts accumulate to reveal larger truths about state violence.

Rather than being simply heroic narratives or resistance, Montejo's writings are preoccupied with the blurring of victim and victimizer, with Mayan complicity in the killing of other Mayans and the consequent estrangement of people from their own communities. The testimonies reveal the widespread routinization of violence in the everyday practices of the counterinsurgency forces. How could betrayals occur in communities where people knew each other so well? How can one make sense of one's survival when others were killed in the same circumstances? The testimonies narrate people's encounters with the representatives of state power, the chains of command and collusion across social institutions, the tactics of indoctrination used to convince Mayans of the legitimacy of the civil patrols, and the reward structures for military and paramilitary forces. They show how some indigenous individuals resisted complicity in small ways, while others grew sympathetic to the army.

For the armed forces, which had mobilized 36,000 soldiers by 1983, the justification for widespread violence was twofold. First, the army needed to vanquish the estimated 6,000–12,000 guerrillas[21] fighting in the western highlands. In practice, this goal proved illusive as dispersed groups of highly mobile rebels operating in rugged terrain proved difficult to extinguish. Second, the army wanted to insure that the guerrilla uprising would not escalate into a mass insurrection of impoverished peasants to challenge the state and its exploitative economics. The danger of mass insurrection was given extraordinary intensity by the political fantasy of indigenous rebellion. This potential had to be fought at all costs because it would inevitably be directed against the ladinos, the mainstream of Guatemala's ethnic hierarchy. The projected fear of uncontrollable ethnic violence justified and necessitated preemptory violence by the state. Montejo's refugee testimonies illustrate the military's discursive transformation of the savage Indian into the subversive communist over the course of the war.[22] As Enrique Sam Colop (1991), Charles Hale (1996), Jennifer Schirmer (1998), Diane Nelson (1999), and Michael Taussig (1987) have demonstrated, the rebellious Indian has long been a central element of Latin American political imaginaries.

Guatemala's civil patrols call into question the utility of the "death squad" as a generalized analytical concept. The patrols appear to fit the profile of paramilitary organizations directly supported by the state, along with the state's conventional disclaimer of its role in their creation and their built-in capacity to operate without accountability to the justice system. Yet the civil patrols were not primarily composed of former counterinsurgency soldiers and police but rather of small farmers and laborers. After the heat of the war, patrols were used by the army to "indigenize pacification" (Schirmer 1998), echoing Aditjondro's findings for Indonesia (this volume). In Guatemala, patrols were forced to monitor their own communities and kill "subversives" or be denounced as subversives themselves. This contemporary form of forced labor further exhausted farmers who were compelled to patrol at night without compensation. Civil patrols fostered the internalization of state violence and the fragmentation of local trust and cooperation, even when they were resisted. In an environment of betrayal and extreme insecurity, everyone faced the existential dilemma of finding ways to coexist and gather news crucial to survival, without necessarily trusting one's family and neighbors (Warren 1998).

It is clear when one examines the country's long awaited "transition to peace" that the process could not be a definitive resolution of violent conflict. Rather there are complex legacies for both civilians and the military that propelled a surge in violence with demobilization.[23] Recently, there have been some indications that, with the postaccord retraining of the police, who are notoriously corrupt and ineffective in pursuing criminals, and the trials of former patrollers who continue to victimize others, the country may be beginning to address some of the institutional bases underlying diffuse interpersonal violence. Yet, peace and democratization do not appear to be rewriting the rules of civilian-military cooperation or the veiled discourse of stability that only the military can guarantee. The continued appointment by the military of former soldiers as military commissioners in rural communities leaves in place the older decentralized structure and its potential for corruption.

Bringing the Project Home

When studies of violence focus on death squads in other societies there is a danger that Western democracies will emerge as if untouched by many of the issues this discussion has generated. The risk is one of perpetuating still another form of orientalism or radical alterity that portrays regions outside the West as backward, nondemocratic, not fully civilized. The inclusion of Spain and Ireland in this collection mitigates against this misstep; yet the question of America's internal violence remains unaddressed.[24] The ironic politics of democratic societies — some well-established, others new — suggests a line of investigation that pursues the limits of democracracy as practiced within and outside electoral politics. Following the ethnographers of state violence, it would be important to ask how *heterogeneous formations of violence* become legitimate, tolerable, or expected, even as they are condemned when revealed to the public. How do formations of violence and technologies of power reproduce themselves in established democracies? For the U.S., even a brief list of spaces of violence demonstrates how controversial it is to raise these questions. In the case of the Guatemalan disapora created by the counterinsurgency war that brought refugees to the U.S., one would have to include, among other issues:

- the foreign policy that has allowed military-economic aid and the training of military officers from Latin America in terrorist counter-insurgency techniques which they used with impunity and often with U.S. support in their own countries (McClintock 1992; Jonas 1991, forthcoming; Commission for Historical Clarification 1999);
- urban policies and policing that seal off Black and Latino "inner cities" from the wider society as spaces where criminal violence, dysfunctional schools, and corrosive poverty are tolerable (Bourgois 1995; Wacquant 1996; Suarez-Orozco 1989); and
- the complicity of state and popular sectors that actively fosters anti-immigrant anxiety in California based on political imaginaries of radical otherness and incommensurate cultures in an attempt to deny residents public education and medical benefits (Suarez-Orozco 1996).

The first of these spaces of violence remained virtually unknown to the public until the 25 February 1999 release of Guatemala's final truth commission report that describes the U.S. training of Guatemalan counterinsurgency officers and the direct and indirect CIA support of state terrorism. On 12 March 1999, during his trip to Central America, President Clinton apologized for the U.S. involvement in widespread repression. Domestically, urban and anti-immigrant policies are arenas in which there is substantial evidence of state and local collusion to create violent forms of exclusion. The ongoing practice of urban politics has made school desegregation particularly difficult to achieve in the U.S. (Hochschild 1994). Nor has there been widespread success in generating inclusive multicultural models of American society.

Guatemalan refugees have come to experience these spaces of violence as interconnected aspects of American social reality, after fleeing the political and economic dislocations of their country's civil war. Once in the U.S., refugees settled illegally or gained residency papers only to find themselves living in highly segregated neighborhoods, facing terrible violence in the public schools, and subject to virulent racism in states such as California, Florida, and Texas.[25] These limits to democratic inclusiveness are likely to grow in importance with the demographic shift in areas like the Los Angeles basin where people of Latin American descent will soon make up the majority of the population. The riots in East Central Los Angeles, sparked by the 1991 Rodney King beating and later acquittal of the police officers who were charged with using excessive force, demonstrate the immense racial and economic tensions just below the surface in impoverished Black and Latino neighborhoods, the police force, and the surrounding working-class and middle-class populace. The issues of displacement, segregation, monocultural state imaginaries, and politicians willing to mobilize constituents through strident anti-immigrant politics, as happened with Proposition 187 in California and the promotion of English-only policies in twenty-two states,[26] resonate with similar formations of violence in long-established European democracies.

As we have seen in this brief overview, the project of identifying spaces of violence and state-civilian complicity—something that lies at the heart of this volume's case studies and the renewal of political anthropology— takes social analysis in many unanticipated directions. The examination of death squads has been an important part of this journey in that it directs attention to important regularities across cultural and political systems, compels us to see the interplay of organized and unorganized forms of violence, raises the question of violence in authoritarian regimes and democracies, and calls on social analysis to contribute to visions of a more inclusive peace. These comparisons also reveal the cultural, historical, and political particularities of violence and the diversity of its manifestations. This is the lesson from the Guatemalan refugees who after fleeing their homeland's war found themselves confronting different formations of violence and a novel place in the political imaginary of their adopted country. Thus, as useful as the comparative project on death squads has been, what becomes most important is to wander off the path to examine spaces of violence wherever they occur as aspects of interpenetrating social fields, many of which are increasingly transnational even as they are locally and intimately experienced.[27]

Notes

This essay benefited greatly from discussions with and generous suggestions from Begoña Aretxaga, Abigail Adams, Jennifer Schirmer, Stephen Jackson, Aykan Erdemir, Stanley Tambiah and the volume contributors — none of whom is responsible for the limitations of my overview. Rather than attempting a grand synthesis of the rich and ethnographically complex essays in this volume, I have chosen to raise issues that crosscut these analyses and my own work on Guatemala.

1. There are, reciprocally , many ways to understand the resistance and violence of armed insurgents. Contrast, for example, Aretxaga (1997), Stoll (1993), and Zulaika and Douglass (1996).

2. For an example of coerced neutrality, see Stoll (1993).

3. See Fox's (1990) discussion of Hindu nationalism as an example of state elites seeking to create a hegemonic national culture and to stigmatize cultural difference and marginalize other groups.

4. See Aretxaga (1998) for a striking conceptualization of the interplay of nationalism and gender in Irish discourse and politics.

5. One would hasten to add that scholarly metanarratives are often transformed by their authors into something more — from critiques of capitalism and imperialism to theoretical exploration of the production of political meaning to arguments for certain policy kinds of interventions.

6. CONAVIGUA is the National Coordinator of Guatemalan Widows, a rural grassroots organization that after the war generated local self-help groups and national leaders active in the peace process.

7. See, for examples, Carmack (1988b), Aretxaga (1997), and Warren (1998).

8. See Escobar and Alvarez (1992), and Alvarez, Escobar, and Dagnino (1998).

9. See Ferguson (1994) and Taussig (1992, 1997).

10. For examples of this painful history, one only has to think of recent revelations about a U.S.-supported attempt to assassinate Fidel Castro or the U.S. training of military officers who became torturers and assassins of Americans and Guatemalans in that country during the later 1970s and 1980s (McClintock 1992).

11. For instance, "pacification" techniques developed with U.S. supervision in Guatemala in the 1960s were thoroughly transnational in their historical development first as weapons of Western colonial expansion and later as Cold War tactics to halt socialist expansion. In this case, the newly refined techniques were reimported by the U.S. into the Vietnam War and later reintroduced into Guatemala with updated surveillance technology in the late 1970s. When the Zapatista insurrection occurred in Mexico in 1994, Guatemalan military advisors offered to

assist the Mexican army with techniques of low intensity warfare. See McClintock for the background of this transnational circulation of military knowledge (1985, 1992).

12. For examples of exogenous influences, see Prunier (1995) and Woodward (1995). For ethnographic examples of the interplay of local and national forms of violence and their hermeneutics, see the case studies in Warren (1993).

13. There are, however, narrative conventions in the disciplines, such as the focus on local issues in anthropology (see Carmack 1988b), and displacement of causation to external forces, common in political science (see Prunier 1995, Woodward 1995). But there are important critiques of and exceptions to these tendencies (see Smith 1990a; Poole and Rénique 1991; Starn 1991; Nordstrom and Martin 1992; Schirmer 1996, 1997, 1998, 1998/99; Wilson 1997).

14. For example, see MINUGUA (1998).

15. Here current Western portrayals of Islam come to mind, such as Huntington (1996).

16. Nevertheless, it is interesting that the hearings selectively focused on Winnie Mandela rather than on the male leadership of the ANC.

17. For information on the Guatemalan peace process, see COMG (1998), Arnson and Quiñones (1997), ASIES (1996), Bastos and Camus (1995).

18. For literature on death squads and the civil patrols, see Americas Watch (1982, 1984, 1986, 1989), Carlsen (1997), Carmack (1988b), Falla (1994), Jay (1993), Jonas (1991, forthcoming), Lovell (1995), Manz (1988), Montejo and Akab' (1992), Painter (1987), Perera (1993), Schirmer (1998), Simon (1986), Smith (1990b), Stoll (1993), Trudeau (1993), and Wilson (1995).

19. Members of CERJ (whose bilingual acronym translates as the Council for Ethnic Communities for the Rights of the Marginal and Oppressed: All Are Equal Rujunel Junam) have been subject to severe repression (Americas Watch 1989).

20. Schirmer challenges this view by noting that after 1983 the army had an explicit policy of dividing the populace from the guerrillas so that neutrality was not an option (1998:82–87).

21. For discussions of the statistics, see Schirmer (1998:41, 47) and Ball et al. (1998).

22. This echoes Aditjondro's finding (this volume) that Indonesian forces justified massacres of civilians as a form of "pest control" of communists and infidels. As one anticommunist put it, "When you clean the field, don't you kill all the snakes, the small and large alike?"

23. This pattern parallels the common escalation of repression after the worst of counterinsurgency wars (see Corradi et al. 1992).

24. In the narrow sense, the KKK and lynchings in the South come to mind as an example of death squads in the U.S.

25. For the experiences of Guatemalan refugees in the U.S., see Suarez-Orozco (1989), Burns (1993), Hagen (1994).

26. Interestingly enough, these policies have not survived court challenges and those that remain on the books have not been fully implemented. Their function, therefore, would seem to be primarily in terms of feeding anti-immigrant hostility, which Suarez-Orozco (1996) argues was most intense in the early 1990s when U.S. citizens faced growing economic uncertainties as work forces were downsized.

27. These points echo Zulaika and Douglass's (1996) insightful analysis of "terrorism" and Appadurai's consideration of the interpenetration of the local and transnational (1996).

Bibliography

Alvarez, Sonia, Arturo Escobar, and Evelina Dagnino (eds.)
    1998 *Cultures of Politics/Politics of Culture: Revisioning Latin American Social Movements*. Boulder, Colo.: Westview Press.
Americas Watch
    1989 *Persecuting Human Rights Monitors: The CERJ in Guatemala*. New York: Americas Watch.
    1986 *Civil Patrols in Guatemala*. New York: Americas Watch.
    1984 *Guatemala: A Nation of Prisoners*. New York: Americas Watch.
    1982 *Human Rights in Guatemala: No Neutrals Allowed*. New York: Americas Watch.
Appadurai, Arjun
    1996 *Modernity at Large: Cultural Dimensions of Globalization*. Minneapolis: University of Minnesota Press.
Aretxaga, Begoña
    1998 "What the Border Hides: Partition and the Gender Politics of Irish Nationalism." *Social Analysis* 42:1, pp. 16–32.
    1997 *Shattering Silence: Women, Nationalism, and Political Subjectivity in Northern Ireland*. Princeton: Princeton University Press.
Arnson, Cynthia, and Mario Quiñones Amézquita (eds.)
    1997 *Memoria de la conferencia: Procesos de paz comparados*. Guatemala: Associación de Investigación y Estudios Sociales (ASIES) and the Latin American Program of the Woodrow Wilson International Center for Scholars.
ASIES
    1996 *Acuerdo de Paz Firme y Duradera: Acuerdo sobre Cronograma para la Implemtación, Cumplimiento y Verificación de los Acuerdos de Paz*. Guatemala: ASIES.
Ball, Patrick, Paul Kobrak, and Herbert F. Spirer
    1998 *State Violence in Guatemala, 1960–1996: A Quantitative Reflection*. AAAS and CIIDH. <http://hrdata.aaas.org/ciidh/qr/english/qrtitle.html>
Bastos, Santiago, and Manuela Camus
    1995 *Abriendo Caminos: Las Organizaciones Mayas desde el Nobel hasta el Acuerdo de Derechos Indígenas*. Guatemala: FLACSO.
Bourgois, Philippe
    1995 *In Search of Respect: Selling Crack in El Barrio*. New York: Cambridge University Press.
Burns, Allen G.
    1993 *Maya in Exile: Guatemalans in Florida*. Philadelphia: Temple University Press.
Carlsen, Robert S.
    1997 *The War for the Heart and Soul of a Highland Maya Town*. Austin: University of Texas Press.
Carmack, Robert
    1988a "The Story of Santa Cruz Quiché." In *Harvest of Violence: The Maya Indians and the Guatemalan Crisis*. Robert M. Carmack, ed. Norman: University of Oklahoma Press.
    1988b *Harvest of Violence: The Maya Indians and the Guatemalan Crisis*. Norman: University of Oklahoma Press.
COMG (Consejo de Organizaciones Mayas de Guatemala)
    1995 *Construyendo un Futuro para Nuestro Pasado: Derechos del Pueblo Maya y el Proceso de Paz*.

Commission for Historical Clarification
  1999 *Guatemala: Memory of Silence Tz'inil Na'tab'al.*
Corradi, Juan E., Patricia Weiss Fagen, and Manuel Antonio Garretón (eds.)
  1992 *Fear at the Edge: State Terror and Resistance in Latin America.* Berkeley: University of California Press.
Davis, Sheldon
  1988 "Introduction: Sowing the Seeds of Violence." In *Harvest of Violence: The Maya Indians and the Guatemalan Crisis.* Robert M. Carmack, ed. Norman: University of Oklahoma Press.
Escobar, Arturo, and Sonia E. Alvarez (eds.)
  1992 *The Making of Social Movements in Latin America: Identity, Strategy, and Democracy.* Boulder, Colo.: Westview Press.
Falk, Richard
  1997 "The Right of Self-Determination under International Law: The Coherence of Doctrine versus the Incoherence of Experience." In *Self-Determination and Self-Administration: A Handbook.* Wolfgang Danspeckgruber with Sir Arthur Watts, eds. Boulder, Colo.: Lynne Rienner.
Falla, Ricardo
  1994 *Massacres in the Jungle: Ixcan, Guatemala, 1975–1982.* Boulder, Colo.: Westview Press.
Ferguson, James
  1994 *The Anti-Politics Machine: "Development," Depoliticization, and Bureaucratic Power in Lesotho.* Minneapolis: University of Minnesota Press.
Fox, Richard
  1990 "Hindu Nationalism in the Making, or the Rise of the Hindian." In *Nationalist Ideologies and the Production of National Cultures.* Richard Fox, ed. Washington, D.C.: American Anthropological Association.
Hagen, Jacqueline
  1994 *Deciding to Be Legal: A Maya Community in Houston.* Philadelphia: Temple University Press.
Hale, Charles
  1996 "Maya Effervescence and the Ladino Imaginary in Guatemala." Paper presented at the American Anthropological Association meetings, San Francisco, 11 November.
Hochschild, Jennifer
  1994 *New American Dilemma: Liberal Democracy and School Desegregation.* New Haven: Yale University Press.
Huntington, Samuel
  1996 *The Clash of Civilizations and the Remaking of the World Order.* New York: Simon and Schuster.
Jay, Alice
  1993 *Persecution by Proxy: The Civil Patrols in Guatemala.* New York: Robert F. Kennedy Memorial Center for Human Rights.
Jonas, Susanne
  Forthcoming. *Of Centaurs and Doves: Guatemala's Peace Process.* Boulder, Colo.: Westview Press.
  1991 *The Battle for Guatemala: Rebels, Death Squads, and U.S. Power.* Boulder, Colo.: Westview Press.
Kim, Karen C.
  1998 " 'From the Bones of Memory': Women's Stories from the South African

Truth and Reconciliation Commission." Unpublished senior thesis, Harvard University, November.

Lovell, W. George
1995 *A Beauty That Hurts: Life and Death in Guatemala.* Toronto: Between the Lines Publishers.

Malamud-Gotí, Jaime
1996 *Game Without End: State Terror and the Politics of Justice.* Oklahoma: University of Oklahoma Press.

Manz, Beatriz
1988 *Refugees of a Hidden War: The Aftermath of Counterinsurgency in Guatemala.* Albany: SUNY Press.

McClintock, Michael
1992 *Instruments of Statecraft: U.S. Guerrilla Warfare, Counterinsurgency, and Counterterrorism, 1940–1990.* New York: Pantheon.
1985 *The American Connection: State Terror and Popular Resistance in Guatemala.* London: Zed Books.

MINUGUA (United Nations Verification Commission in Guatemala)
1998 "The Situation in Central America: Procedures for the Establishment of a Firm and Lasting Peace and Progress in Fashioning a Region of Peace, Freedom, Democracy and Development." A/52/757. New York: United Nations.

Montejo, Victor
Forthcoming. *Elilal: Mayan Exile and Survival.* Norman: University of Oklahoma Press.
1993 "The Dynamics of Cultural Resistance and Transformations: The Case of Guatemalan-Mayan Refugees in Mexico." Ph.D. diss., University of Connecticut.
1987 *Testimony: Death of a Guatemalan Village.* Willimantic, Conn.: Curbstone Press.

Montejo, Victor, and Q'anil Akab'
1992 *Brevísima Relación Testimonial de la Continua Destrucción del Mayab' (Guatemala).* Providence, R.I.: Maya Scholars Network.

Nelson, Diane
1999 *The Finger in the Wound: Ethnicity, Nation, and Gender in the Body Politic of Quincentennial Guatemala.* Berkeley: University of California Press.

Nordstrom, Carolyn, and JoAnn Martin (eds.)
1992 *Paths to Domination, Resistance, and Terror.* Berkeley: University of California Press.

Ortner, Sherry
1995 "Resistance and the Problem of Ethnographic Refusal." *Comparative Studies in Society and History*, 135, no. 1 (January), pp. 173–193.

Painter, James
1987 *Guatemala: False Hope, False Freedom.* London: Catholic Institute for International Relations (CIIR) and Latin America Bureau.

Paul, Benjamin D., and William J. Demarest
1988 "The Operation of a Death Squad in San Pedro la Laguna." In *Harvest of Violence: The Maya Indians and the Guatemalan Crisis.* Robert M. Carmack, ed. Norman: University of Oklahoma Press.

Perera, Victor
1993 *Unfinished Conquest: The Guatemalan Tragedy.* Berkeley: University of California Press.

Poole, Deborah, and Gerardo Rénique
1991 "The New Chroniclers of Peru: U.S. Scholars and Their 'Shining Path' of Peasant Rebellion." *Bulletin of Latin American Research*, 10:1, pp. 133–191.
Prunier, Gerard
1995 *The Rwanda Crisis, 1959–1994: History of Genocide.* London: Hurst.
Sahlins, Marshall
1961 "The Segmentary Lineage: An Organization of Predatory Expansion." *American Anthropologist*, 63, pp. 322–345.
Sam Colop, Luis Enrique
1991 *Jub'aqtun Omay Kuchum K'aslemal: Cinco Siglos de Encubrimiento.* Seminario Permanente de Estudios Mayas, cuaderno no. 1. Guatemala; Editorial Cholsamaj.
Schirmer, Jennifer
1998–99 "Prospects for Compliance: The Guatemalan Military and the Peace Accords." David Rockefeller Center for Latin American Studies, Working Papers on Latin America. Paper no. 98/99-1.
1998 *The Guatemalan Military Project: A Violence Called Democracy.* Philadelphia: University of Pennsylvania Press.
1997 "Universal and Sustainable Human Rights? Special Tribunals in Guatemala." In *Human Rights, Culture and Context: Anthropological Perspectives.* Richard Wilson, ed. London: Pluto Press.
1996 "The Looting of Democratic Discourse by the Guatemalan Military: Implications for Human Rights." In *Constructing Democracy: Human Rights, Citizenship, and Society in Latin America.* Elizabeth Jelin and Eric Hershberg, eds. Boulder, Colo.: Westview Press.
Sikkink, Kathryn
1996 "The Emergence, Evolution, and Effectiveness of Latin American Human Rights Networks." In *Constructing Democracy: Human Rights, Citizenship, and Society in Latin America.* Elizabeth Jelin and Eric Hershberg, eds. Boulder, Colo.: Westview Press.
Simon, Jean-Marie
1986 *Civil Patrols in Guatemala.* New York: Americas Watch.
Smith, Carol (ed.)
1990a *Guatemalan Indians and the State: 1540–1988.* Austin: University of Texas Press.
1990b "Conclusion: History and Revolution in Guatemala." In *Guatemalan Indians and the State: 1540–1988.* Carol Smith, ed. Austin: University of Texas Press.
Starn, Orin
1991 "Missing the Revolution: Anthropologists and the War in Peru." *Cultural Anthropology*, 6:1, pp. 63–91.
Stoll, David
1993 *Between Two Armies in the Ixil Towns of Guatemala.* New York: Columbia University Press.
Suarez-Orozco, Marcelo
1996 "State Terrors: Immigrants and Refugees in Post National Space." Paper given at the American Anthropological Association meetings, San Francisco, 20 November.
1989 *Central American Refugees and U.S. High Schools: A Psychosocial Study of Motivation and Achievement.* Stanford: Stanford University Press.

Tambiah, Stanley
  1996 *Leveling Crowds: Ethnonationalist Conflicts and Collective Violence in South Asia.* Berkeley: University of California Press.
Taussig, Michael
  1997 *The Magic of the State.* New York: Routledge.
  1992 *The Nervous System.* New York: Routledge.
  1987 *Shamanism, Colonialism, and the Wild Man: A Study in Terror and Healing.* Chicago: University of Chicago Press.
Trouillot, Michel-Rolph
  1999 "Close Encounters of the Deceptive Kind: The Anthropology of the State in the Age of Globalization." Paper delivered at the "Close Encounters" conference, Stanford University, 10 April.
Trudeau, Robert
  1993 *Guatemalan Politics: The Popular Struggle for Democracy.* Boulder, Colo.: Lynne Reinner.
Wacquant, Loïc
  1996 "The Rise of Advanced Marginality: Notes on Its Nature and Implications." *Acta Sociologica,* 39:2, pp. 121–139.
Warren, Kay B.
  1998 *Indigenous Movements and Their Critics: Pan-Maya Activism in Guatemala.* Princeton: Princeton University Press.
  1993 *The Violence Within: Cultural and Political Opposition in Divided Nations.* Boulder, Colo.: Westview Press.
Wilson, Richard
  1997 *Human Rights, Culture and Context: Anthropological Perspectives.* London: Pluto Press.
  1995 *Mayan Resurgence in Guatemala: Q'echi' Experiences.* Norman: University of Oklahoma Press.
Woodward, Susan
  1995 *Balkan Tragedy: Chaos and Dissolution after the Cold War.* Washington, D.C.: Brookings Institution.
Zulaika, Joseba, and William Douglass
  1996 *Terror and Taboo: the Follies, Fables, and Faces of Terrorism.* New York: Routledge.

Contributors

George J. Aditjondro is a Lecturer in the Department of Sociology and Social Anthropology at the University of Newcastle, Australia. An Indonesian activist who has been an outspoken critic of that country's rule in East Timor, West Papua, and Aceh, he is now in indefinite exile in Australia to avoid a long jail term for criticizing President Suharto in comments he made at an academic conference. He continues to speak out against Indonesian government policies, and reflects that "I see myself as an independent academic, a free-floating academic whose role is to say what's right and what's wrong, based on what I have observed and what I have studied" (correspondence).

Frank M. Afflitto is an Assistant Professor in the Department of Criminology and Criminal Justice at the University of Memphis. His Ph.D. dissertation was a study of state-terror survivors in Guatemala and their perceptions of justice and impunity. He comes from a multidisciplinary background including anthropology, social psychology, and criminology, and is an ethnographer with extensive fieldwork experience in Latin America and the West Bank.

Begoña Aretxaga is an Assistant Professor in the Department of Anthropology at the University of Texas, Austin. She has published widely on aspects of gender, political culture, violence, and ethnic nationalism among Basques and in Northern Ireland, and is the author of *Shattering Silence: Women, Nationalism, and Political Subjectivity in Northern Ireland* (1997).

Cynthia Keppley Mahmood is Associate Professor of Anthropology at the University of Maine, and author of *Fighting for Faith and Nation: Dialogues With Sikh Militants* (1996).

Thomas M. McKenna is an Associate Professor in the Department of Anthropology at the University of Alabama, Birmingham, and the author of *Muslim Rulers and Rebels: Everyday Politics and Armed Separatism in the Southern Philippines* (1998).

Joyce Pettigrew is a Reader in Social Anthropology at the Queen's University of Belfast. She is the author of *Robber Noblemen: A Study of the Political System of the Sikh Jats* (1975) and *The Sikhs of the Punjab: Unheard Voices of State and Guerrilla Violence* (1995), and edited *Martyrdom and Political Resistance* (1997).

Antonius C. G. M. Robben is Professor of Anthropology in the Department of Cultural Anthropology at Utrecht University, the Netherlands. He is the author of *Sons of the Sea Goddess: Economic Practice and Discursive Conflict in Brazil* (1989), edited (with Carolyn Nordstrom) *Fieldwork Under Fire: Contemporary Studies of Violence and Survival* (1995), and is currently writing a book on political violence in Argentina during the 1970s.

Jeffrey A. Sluka is a Senior Lecturer in Social Anthropology at Massey University, New Zealand, and the author of *Hearts and Minds, Water and Fish: Popular Support for the IRA and INLA in a Northern Irish Ghetto* (1989).

Kay B. Warren is Professor of Anthropology at Harvard University. She is the author of *Women of the Andes: Patriarchy and Social Change in Two Peruvian Towns* (with Susan Bourque, 1981), *The Symbolism of Subordination: Indian Identity in a Guatemalan Town* (1989), and *Indigenous Movements and Their Critics: Pan-Maya Activism in Guatemala* (1998), and editor of *The Violence Within: Cultural and Political Opposition in Divided Nations* (1993).

Index